University of Plymouth
Charles Seale Hayne Library
Subject to status this item may be renewed
via your Voyager account

http://voyager.plymouth.ac.uk
Tel: (01752) 232323

ECONOMIC CONVERGENCE IN A MULTISPEED EUROPE

Also by E. Karakitsos

MACROSYSTEMS: The Dynamics of Economic Policy

Economic Convergence in a Multispeed Europe

K. B. Gaynor
The Management School
Imperial College
University of London

and

E. Karakitsos
The Management School
Imperial College
University of London

Forewords by

Norbert Kloten
Chairman, Academic Economic Advisory Council
German Federal Ministry of Economics, Bonn

and

Farhan Sharaff
Global Chief Investment Officer, Citibank – Private Bank, New York

First published in Great Britain 1997 by
MACMILLAN PRESS LTD
Houndmills, Basingstoke, Hampshire RG21 6XS and London
Companies and representatives throughout the world

A catalogue record for this book is available from the British Library.

ISBN 0–333–66197–4

 First published in the United States of America 1997 by
ST. MARTIN'S PRESS, INC.,
Scholarly and Reference Division,
175 Fifth Avenue, New York, N.Y. 10010

ISBN 0–312–16534–X

Library of Congress Cataloging-in-Publication Data
Gaynor, K. B.
Economic convergence in a multispeed Europe / K. B. Gaynor and E.
Karakitsos.
p. cm.
Includes bibliographical references and index.
ISBN 0–312–16534–X (cloth)
1. European Union countries—Economic policy. 2. Europe—Economic
integration. I. Karakitsos, Elias. II. Title.
HC240.G32   1996
338.94—dc20   96–34660
                                                                                    CIP

© K. B. Gaynor and E. Karakitsos 1997
Forewords © Farhan Sharaff and Norbert Kloten 1997

This book is printed on paper suitable for recycling and made from fully managed and
sustained forest sources.

10   9   8   7   6   5   4   3   2   1
06   05   04   03   02   01   00   99   98   97

Printed and bound in Great Britain by
Antony Rowe Ltd, Chippenham, Wiltshire

To my family

K.B.G.

To Chloe

E.K.

So we grew together...
But yet an union in partition.
(Shakespeare, *A Midsummer's Night Dream*)

Contents

List of Figures

x   *List of Figures*

List of Tables

Foreword

In the last ten years financial markets in Europe have been predominantly affected by the policies which have been pursued for the goal of economic and monetary union. In the last five years to the breakdown of the ERM asset prices increasingly reflected the belief that European economies were converging. Contrary to the common belief that financial markets are most of the time, or even occasionally, destabilizing, the truth is that in the period preceding the ERM crisis financial markets, if anything else, were stabilized in thoroughly adopting the convergence theory. But large movements in asset prices invariably reflect inconsistencies in economic policies. The ERM crisis reflected the inconsistent policies which were pursued in Europe after the German reunification which represented an asymmetric shock to the system, as this book so well explains. This resulted in desynchronization of the business cycles between Germany and the rest of Europe, and hence revealed the inconsistencies in policies prompting the response of financial markets which caused the collapse of the ERM.

Asset prices reflect investors' expectations of the future path of key macro-variables which are, in turn, determined by changes in fiscal and monetary policies. The optimal mix in terms of fiscal and monetary policies is chosen so that it would satisfy the policy-makers' targets. These are encapsulated in their objective function. This objective function is optimized subject to the feasible set which describes the way economic policy affects these targets. Hence, in order to arrive at an estimate of the optimal policy mix, the modern investor must solve the policy design optimization problem. This means that she/he must form expectations of the policy-makers' objective function.

The large volatility in asset prices is due to frequent revisions of investors' expectations. Asset prices are fluctuating as investors' expectations are altered in response to actual or perceived changes in the policy-makers' objective function or to the optimal policy as the actual current state of the economy turns out to be different than expected. This book explains what are the policy choices for not only existing but also prospective members of monetary union, hence providing a framework of how investors' expectations are formulated. The book also provides an innovative approach for analyzing the risk premia in the foreign exchange and bond markets. With respect to the latter this is extremely important for relating the pricing of the high yielders, like Italy, Spain and Sweden, to the core countries, such as Germany. The methodology is based on the implications of the stock–flow equilibrium relationships for the dynamic adjustment of key macro-variables which are determinants of the risk premia.

The book describes the widening and deepening process of monetary union by identifying the policy options in three separate stages. In the first stage, which is a model for the widening process, are countries which belong to the periphery and have a long way to go in achieving convergence. The policy issue is how to combine disinflation with a debt-reduction package and what is the optimal time for entry to the ERM while minimizing the cost in terms of output. The analysis clearly demonstrates the conditions under which such policies may be inconsistent and hence unsustainable, thereby causing large swings in asset prices by altering the value of the risk premium. These are the conditions which cause the vicious circle where disinflation causes output losses, while output losses and disinflation result in larger deficits.

The second stage characterizes the deepening process of monetary union. The analysis applies to the median group which consists of countries which have achieved some convergence but have still a way to go. The possibility of inconsistent and hence unsustainable policies arises from the conflict between policies which promote convergence according to the Maastricht criteria and policies which stabilize output. The vicious circle which will cause large swings in asset prices stems in this case from the fact that policies which promote nominal convergence do so at the expense of fiscal stability.

The third stage concerns the core countries which have achieved nominal convergence, are ready to form a monetary union, but have not sorted out what type of fiscal policies should be pursued once they form it. Policies which do not attempt to stabilize output will be very damaging for the equity market in Europe with disastrous effects for the growth potential of the region.

For a decade or so now Professor Karakitsos has provided the Global Investment Strategy Committee of Citibank Private Banking Group with this type of analysis as a background of the likely movements of asset prices. This type of analysis has been at the core of deriving an optimal asset allocation for globally diversified portfolios.

In short, the book is useful to all those who are interested in the prospects for Europe, the types of economic policies which should be pursued in the widening and deepening process of monetary union and their implications from many different angles including that for financial markets.

FARHAN SHARAFF
Global Chief Investment Officer
Citibank–Private Bank, New York

Foreword

The disparity of views concerning the structures within which the realization of the European Monetary Union will take place has intensified. A considerable battle is in progress regarding the application of the convergence criteria and the date of entry into the third (final) stage of monetary union, and furthermore regarding the circle of participating countries and the status of latecomers as well as the regulation of the relationship between these different groups of countries. There is also the question about the possible implications of monetary union. The wide spectrum of these issues – some of which I highlighted in two recent papers (Kloten, 1995) – is reflected in an overflowing amount of literature. Only few of the publications convey a secure foundation, separating the irrelevant from the relevant and providing a lead to the political search for decision making. To the rare publications which do offer orientation in this labyrinth belongs the book by Kevin Gaynor and Elias Karakitsos. This elaborate study considers the widening and deepening process of European integration as earmarked by a *de facto* multi-speed approach in terms of convergence. While the literature has concentrated on issues such as transitional mechanisms to monetary union, convergence, debt sustainability and the Maastricht criteria themselves, the book integrates each of these elements into a dynamic general equilibrium model with a specified demand and supply side which satisfies stock–flow relationships. Since Maastricht neglects fiscal policy issues both during transition and in the monetary union, and since the convergence criteria explicitly ignore relevant aspects of stabilization, (neither output nor unempoyment), the authors try to close the gap. They consider the optimal timing of ERM entry as well as useful coordination mechanisms and federal co-insurance schemes.

Using cluster analysis Gaynor and Karakitsos – picking up Dornbusch's taxonomy – identify three groups of member states: "core", "median" and "periphery". A representative country of the periphery is Greece, which the authors regard as a model of the widening process of European integration for all Eastern European countries. Spain is considered as a model of the deepening process representing the median group of countries which have already achieved some nominal convergence. The core comprises countries which to a large extent have accomplished nominal convergence (such as France and Germany). The theoretical reasoning leads to clear-cut political recommendations.

In general, European integration has to be based upon a multi-speed strategy. To maximize the likelihood of achieving the ultimate target more (and not less) flexible domestic policies (than it is asked in Maastricht) and a more flexible convergence time-table (than is scheduled) is required. "It is better that member states arrive at the destination late than to not arrive at all."

In particular, Countries such as Greece should solve their domestic problems before joining the ERM. Not the "cold turkey" but the "gradualist" option offers better chances to enter the ERM at the least cost in terms of lost output, even at the temporary expense of the loss of credibility.

Countries such as Spain should use the full width of the ERM, which does not imply easing monetary policy and would not endanger the convergence achieved to date. A narrow-band ERM with a risk premium dependent on relative inflation rates, unemployment rates, debt levels and the current account would perform worse in terms of both stabilization of output and nominal convergence.

The core countries who are potential first-hour members of the monetary union should bear in mind that a flexible domestic fiscal policy scheme which allows for some role for stabilizing output outperforms a tight policy scheme where the sole target is the debt ratio. A flexible policy can be useful, and stable, only if its implementation will be considered with care. A modest federal budget will provide useful service in redistributing resources when asymmetric shocks occur. Therefore, core countries are advised to install a well designed federal co-insurance scheme.

The messages of the book are derived from an innovative modelling approach, distinguished by a dynamic setting and an explicit consideration of inconsistencies in the targets of economic policy and of the impact of expectations, but also by a sound empirical basis. The practical implications of this remarkable piece of applied economics are of great value for all policy makers. Yet the political conclusions reflect the structure of the models and the adhering sets of assumptions. Therefore, the models or the results may not be accepted, either partly or as a whole. Political reflections and deliberations may speak against substantial concessions of policy performance with regard to the convergence criteria or against the high-ranking virtues of a federal co-insurance scheme. Whereas objections could be raised, the book of Gaynor and Karakitsos has to be regarded as a markstone, providing at the very least a well-structured and well equipped platform for opinion-forming and political path-finding.

Note. See the two papers by Norbert Kloten in *Financial Decision-Making and Moral Responsibility* (ed. Stephen. F. Frowen and Framis. P. McHugh): "European Monetary Union: Sovereignty and Hegemony" (pp. 197–206) with comments by Wim Kösters (pp. 207–212), and "The Economic and Political Environment of Economic and Monetary Union" pp. 213–25).

NORBERT KLOTEN

Former President, Land Central Bank in Baden–Württemberg and ex officio
Member of the Bundesbank's policy–making Council

Chairman, Academic Economic Advisory Council at the German Federal
Ministry of Economics, Bonn

Acknowledgements

This research is an extension of an earlier work conducted for the European Commission while Elias Karakitsos was acting as adviser to DG II. This financial support is gratefully acknowledged; however, the views expressed in this book are those of the authors alone. The work has benefited from the study of the reaction of financial markets to the process of European integration while Elias Karakitsos has been acting as an advisor to the Global Investment Strategy Committee of Citibank Private Banking Group.

Introduction

The late 1980s and early 1990s will be remembered by history as a turning point; decisions were made which dramatically changed the face of European politics and economics. The fall of the Soviet empire, the re-unification of Germany and the signing of the Maastricht Treaty have all had an important impact on the way Europe is perceived and the way Europe perceives itself. An opportunity now exists for unparalleled integration and cooperation, stretching uninterrupted from the Atlantic to the Urals. The problem, of course, is how to achieve this.

THE PATH TO MU

The two competing dynamics are deeper or wider integration. Two extreme options are to limit the amount of full European Union (EU) members and push on to monetary union (MU), or to widen membership at the expense of closer monetary and economic cooperation. Unsurprisingly, in an EU of fifteen members, unanimity on which path to take is not forthcoming. The intergovernmental conference of 1996 is meant to address these questions, and formulate and clarify the steps to be taken next. Unfortunately, the economics literature has not produced clear and practical policy prescriptions; it often reaches conflicting conclusions on issues for which decisions are ultimately based on political considerations, for example floating or MU. Moreover, the reasons for the conflicting results are either unclear or arcane, and are thus of little use in aiding decision making. The aim of this book is to provide clear comparisons between the relevant options, based on a transparent and easily understood modelling framework.

As things stand EU policy makers have committed themselves to forming a MU before the end of the decade, according to the timetable set out in the Maastricht Treaty. In order to qualify for membership a country must satisfy the criteria set out in the Treaty. The Treaty's criteria represent two forms of test: fiscal stability and nominal convergence. Applying the criteria tests to the present member states indicates the level of nominal convergence and the amount of fiscal consolidation which remains to be achieved by some

2 Economic Convergence in a Multispeed Europe

members. A large proportion of the current members would fail to qualify for membership based on their 1994 performances. The situation has deteriorated in 1995, with even Germany failing the budget deficit criterion. However, some members are closer to passing than others, whilst a small group have serious problems. In practice, therefore, Europe finds itself facing a *de facto* multi-tier system in terms of convergence.

If this is the case then each member state (or prospective member), has a different set of problems and objectives. For example, it makes little sense to ask how Greece should go about ensuring MU membership in the short term, whilst questions of large-scale nominal convergence are inappropriate for France and Germany. Instead, it is more useful to group together countries with common problems, and to address these problems for that group only. Thus, robust policy mixes which are appropriate for promoting convergence, stabilizing debt, or making MU successful, for example, need to be examined for the relevant group.

This is the subject matter of this book. The book covers each point on the road to MU, from countries which need to undertake large amounts of adjustment, through countries which need to make the final step, to the core countries, where the examination is directed at MU itself. The issue is not whether MU is desirable, but rather how to achieve it amongst a multiplicity of countries, and once there how to make it work effectively. In the light of this coverage, the book is important not only to current members but also to new and prospective members of the EU.

Following Dornbusch's (1991) taxonomy there are three identifiable groups of member states within the European Union. We define these groups as "core", "median", and "peripheral". The core group comprises countries which have similar inflation and interest rate performance, reasonably stable exchange rates, and sustainable public sector debts and deficits. These are countries which one could reasonably assume would form the basis of any MU in the near future. The median group is made up of countries with an inflation differential from the core average, less credibility in the exchange rate target, and perhaps debt and deficit problems, all of which are reflected in higher nominal interest rates.

The peripheral have, for one reason or another, a relatively large inflation and interest rate differential, weak currencies, high deficits and debt, and may not have taken part in full Exchange Rate Mechanism (ERM) membership. For this group, the issue is how to combine disinflation with a debt reduction package with joining the ERM whilst limiting the cost in terms of output. Since the original motivation for the ERM stemmed from the Common Market and the Common Agricultural Policy (CAP), if new members are allowed to take part in these, the next issue is surely exchange rate stability for these countries. Therefore, this analysis pertains not only to non-ERM EU members but also to non-EU members.

For the median countries the question is how to proceed with convergence in a free capital ERM. The opportunity offered by wider ERM bands is examined with the distinction between policies which stabilize and policies which produce convergence forming the backdrop. Finally, for the core countries three options for fiscal policy in MU are compared, and, as it appears likely some EU states will not be in the founding MU group, the impact of the core's decision on fiscal policy on ERM members is indicated.

Each of these research topics has received attention in the literature, yet a full appreciation of the questions requires a number of effects and interactions to be taken into account. The issues have been largely addressed in an analytical, static, partial equilibrium setting. What is required instead is a general equilibrium approach in a dynamic setting with a sound empirical basis. However, the current models available for the peripheral countries are limited in their use for policy analysis, and they are single country only,[1] whilst large multi-country econometric models often lack consistent stock-flow relationships. This book goes some way to redressing the paucity of work which uses this approach, by developing multi-country numerical simulation models for Germany, France, Spain and Greece which capture the stylized facts of the interactions and processes defined as being important. These are models were used in a joint research project for DG II of the European Commission[2] to assess the current dynamic convergence paths of selected peripheral countries.

The modelling approach used is innovative in that it is based on theoretical and well understood models which incorporate empirical estimates garnered from numerous sources, and in its treatment of risk premia for ERM members. These models offer a flexible approach which allows the investigation of a wide variety of questions under clear assumptions about the critical aspects of the model, for example the speed of expectations adjustment, or the extent of nominal wage rigidity. It is argued that the approach used here is the more appropriate and that it gives clearer answers than have hitherto been available. Moreover, the spirit of the book is to present policy makers with practical and easily understood implications for policy, and so optimal control techniques were avoided.

There has long been a feeling in European policy circles that the issue of multiple geometry, or multispeed convergence, is somehow *anti-communautaire*. We would argue the opposite: imposing a unitary Europe, where all must take part in each step and policy, is a recipe not only for economic pain, but also for conservatism in policy making since unanimous agreement is so hard to achieve. If the ideal end point is a single market and a single currency, but all members start from different points, it is surely infeasible to expect them to all arrive at the same time. Thus, rather than being *anti-communautaire*, flexibility should be seen as promoting convergence, since it increases the chance of convergence taking place by reducing the self-imposed tensions in the system.

As the EU contemplates the accession of new members, both rich and poor, and the transition to MU, this book offers lessons from existing members for new members, and some new evidence and advice about the path to and operation of MU itself.

OUTLINE OF THE BOOK

Chapter 1 reviews the history and development of European integration in general, and monetary integration in particular. This sets the scene by introducing the provisions of the Maastricht Treaty and reviewing the functioning of the ERM over its history. From this review several lessons are drawn for the way in which the ERM and MU are modelled.

Chapter 2 presents evidence indicating the multispeed nature of monetary integration in Europe. The recent experience and convergence of the member states is evaluated before cluster analysis is used to distinguish the groups. Finally the Maastricht criteria performance of the member states is reviewed. Chapter 3 considers the issues discussed above in more detail, and examines the coverage these areas have received in the literature to date.

Chapters 4, 5 and 6 present the results for the peripheral country, Greece, the median country, Spain, and the core countries, France and Germany, respectively. Chapter 7 draws together the conclusions of the research, identifies the weaknesses inherent in the approach, and discusses suggestions for further research and the implications of the work for European macroeconomic policy. Appendix 1 introduces a representative version of the model used in the research, justifies the functional forms used and discusses the calibration of the model, while Appendix 2 presents the parameters and data used.

1 European Integration, the ERM and Maastricht

1.1 INTRODUCTION

Chapter 1 presents a brief review of the main post-war integration efforts in Europe, up until the Maastricht Treaty. The various phases of the ERM are also discussed. The purpose is to draw lessons about the functioning of the ERM over the period, for example its asymmetric nature, and to introduce the framework within which policy will be conducted in MU.

1.2 A BRIEF HISTORY OF EUROPEAN INTEGRATION

Foundations

The modern vision and form of the European convergence ideal can be traced back to the early post-war years and the Marshall Plan. The deteriorating European political climate prompted the US Secretary of State, George Marshall, to propose a plan of aid for Europe.[1] It was to be based on the simple, unifying principle that the US' role "of friendly aid" should be dependent on Europe acting in concert, not individually. The aid was for Europe, not individual countries.

Marshall aid served several purposes. It helped alleviate the "dollar shortage", it allowed Europe to acquire the production capacity and raw materials needed to regenerate industry, and it allowed the dismantling of trade and payments controls which had been in place to conserve dollars.[2]

The Organisation for European Economic Cooperation (OEEC), the forerunner of the OECD, was created to coordinate the distribution of the aid and promote economic recovery through trade. One of the OEEC's more important steps was the formation of the European Payments Union (EPU), a credit network which allowed the settlement of intra-European trade imbalances without using precious dollars.

The Marshall Plan also acted as a catalyst in the search for a solution to the "German problem" (Somers, 1992). As the West German economic recovery began, a working relationship needed to be found between the old allies and the new Germany. A strong, united Europe was required, one that embraced the semi-nation of West Germany, but did not allow it to dominate its new partners, either politically or economically.

Jean Monnet, then French Minister of Foreign Affairs, identified a way forward, the so-called Schuman plan of 1950. The coal and steel industries were of such strategic importance that European cooperation in the control of these industries would be an important step in cementing the tenuous new balance.

As a result the Treaty of Paris (1951) established the European Coal and Steel Community (ECSC).[3] A supranational body would have the ability to impose minimum prices, production quotas, taxes and to affect investment decisions in these industries. This sectoral approach to integration, the "Community Method", was based on the belief that common solutions could be found to common problems (Collins, 1994). It was to become a recurrent theme in the years ahead.

This single step laid the foundation for much wider cooperation in the economic field; it was also, as Haas (1958, p. 106) indicates, the beginning of a quest for a "political federation of Western Europe". Furthermore, as Tsoukalis (1993, p. 19) points out, the "Schuman plan laid the foundations of Franco–German reconciliation which later developed into close co-operation, thus providing the cornerstone and the main driving force to regional integration."

The formation of the ECSC coincided with what is generally agreed to be the end of the reconstruction period. Output had reached its pre-war levels in most Western economies (Mayne, 1970), resulting in the cessation of Marshall Aid. The comparative success of the ECSC and the buoyant economic environment led to new efforts at integration. June 1955 saw the six ECSC members meet at Messina to discuss general integration and new communities based on the sectoral approach.

The aspiration of more general integration was clearly in the direction of some form of political union (Haas, 1958). This, after the collapse of the European Defence Community initiative, was seen as too sensitive an issue, and was left to future negotiations. Instead, economic integration became the primary goal. The six ECSC members duly formed the European Economic Community (EEC) and the European Atomic Energy Commission (EURATOM) via the 1957 Treaty of Rome.

The aim of the EEC was to create a common market within twelve years. This went beyond any free trade area or customs union to include common external tariffs (CETs) and the free movement of factors of production. A broadly common set of economic policies was also envisaged as being important. However, little concrete action was taken to encourage cooperation on the economic policy front beyond statements about the desirability of policy being of common interest to the Six.

The year of the Treaty's implementation (1958) brought widespread currency convertibility, at least for current account transactions, and the abolition of the EPU. Capital account transactions remained, in the most part, unconvertible. This reflected statements in both the Treaty of Rome and the Articles of the IMF about their potentially destabilizing effects.

The perceived danger of large-scale private capital flows was identified in the League of Nations report *International Currency Experience*, published in 1944 (quoted in Kenen, 1994) which attempted to explain the collapse of the international monetary order between the wars.[4] The lesson of that period remained fresh in the mind of many policy makers and, accordingly, capital controls remained in place for some time, and were often re-imposed in times of crisis. Convertibility for current account transactions was seen as a prerequisite for the creation of the Common Market, whilst continued capital controls gave governments the ability to set domestic monetary policy independently (Tsoukalis, 1993; Padoa Schioppa, 1984).

The Bretton Woods agreement provided the main exchange rate apparatus of the period. Whilst it functioned there was no real need or desire for a regional monetary or exchange rate bloc (Eichengreen, 1993). Hence, European macroeconomic policy remained under the purview of national governments within the framework of the international monetary agreement. The comparative tranquillity of the Bretton Woods system was not to last long.

The decade between the signing of the Treaty of Rome and the next major steps on the road to full integration, the Common Agricultural Policy (CAP) and the Werner Report, brought increased tension in the Bretton Woods system. The US policy of "benign neglect" coupled with large capital outflows from the USA to Europe led to downward pressure on the dollar and intense pressure in the system.[5] The international economic order was changing with Europe becoming increasingly integrated on the trade front, and finding its feet in the international arena, for example at the Kennedy Round of the GATT. New members were applying for membership of the club, and the instigation of the CAP was seen as a reaffirmation of political support for closer convergence. This positive environment was threatened by the deteriorating international monetary order.

Even before the Nixon policy changes of August 1971, these events had acted as a stimulus for Europe to examine ways to ensure exchange rate stability for the member states. The European Summit held at the Hague in 1969 produced a solemn statement that Europe should become an economic and monetary union (Papademos, 1993, identifies this as the start of European monetary integration). Pierre Werner, the then Prime Minister of Luxembourg, chaired a committee to investigate how this could be achieved.

Werner reported in October 1970,[6] calling for a monetary union to be achieved via three stages and within ten years. Stage One was to be spent reducing exchange rate fluctuations and beginning the process of monetary and fiscal policy coordination. Stage Two would be a consolidation stage where inflation differentials and exchange rate variance would both decline further. The final stage, Stage Three, would see the irrevocable fixing of exchange rates, the removal of capital controls, the emergence of a system of European central banks to operate monetary policy, and much closer coordination of fiscal policy at the EC level (Eichengreen, 1993; Papademos, 1993; El-Agraa, 1994).

Events overtook this grand and ambitious plan. The result of the Nixon measures was to create a short period of floating until the late 1971 Smithsonian Agreement, an effort to shore up the crumbling Bretton Woods system. The agreement was to return to the pegged system, but with some fundamental changes. The size of the fluctuation bands were increased to 2.25% around the dollar, the dollar was devalued against gold, and the US Treasury's gold window would remain closed. As (Kenen, 1994, p. 501) put it, ''In other words, the new official gold price was the one at which the United States would *not* buy or sell.''

The new fluctuation bands would mean that European currencies could fluctuate by up to 4.5% against each other. This was felt to be excessive in the context of the CAP and Common Market, and thus, against the backdrop of the Smithsonian Agreement and the Werner Report aims, steps were taken to form a regional bloc of exchange rate stability. The ''Snake in the Tunnel'' was formed in March 1972; the member currencies were to have fluctuation bands of 2.25% against each other, whilst as a whole they would move within the 2.25% band against the dollar. The latter formed the tunnel, the former the snake.

Unfortunately the tunnel only lasted until 1973, when generalised floating began. The snake itself was not without problems either. Sterling, the punt, and the lira left early on. The krone and the franc left and rejoined, the franc repeating the process again until it finally left in January 1974 (see Mayes, 1994). Finally, the first oil shock left the snake as a DM zone, as the original members elected to follow different policies in response to it.

The snake clearly failed to deliver its promise: stable exchange rates (Eichengreen, 1993). This failure has been explained by two factors. First the system was dominated by Germany and second, decisions on parity settings were unilateral (much as under Bretton Woods). Faced with a shock the size of OPEC I, the system was unsustainable as members failed to coordinate their policy responses (Tsoukalis, 1993). In this climate it is unsurprising that the basic elements of exchange rate and monetary policy coordination agreed on at the Hague Summit were abandoned by the members. The Werner Report and its version of MU were effectively dead.

The period up until the first oil shock was in many ways a "golden era" (Tsoukalis, 1993; Hobsbawm, 1994). Low inflation, good growth rates, low unemployment, success in implementing the common market, and the beginnings of a real international presence combined to give Europe a positive outlook on the process of integration. This atmosphere encouraged new applicants. The UK, Ireland and Denmark joined in January 1973, the first and last enlargement until Greece joined almost a decade later.

The breakdown of the Snake as a truly European initiative, the oil shock and a return to generalized floating heralded a period of stagnation and lack of regard for international policy cooperation. The golden age was over.

The modern era

Roy Jenkins, in his role as President of the Commission, revived the issue of European monetary cooperation in his Jean Monnet speech of October 1977: "We must now look afresh at the case for monetary union because there are new arguments, new needs, and new approaches to be assessed" (quoted in Vaubel, 1979). By 1979 the new approach was in action, the EMS was born[7] amidst derision and cynicism from both economists and central bankers.

Vaubel (1979) in an entertaining, and sometimes caustic, lecture is representative of the level of confidence in the new system at the time.[8] He saw the new system as merely an extension of the last, with the snake currencies of the time fixing parities with three non-snake currencies, the French franc, Italian lira, and Irish punt. The changes to the financing facilities, in his opinion, were minor and would not be enough to halt frequent re-alignments and turbulence. Whilst he acknowledged that one of the reasons for the EMS being introduced was to "dampen inflation expectations", Vaubel felt that any attempt to reduce inflation to German levels would result in an unnecessary loss of employment, following from too fast a stabilization. In an uncannily accurate look to the future he predicted that the first years of the system would be characterized by large-scale interventions, abrupt parity changes, and new capital, and possibly trade, controls.

Why were the Europeans willing to return to a pegged exchange rate system after the breakdown of the Snake and Bretton Woods? The answers given in the voluminous literature usually centre around the functioning of the CAP and the Common Market, which required stable exchange rates to function properly, and the level of intra-European trade.

The latter point is interesting. Giavazzi and Giovannini (1989) point out that whilst the EC economy as a whole is not much more open than the USA or Japan, its individual members are, in large part, very open. Therefore intra-European trade is by far the more important. If, as has been suggested (Krugman, 1990; Kenen and Rodrik, 1986), volatile exchange rates impede the growth of trade and foreign investment, then stabilizing intra-European trade is extremely important to the growth prospects of the member states. However, the existence of this effect is neither clear nor overwhelming. Brada and Mendez (1988) find that exchange rate uncertainty does have an impact regardless of the exchange rate regime, but that its effects are much smaller than those caused by restrictive trade practices. Krugman (1990) makes the important distinction between what might have happened and what has happened; just because econometric results show that trade has increased despite the presence of volatility, this does not necessarily tells us anything about how it would have reacted without volatility or, indeed, the costs of that volatility. In any event exchange rate volatility was felt to be unacceptable in the EC, and this was the driving force for the ERM, not inflation convergence (Artis and Taylor, 1994) or longer-term views about MU (at least not explicitly) as evidenced by the experience of the first period of the ERM.

1.3   THE FIRST THREE PHASES OF THE ERM

The ERM is normally said to have been characterized by at least three historic periods of functioning (see Table 1.1), with the current phase of wide fluctuation bands, making a distinct fourth phase (Goodhart, 1990; Artis and Taylor, 1988; Mastropasqua *et al.*, 1988; Russo and Tullio, 1988; Padoa Schioppa, 1988; Rieke, 1990; Giavazzi and Giovannini, 1989; Giovannini, 1990; Karakitsos, 1994).

The first phase, from the inception of the system in March 1979 through to March 1983, was characterized by frequent realignments, little policy coordination, and low convergence in key macroeconomic variables (c.f. Vaubel, 1979) (see Table 1.1). The turnaround came when the French Socialist government switched policy emphasis to controlling inflation, with the ERM providing an additional nominal anchor. From this point on the French real exchange rate began to appreciate, a sign that the nominal exchange rate was no longer offsetting wage and price differentials. Italy had a similar, if not as pronounced, change in policy view slightly earlier, after the realignment of 1981 (Goodhart, 1990).

From March 1983 through to January 1987, the second phase, consolidation took place with declining inflation differentials and fewer realignments. However, the shift in policy observed in the ERM countries

Table 1.1 Realignments in the ERM, 1979–87

1979–83	No. of realignments	Average size of realignment (%)	Degree of offsetting (%)
Narrow Band	22	5.1	101.2
All ERM	27	5.3	89.7
1984–7			
Narrow Band	9	3.5	52.7
All ERM	12	3.8	52.1

Note: All data refer to bilateral DM exchange rates. Offsetting of inflation differentials is measured by the ratio of central rate variation to the price differential by the time of realignment.
Source: *One Market, One Money* (Commission of the European Communities, 1990), p. 42.

had not convinced the private sector. Speculative attacks continued and capital controls were often used to beat them off (Giavazzi and Giovannini, 1989).

This period also brought about a clear division of work in the system. The change in French policy highlighted the shift in views. Adhering to the exchange rate peg brought the $n-1$ problem to the fore. In any group of n countries there are only $n-1$ exchange rates. This creates a fundamental indeterminacy in the system,[9] which can be solved through either letting one country set monetary policy, with the rest then setting their monetary policy to maintain the exchange rate target, or cooperation in setting monetary policy for the region as a whole.

1.3.1 Asymmetry in the ERM

There are two views of Germany's role in the ERM during this period, outlined and tested by, amongst others, De Grauwe (1990), Collins (1988), Obstfeld (1988), Hughes Hallett *et al.* (1993), Giavazzi and Giovannini (1989), Cohen *et al.* (1988), Fratianni and von Hagen (1990) and Weber (1992). The conventional view is that Germany has played the hegemonic role of monetary leader, much as the USA did in the Bretton Woods era (Krugman, 1990). Other members peg their currency to the DM and are therefore forced to follow German monetary leadership. In this respect, the EMS is a DM zone.

The second view is perhaps more in tune with recent empirical evidence, for example that of Fratianni and von Hagen (1990) and Cohen and Wyplosz (1989). It finds that more symmetry exists in the system than was previously thought. Germany is the most important member, but monetary developments in other countries, most notably France, do affect German policy. Granger causality tests (De Grauwe, 1989), reaction function estimates (Giavazzi and Giovannini, 1989), analysis of marginal and intra-marginal intervention differences and vector autoregressions of money growth rates and interest rates (Cohen and Wyplosz, 1989), indicate, to a varying degree, that there is some two-way causality.[10]

However, reconciling these analytical results with observation of the system's actual day-to-day functioning is a vexed issue. Observation of member states' responses to German interest rate changes clearly demonstrates the asymmetric nature of the system (Goodhart, 1990). Giavazzi and Giovannini (1989), and Mastropasqua *et al.* (1988) show that the relative volatility of French and Italian off shore and on shore interest rates were much higher than Germany's during periods of speculative pressure, indicating the market's perception of the respective roles of the members.[11] Karl-Otto Pohl in a 1990 speech (quoted in Goodhart, 1990) explicitly accepted the Bundesbank's role as monetary leader.

Goodhart (1990) interprets the system in the following way: Germany does act as monetary leader, but it does not set monetary policy with internal price stability exclusively in mind. At times the Bundesbank will take the situation of its partners into account. Draghi (1989) takes a stronger line: "I see one country running its own monetary policy without too much regard for the rest of the area ... In other words, monetary policies are not independent."

Which view is adopted has important implications for the modelling of the ERM, and the results obtained. In this book the Bundesbank's role is seen as one of hegemonic leadership in the monetary field; it sets monetary policy with purely domestic targets in mind. The only impact the other member states' economic situation has on that decision is through the normal trade and financial linkages of the system. An example may help to clarify this.

Starting from a position of equilibrium in the product market, if there is an autonomous decrease in French demand this feeds into all other members' demands through the trade multiplier. Germany will experience a decline in exports to all of Europe, and consequently a fall in German demand. This may prompt the Bundesbank to reduce interest rates from which the view could be formed that the Bundesbank is helping to "bail out" a partner country, whereas in fact it is merely reacting to a foreign disturbance which has impacted on domestic variables.

The third phase

The third stage ran from January 1987 through to the beginning of 1991. This was a period of tranquillity, inflation convergence proceeded and realignment pressure was low, reflected in a narrowing of both the short- and long-term interest rate differentials (Artis and Taylor, 1988).

This phase coincided with the Single European Act (SEA) of 1986, which enshrined the general objectives of the newly expanded EC. The entry of Greece, Spain and Portugal, slow growth and high unemployment combined to make the prospect of further convergence appear precarious. EC budgetary issues and a lack cohesion amongst the (now twelve) members were the main problems of the day. The SEA brought settlement and agreement through its definition of common aims (Collins, 1994).

The main thrust of the Act was a single market for capital, labour, services and goods, which was to be in operation by the end of 1992. As a support structure for this aim other policy targets were set concerning the environment, health and safety at work, research and development in technology fields, and, perhaps, most important in the long run, cooperation in economic policy. In addition important steps and declarations were made in areas such as aid for weaker members and foreign policy collaboration. The SEA also introduced qualified majority voting in certain policy areas. The SEA brought Europe to an impasse. Its free market requirements made for an uneasy alliance with the realignment adverse late 1980s' ERM. The literature written soon after its signing focused on the ability of the ERM to survive under these conditions.

1.4 A FOURTH ERM PHASE

An ambitious directive in 1988 announced the elimination of all exchange controls in eight members by July 1990. This target was met. The SEA committed the members to the creation of a single financial market in Europe by 1992. Much of the literature at the time of the second and third stages was pessimistic about the ERM's ability to survive without capital controls, for example Kenen (1989), Driffill (1988), Bini Smaghi and Micossi (1990), Giavazzi and Giovannini (1989), Giavazzi (1989), and Obstfeld (1988).

What Padao Schioppa (1988) called the "inconsistent quartet" – free trade, full capital mobility, fixed exchange rates, and national monetary policy autonomy – meant that one element of the quartet had to give way if progress was to be made. Padoa Schioppa counselled that autonomous monetary policy should be the element to go. Others suggested that wider bands, modified exchange controls or random realignments should appear (Driffill, 1988; Goodhart, 1990; Giavazzi, 1989).

In fact the stripping away of general capital controls amongst members in 1990 did not have an instant destabilizing effect. This is partly to do with the provisions of the Basle–Nyborg agreement in 1987 which allowed access to the Very Short-Term Financing Facility (VSTFF) for intra-marginal intervention.[12] These provisions were tested in the autumn of 1987 when there was a run on the franc. The Bundesbank lent heavily to France, successfully abating the speculative pressure for devaluation. France repaid Germany after the pressure eased, and well within the new 75-day repayment window (Mayes, 1994). It has been suggested (Currie, 1992) that the agreement was a major step in increasing the credibility of the system.

However, this experience was not shared by all, with Italy providing a particularly good example. Removal of some capital controls in 1987 led to almost immediate speculative pressure, but the size and maturity profile of the Italian debt stock meant that interest rates could not be increased by enough to ward off the attack. The choice was between re-imposition of capital controls or an unjustified devaluation; re-imposition of capital controls won out (Giavazzi, 1989).

Thus the dangers of free capital in a managed exchange rate regime are clear, and were clear at the time. In fact the critics have been proved correct by later events. The bands did have to be increased, but there is still no clear explanation as to why the pressures appeared at the time they did and why the pressures were so widespread (Rose and Svensson, 1993). For an explanation we need to understand the process which led to the Maastricht referenda, and the impact of German re-unification.

German re-unification

The sweeping changes seen in Eastern Europe in the late 1980s had some dramatic impacts on the EC. Beyond the obvious changes in the defence situation, the most important in terms of European monetary integration was the re-unification of Germany.[13]

The way in which shocks are transferred between countries depends on the exchange rate regime in use (Kenen, 1989). In the ERM of the time members were tightly bound together, since the exchange rate was seen as an important aid to disinflation, and was essentially fixed. Therefore as the EC's largest economic member, and hegemon, began to diverge from the average, the consequences for other members were extremely serious. With the reduction in capital controls, the two-way insulation felt by Germany and the rest over monetary policy had diminished.

Siebert (1991) and Owen (1991) explain the general outcomes of re-unification on the ERM countries. On the one hand the expansion of the German economy acted as a "locomotive" to the rest of the Community, whilst on the other the combination of increased government deficits and tight monetary policy increased German interest rates, creating a "brakes-man" effect. Siebert reaches the conclusion that the net effect is a positive spillover for the world economy *in toto*, whereas Owen, using econometric results and data available at the time, shows how the net effect depends on the trade shares and multipliers of each EC country with Germany. Therefore the impact is country specific.

In order to finance the re-unification (without large tax increases) German interest rates increased (see Chauffour *et al.*, 1992, for a discussion of the inconsistency of the fiscal and monetary policy mix at the time), and this coupled with the DM's long-term tendency to appreciate had two main consequences.

First, as realignments were, according to the Delors Committee's gradualist approach to MU, to become less frequent, EMS countries experienced an increase in their interest rates to protect their currency pegs. Secondly, the DM's appreciation tended to drag the ECU zone with it *vis-à-vis* non-EMS currencies, causing a reduction in international competitiveness for the EMS area as a whole.

Giavazzi and Spaventa (1989) point out that initial conditions are important when a disinflation is to occur. The Italian economy disinflated relatively painlessly because companies faced disinflation from a high level of profits, and were able, therefore, to take a reduction in profit margins, without going out of business. The same point applies here. At this stage on the path to MU, member states had achieved convergence to a low level of inflation and interest rates. Therefore the further deflationary forces outlined above were extremely painful for some member states. Chauffour *et al.* (1992) suggest, using the MIMOSA econometric model, that the ERM of the time was the worst possible choice of exchange rate regime, as compared to floating or MU.

The events in Germany, recession, and the perceived popular swing against MU in some member states forced a re-evaluation of the timetable and targets of the Maastricht Treaty whilst the abolition of capital controls created the perfect environment to exploit any weakness.

After the Danish referendum on the Maastricht Treaty in June 1992, the Treaty as a practical vehicle for MU was questioned by financial markets. Prior to the referendum markets assumed convergence of members' economies under the Stages One–Three outlined in the Treaty and the Delors Report. The currency crisis in September 1992, which resulted in the suspension of sterling and the lira from the ERM, and the realignment of the peseta and escudo in November, demonstrated the market's perception regarding the political momentum for MU. 1993 brought continued turbulence in the markets. 30 January saw a 10% devaluation of the punt, to help offset sterling's depreciation. The Bundesbank began to ease key money market rates, but too slowly to help other ERM members as far the markets were concerned. The centre-right victory in the French general elections brought an attempt to reduce French interest rates below their German counterparts, highlighting the French economy's need for lower rates. The market response from around mid-June onwards was to sell francs, the view being that the French would have to lower interest rates and devalue. The result was pressure on other members, resulting in another devaluation for the escudo and peseta on 13 May, and finally a relaxation of the ERM rules on Monday 2 August, with new wider bands of 15%. Following the responses of the central banks to the crisis, the markets had imposed a *de facto* two-speed Europe with core countries seen to be ready for MU, while all other members would have the option to converge at their own speed (Karakitsos, 1994). The relative calm which had prevailed in the ERM for some time was shattered, a fourth ERM phase had begun.

A stark choice was available: either move backwards to looser exchange rates or press on to MU. The former, as Eichengreen (1993) points out forcefully, was viewed as unthinkable because of damage to the CAP, the very idea of integration, and the political economy of the single market.[14] Therefore the only way was forward to MU.

1.5   DELORS AND MAASTRICHT

A year after the SEA became law an EC Summit held at Hanover declared that in adopting the SEA the member states had clearly accepted the aim of economic and monetary union. An agreement was reached to discuss ways of achieving this at the next major summit, to be held in Madrid in 1989. In much the same way as Pierre Werner sixteen years before, Jacques Delors, the then President of the EC Commission, was asked to chair a committee charged with defining the process by which economic and monetary union should be achieved. The resulting report (Committee on the study of Economic and Monetary Union, 1989, hereafter the Delors Report), suggested a detailed plan of action by which MU would be implemented.

Three stages were outlined. Stage I would be concerned with the initiation of the process and greater convergence of economic performance. This was to be achieved through closer coordination within the current framework.

Economic union was to be fostered by the completion of the internal market and more effective regional and structural policies. The process of monetary union was to be begun by the removal of all obstacles to a free single financial market, and by closer cooperation on macroeconomic policies. Exchange rate realignments, whilst still possible, were to be avoided; instead the onus would be on improving the efficacy of other adjustment mechanisms. Furthermore, the report found that it was important to have all members in the ERM by this stage.

The proposals for Stage I required alterations to be made to the Treaty of Rome. Stage II could only begin when this was completed. The focus of Stage II was to set up institutions to facilitate the transition to MU. Policy decision making would remain with the members, but preparations would be made for the final stage when some policy making would be centralised. A European System of Central Banks (ESCB) would be established, which would help coordinate the independent monetary policies through the Committee of Central Bank Governors. At this stage, realignments would occur only in exceptional circumstances. Stage II would also require some foreign exchange reserves to be lodged with the ESCB for intervention purposes, and the ESCB would take over the regulation of the monetary and banking sectors to achieve harmonization.

Stage III would begin with the irrevocable fixing of exchange rates, and the hand over of monetary policy to the ECSB, including foreign exchange interventions in external currencies. The ECSB would further be charged with achieving the required technical changes involved in the transition to a single currency, if the decision to form one was made. Fiscal policy was to be constrained through the use of binding rules on deficits and financing, whilst the fiscal policy of the region as a whole would be a common matter, decided on a majority basis.

The report proffered a step-by-step transition to monetary union, but stressed that acceptance by a member of Stage I implied acceptance of the whole, "the decision to enter upon the first stage should be a decision to embark on the entire process" (Delors Report, 1989, p. 31).[15] It was to be a single process, albeit made up of three steps.

The similarities between the Werner and Delors Reports are obvious, and not surprising, given the nature of their tasks. Delors is more specific about the transition periods, perhaps reflecting the uneasy compromise between the "monetarists" and "economists" of Werner's committee, as opposed to the unanimity of Delors', and more strict about limiting fiscal policy autonomy.

The report was submitted in April 1989, and within two months a date for Stage I (1 July 1990) was agreed (at the Madrid Summit). This date coincided with the removal of capital controls amongst eight of the members.

December 1989 brought the decision for a new intergovernmental conference in order to facilitate the changes required to the Treaty of Rome as a result of the report. The European Council next agreed that the date of the commencement of Stage II should be 1994.

By the time the intergovernmental conference met in December 1990 a great deal of work had already been done. The Committee of the Governors of Central Banks and the Monetary Committee had drafts for the statutes of the European Central Bank (ECB). Two months before the meeting the Commission had published *One Market, One Money* (Commission of the European Communities, 1990), an influential and comprehensive study of the benefits and costs of moving to MU. An impressive momentum had gathered to push through the required legislation, and to begin the process.

The intergovernmental conference concluded with the signing of the Maastricht Treaty in December 1991. The Treaty's provisions for MU echoed the Delors Report relatively closely, although there were some important differences and clarifications. The sheer speed of the Treaty's formation is impressive given the pace traditionally associated with European policy discussions. But this pace has been blamed for creating a ''democratic deficit'' between the technocrats who drafted the Treaty and the public who would have to live under its provisions. Ultimately, after several referenda, the Treaty was ratified by all members.

Stage II began on 1 January 1994. At this time all capital controls were to be removed, and the European Monetary Institute (EMI) set up. The removal of all remaining capital controls was an important step, which has been discussed extensively in the literature. However the Treaty allowed members with a derogation to continue capital controls until the end of December 1995 at the latest.[16]

The EMI was formed to ''strengthen cooperation between the central banks'' of the member states to ensure stable prices. However, unlike the suggestions in the Delors Report for the ESCB's role in Stage II, the EMI's opinions and recommendations are not binding and fiscal discipline is not enforceable.

Stage III is envisaged to occur any time after 31 December 1996. This is the final part of the process, where the issues of interest here are the irrevocable fixing of intra-EC exchange rates, the criteria for selection to be part of MU, and the institutional framework for monetary and fiscal policy within MU.

The Maastricht Treaty makes it clear that MU will begin on 1 January 1999 if no agreement has been reached prior to that date, or the conditions are wrong for an earlier move. The French intention was to bind Germany to a specific date (Tsoukalis, 1993; Goodhart, 1994). The German intention was to ensure that any prospective member of MU had achieved sufficient convergence and displayed the requisite amount of fiscal propriety. The affinity with the earlier arguments between the "monetarists" and "economists" is clear.

The Treaty therefore represented a compromise between a concrete date and clear convergence measures. The so-called "Maastricht convergence criteria" refer to inflation, long-term interest rates, government debt and deficits and the exchange rate. The criteria are unusual in that they have actual reference values attached to them; it is therefore easy to compare a country's performance with what is required.

On the exchange rate front, the Treaty states that in order to make MU a member's exchange rate will have participated in the ERM (narrow band) for two years without "severe tensions". This has been widely regarded as a euphemism for "no unilateral devaluations", although what to make of this requirement is now less clear.

Inflation is meant to follow a path which is no higher than 1.5% of the three best performers for one year before the examination. Interest rates follow the same sort of format: average long-term interest rates must not exceed 2% of the three best inflation performance members for one year. Government deficits and debt levels have absolute reference values of 3% and 60% of GDP respectively, although higher values are permissible if they moving at a "satisfactory" rate toward the reference values.

These reference values have been widely discussed in the literature. The areas which have received most attention have been the fiscal policy measures. There are two facets to the literature, first discussions about the usefulness of these criteria for describing the underlying phenomena, and second the reference values themselves (Buiter *et al.*, 1993; Goodhart, 1994; Eichengreen, 1993). The beauty of the criteria is their interaction: having high interest rates to defend an ERM central parity may well allow one of the requirements to be passed, but is just as likely to break two others – deficit levels and the interest rate measure. This interaction of variables is precisely what make the analysis of convergence non-trivial, especially if non-linearities, for example interest payments on debt, are included, since these affect the path of adjustment over time.

Monetary policy in MU

Monetary policy will be set by the newly formed and independent ECB, although concern was voiced prior and during the intergovernmental conference about the ECB's independence.

The ECB's decision making bodies are the Governing Council and the Executive Board. The Governing Council includes the members of the

Executive Board and the Governors of the national central banks. The President and Vice-President are appointed by "common accord" of the members on the recommendation of the Governing Council, after consultation with the European Parliament and the Governing Council. The appointments will last eight years, and are not renewable.

The ECB will have control over the management of any exchange rate systems with non-Community countries decided upon by the Council of Ministers, and will be able to take part in the formulation of "general orientations" for exchange rate policy with non-Community countries, but these controls are considered secondary to price stability.

Fiscal policy in MU

The prospect of fiscal policy coordination in MU has spawned many papers in the literature on what form it should take, for example Giavazzi and Spaventa (1991), Wyplosz (1991), and Giovannini (1990). Maastricht clarified the form. If a member exceeds the reference values outlined above there are certain steps that will be taken by the Commission. First a report will be compiled, followed by recommendations as to what action is necessary. If these are ignored, the Commission will give notice for action to be taken within a specified time to remedy the situation. If the member still ignores these "requests" then punitive action can be taken. These measures include:

- To require the member to provide additional information, to be specified by the Council, before that member can issue bonds and securities.
- Reconsideration of the European Investment Bank's lending policy towards the member.
- Forcing the member to make a non-interest bearing deposit of an appropriate size with the Community until the deficit has been corrected.
- To impose on the member fines of an appropriate size.

One Market, One Money gives an insight into the Commission's view on the role of fiscal policy in MU. It can be summed up in three words: discipline, autonomy, and coordination. Discipline has been outlined above and takes the form of the limits placed on debts and deficits. The reasoning behind these rules is that financial markets may not be able to successfully limit excessive government spending through increased yields on bonds, and hence may not enforce discipline.

Autonomy is considered important and warranted while asymmetries exist and when country-specific shocks occur. What then of coordination?

One Market, One Money comes to the conclusion that there is no compelling evidence for day-to-day fiscal policy coordination. However it suggests that coordination would be required in two cases: to ensure an appropriate policy mix for the Community in the context of the world economy, and to correct medium-term tendencies for excessive budget deficits.

The Maastricht Treaty is rather vague in this area, reflecting perhaps a general feeling at the time that due to the priority given to convergence, "genuine coordination issues have so far been left in the shade" (*One Money, One Market*, p. 113).

Transition to MU

Clauses 109j(3) and 109j(4) of the Treaty summarize in a few words what could turn into a major disagreement between the member states. No later than 31 December 1996, heads of state or governments will meet, and taking into account reports by the EMI and the Commission (and referring to the Maastricht criteria) decide, by qualified majority, whether a majority of member states fulfil the necessary conditions for the adoption of a single currency, whether it is appropriate to proceed, and if so set a date for Stage III.

Paragraph (4) states that if no date has been set by the end of 1997 the date will be set automatically for 1 January 1999. If this is the case the Council will meet before 1 July 1998 to confirm which members fulfil the conditions. If a state does not fulfil the conditions it does not join Stage III, and becomes a member state with a derogation. At least once every two years, or by request of the member, the Council will examine states' performance, and if by qualified majority[17] it is decided that the state is in accordance with the requirements the derogation will be abrogated, and the state may join MU. So, in summary, if a member does not pass the initial requirements at mid-1998, they will more than likely not make MU by 1999; however they can go on applying *ad infinitum*.

1.6   CONCLUSIONS

Europe has set itself an ambitious agenda: MU by the end of the decade with tough membership requirements. MU is an old aspiration, with a lineage traceable to at least the 1950s. The re-emergence of the idea, set out at Maastricht, grew out of the positive experience of the third ERM phase, evidenced by the gradually tightening ERM approach of Delors. The 1990s'

MU differs little from that on offer in 1970, even though much has changed in the interim. There are two exceptions. The first is the proposal for the transition to MU. The second difference are the concrete membership criteria.

Padoa Schioppa's "inconsistent quartet" created the environment for the collapse of the Delors path, while Germany's re-unification provided the catalyst. If the path itself has been undermined, is it still usable? As discussed in this chapter, the ERM has been seen as many things over its sixteen-year history. It has proved remarkably flexible, and there is no reason to presume that the system will break down totally with a reversion to floating rates; it has merely entered another phase. In a sense, the wide bands confirm the two-tier nature of Europe; some states have taken up the option of using the wider bands, others have continued as if nothing has changed. As long as ERM membership is a requirement for MU selection, then whether a state uses the full width of the new bands or not is irrelevant. What is more important is that all the criteria are met. A tight exchange rate band is one way of converging, but there are others.

The path is thus still usable, but what destination has Maastricht produced? The haste with which Maastricht was created led to the neglect of fiscal policy issues both during the transition and in MU. Stabilization issues, coordination mechanisms and federal coinsurance proposals were all essentially ignored. Instead rigid reference values and punishment protocols were put in place.

The fiscal criteria are explicit, clear and, unfortunately, ad hoc. As Buiter *et al.* (1993) explain in detail, criteria pay no attention to cyclical or national factors. The reference values themselves are also open to criticism – why 3% and 60% for deficits and debts? A 3% deficit with nominal output growth of 5% produces a debt:GDP ratio of exactly 60% (with continuous compounding). The average EU debt ratio in 1991 was around 61%, whilst the Commission's fiscal policy "golden rule", that only capital projects should be financed with borrowing, would have produced a deficit of around 3% of EC GDP on average over the period 1974–91. Applying such a mechanical rule to both membership selection and post-MU fiscal policy would seem both naive and unnecessarily restrictive. A more appropriate selection criterion may be the sustainability of a member's debt position, according to agreed measures and assumptions about growth and inflation, perhaps like those proposed in Blanchard *et al.* (1990).

Furthermore, the criteria ignore stabilization; neither output nor unemployment explicitly appear in Delors' plan, or Maastricht. Ultimately it was excessively tight monetary policy and the resultant recession which brought about the ERM crisis of the early 1990s, essentially a stabilization issue. However, the criteria are in place, and in order to qualify members must satisfy them. They therefore represent the ultimate policy targets of the converging states considered in this book. Chapter 2 considers the initial conditions members are faced with, and demonstrates the wide variation of adjustment required for these targets to be met.

2 Convergence in the EU – A Multispeed Europe?

2.1 INTRODUCTION

The purpose of Chapter 2 is to examine the varying amount of convergence which has taken place amongst EU members since the inception of the ERM in 1979, and to differentiate between members' performances in order to determine whether it is fair to state that Europe is truly multispeed. The chapter does not attempt to explain convergence as a by-product of ERM membership or credibility; it merely attempts to examine the current state of the members, to indicate the amount of adjustment left to do, and to cluster the members into the core, median and peripheral groups discussed in the Introduction to the book.

A working definition of "convergence" for a system of variables is discussed, before the evidence for EU members is examined. The variables examined are the Maastricht criteria, and as a supplement real income convergence receives some attention. The chapter then moves on to group the member states using cluster analysis and pass–failure of the Maastricht criteria as selection tools.

2.2 CONVERGENCE IN THE EU

Anderton *et al.* (1992) define "convergence", in general terms, as "the narrowing of international differences in the development of certain economic variables". It is therefore a vague term which, although easily understood intuitively, tells us little about causation, measurement or, indeed, the variables of importance. It is context-sensitive – for example, the majority of work in the area of the EMS has centred around nominal convergence.

Hall *et al.* (1992) discuss more rigorous measures and define the difference between "strong" and "weak" convergence in a system. An example they give is that of buying exchange rate convergence to a baseline rate by operating sufficiently active interest rate policy; to them this is not convergence in "any meaningful sense" – whilst one element converges

24

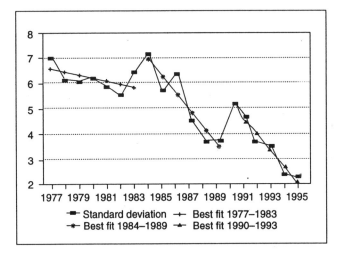

Figure 2.1   Standard deviation of inflation amongst EU-12, 1977–95

the other elements of the system do not. Thus, if there is a vector of variables, X, for countries i and j, Hall *et al.* define strong system convergence to be

$$\lim_{t \to \infty}(X_i - X_j) = \alpha_x \qquad (2.1)$$

for all X over time, where is some arbitrarily small constant. Weak system convergence occurs when some elements of X satisfy the condition, whilst the relationship between the other variables does not change. Therefore when considering convergence in Europe one cannot simply examine single variables.

Figure 2.1 depicts the unweighted standard deviation of the EU-12 member states' inflation rates for each year since 1977. Best fit lines are shown for each of the phases identified in Section 1.3. At first glance, the graph would appear to confirm the anecdotal and econometric evidence in the literature. Phase 1 of the ERM, from 1979 to 1983, is traditionally held to have exhibited very limited convergence, either in nominal or real variables or in policy stances. The best fit line would appear to support this evidence, with the standard deviation amongst members showing some downward trend but nothing very pronounced. The second stage, from 1983 onwards, exhibits a more marked and sustained downward movement, which, after a blip between 1989 and 1990 is continued with an almost identical slope until 1995.

Hence, one might assume that the phases outlined above do explain the stylized facts for the inflation convergence "effect" of the ERM. However, there are two problems with this view. First, the initial period is dominated by the second oil shock, and as Hall *et al.* (1992) point out, "the degree of dispersion may be affected by an external factor which is so strong that it obscures the processes at work on convergence. Examples are an oil price shock and stock market collapse."

Whether the relatively high dispersion observed is caused by differential policy responses, low credibility of a frequently realigned exchange rate target, or by the shock itself is unclear. Secondly, the disinflation following the oil shock was common to most of the industrialised economies, not exclusive to Europe. Again explaining the phenomenon as being a direct by-product of ERM membership is unsound.

Figure 2.2 depicts the same inflation dispersion measure, this time for the G-7. In common with work by, for example, Collins (1988), the phenomenon of inflation convergence is not limited to Europe alone, and in fact best fit lines for the same time periods, produce similar results, albeit that the EU-12 lines are steeper.

However, this slightly negative view about the causes of inflation convergence should not be allowed to obscure the basic fact that the variation of inflation rates amongst the EU-12 is lower now than it has been for at least sixteen years, despite the exchange rate crises in 1992 and 1993. But is this performance spread equally amongst members and has it been reflected in other macroeconomic variables?

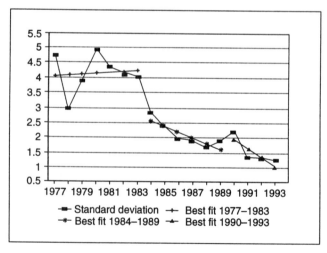

Figure 2.2   Standard deviation of inflation amongst G-7, 1977–93

This first question can be answered by referring to Figures 2.3 and 2.4 which display inflation differentials with respect to Germany for the EU-12.

It is clear from the two graphs that all EMS members have experienced a steadily improving inflation performance *vis-à-vis* Germany, up to the stage

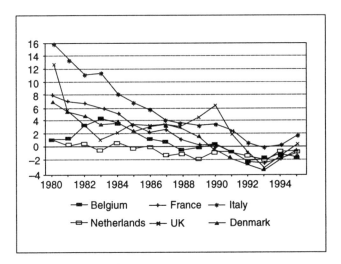

Figure 2.3   Inflation rate differential with Germany (EC-6), 1980–94

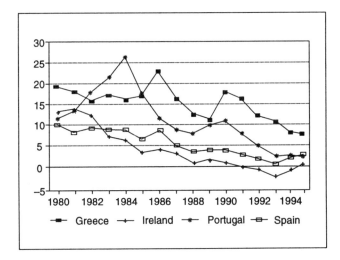

Figure 2.4   Inflation rate differential with Germany (Greece, Ireland, Portugal and Spain), 1980–94

where in 1992 several had lower inflation than Germany. It is also clear that to a certain extent these inflation rates are moving in broadly similar directions. Hence under a fixed exchange rate regime, one might not expect real exchange rate misalignments to increase, although of course they may not improve. However the graphs also indicate that some countries have not succeeded in matching this inflation performance quite so successfully, Greece being the most obvious case.

Hence the first point can be answered; it would appear that in general the reduction in inflation dispersion has been widespread amongst the member states, with some exceptions.

On the second issue, it is instructive to examine a variety of other variables – interest rates, debt: GDP ratios, deficits, and unemployment (see Figures 2.5–2.12). Finally some consideration is given to *per capita* GDP as an indication of the level of real convergence which has been achieved.

The general pattern discerned for inflation is repeated for both long-and short-term interest rates, which mirrors econometric work done by Artis and Taylor (1988). However, the distinction has to be made between interest rate convergence and short-term volatility. Hall *et al.* (1992) find evidence that exchange rate stability and inflation convergence have been gained at the cost of higher interest rate volatility.

This is not the issue in the context of this section; what is important is that there are discernible groups of countries which have differing levels of

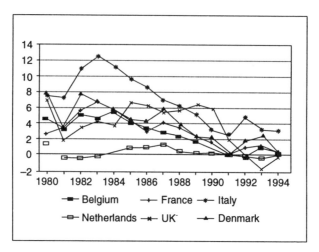

Figure 2.5   Short-term interest rate differential with Germany (EC-6), 1980–94

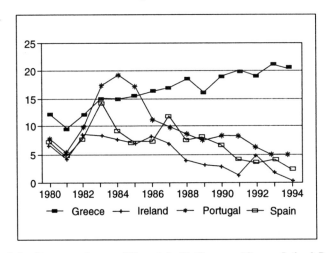

Figure 2.6   Short-term interest differential with Germany (Greece, Ireland, Portugal and Spain), 1980–94

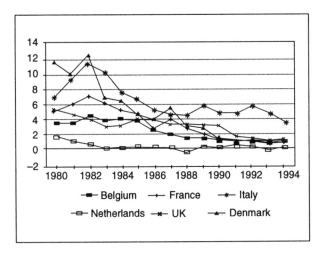

Figure 2.7   Long-term interest rate differential with Germany (EC-6), 1980–94

interest rate convergence with German rates. Once again some member states have not achieved this level of convergence; Greece stands out for both variables, whilst Italy, Spain and Portugal are also outside the high performance group. The difference between the short-and long-term rates around the time of the exchange rate crises is interesting. Whilst short-term rates for the previously high convergence members began to diverge, long-term differentials remained mostly unaffected.

Comparing these data with the inflation graphs in Figures 2.3 and 2.4 is also instructive. Inflation convergence proceeded throughout the period

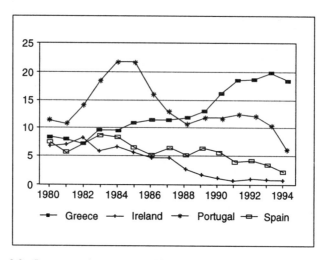

Figure 2.8   Long-term interest rate differential with Germany (Greece, Ireland, Portugal and Spain), 1980–94

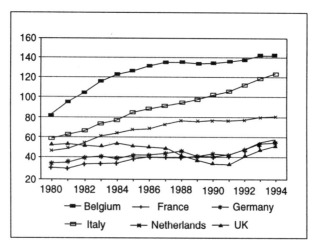

Figure 2.9   Government debt: GDP ratio (EC-6), 1980–94

(although of course the increase in German inflation helped), whilst after 1991 short-term interest rates began to diverge for France, Denmark, Italy, Belgium and Ireland. The Netherlands, the UK and Portugal, Spain and Greece were mostly unaffected, according to this annual data, and for obviously different reasons. Countries which defended their currency pegs

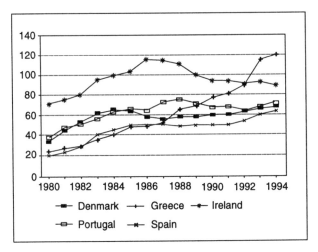

Figure 2.10   Government debt: GDP ratio (Denmark, Greece, Ireland, Portugal and Spain), 1980–94

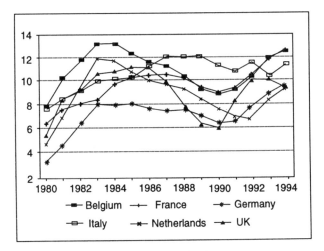

Figure 2.11   Unemployment rate (EC-6), 1980–94

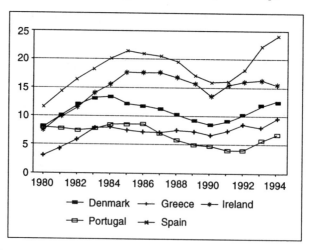

Figure 2.12   Unemployment rate (Denmark, Greece, Ireland, Portugal and Spain), 1980–94

strongly paid the price of higher short-term rates; countries which either devalued (except Ireland) or had very high credibility (the Netherlands) did not. However the divergence experienced in short-term rates around the time of the crises is much lower, for most countries, than the historic difference. Thus, although there was an increase in short-term interest rate differentials, in an historic sense these were small. The fact remains, as for inflation, that interest rate differentials are generally lower than previously.

This general nominal convergence has also been accompanied by a certain amount of convergence in unemployment and government debt. The problem is that the tendency has been for both to grow. Figures 2.9–2.12 depict debt : GDP ratios and standardized unemployment figures for the EU-12 from 1980 to 1994.

Some member states have very high levels of government debt, which, in some cases, do not appear to be stable. Belgium and the Netherlands (Blanchard *et al.*, 1990), according to Figure 2.9, have managed to slow, or halt, the growth rate of debt, whilst Ireland (encouragingly for others) has begun a downward trend. However, to varying degrees, and from varying starting points, the other members (excluding Luxembourg) are experiencing growing debt ratios, although these increases are partially cyclical. According to OECD (1994) data for structural balances, many of these countries would still have been running significant deficits without the downswing in output during the last recession.

Table 2.1 shows the progress made in terms of real convergence as measured by *per capita* GDP in ECU for 1980 and 1992. Since the measure is based on the EU average the closer all members are to 100 the closer the convergence of real incomes is. As can be seen from Table 2.1, this target is some way from being achieved; nevertheless some convergence has occurred. The standard deviations for each of the two years are 24.15 and 22.51 respectively, indicating a slight decrease in the variation across countries.

The evidence suggests, then, that some members have been more successful at achieving convergence than others. In addition, some members have more pressing deficit and debt problems than others, implying a constraint on the conduct of policy. Earlier we asked if the two were linked by applying cluster analysis to the members using the Maastricht criteria data for 1994, and suggested that there was a *de facto* multispeed Europe based on the members' current macroeconomic performance.

Table 2.1 Per capita GDP, 1980 and 1992 and unemployment in Europe, 1980 and 1994

| Year/Country | Per capita GDP | | Index[1] | | Unemployment | |
	1980	1992	1980	1992	1980	1994
Austria	14128	17466			1.6	4.4
Belgium	14158	17435	114.6	113	7.9	12.6
Denmark	14233	17624	115.2	114.2	7	12
Finland	12840	14857			4.7	18.3
France	15371	18298	124.4	118.6	6.3	12.6
Germany	15635	17265	126.5	111.9	3.2	9.6
Greece	8486	9608	68.7	62.3 ·	2.8	9.7
Ireland	8399	12496	68	81	7.3	15.8
Italy	13729	17290	111.1	112.1·	7.7	11.4
Luxembourg	15088	21059	122.1	136.5·	0.7	2.4
Netherlands	14050	16547	113.7	107.2	4.7	9.3
Norway	13504	17236			1.7	5.5
Portugal	6869	9230	55.6	59.8	8	6.8
Spain	9662	12786	78.2	82.9	11.5	24.3
UK	12592	15520	101.9	100.6	5.3	9.4

Note: 1. Index of Average of EU-12 for each year.
Source: OECD.

2.3   A MULTISPEED EUROPE?

The provisions of the Maastricht Treaty allow some member states to opt out of the 1999 "automatic" MU, whilst others will be excluded if they do not meet the criteria in time. The EMS functioned for many years with members not taking part in the ERM or taking part with differing band widths. The SEA provisions to promote regional homogeneity bear testimony to the fact that Europe is made up of economies with differing performances and economic structures. It is clear, therefore, that the idea of a multispeed Europe has been implicitly and explicitly recognized for some time. The above examples and debates about variable geometry and two-tier systems all point to the acceptance that not only do members differ in their economic performance and structures, but that this difference must allow them different speeds of adjustment. This view was endorsed in the Delors Report, which recommended "allowing a degree of flexibility concerning the date and conditions on which some members would join certain arrangements" (para 44).

Dornbusch (1990, 1991) drew attention to, what for him, was an obvious fact, that there are three groups of members in the EU. This view is echoed elsewhere, for example Tsoukalis (1993) and Russo (1989). Dornbusch uses inflation as the quantitative knife to carve out his groups; he has a core group of hard currency nations – Germany, the Netherlands, Austria and Switzerland (and presumably France although it is not explicitly stated) – a second tier where inflation is moderate, but higher than the first group, made up of Belgium, Ireland, the UK and possibly Italy. Finally his third group consists of high inflation countries – Greece, Portugal and Spain.

Tsoukalis grades his groups by a mix of inflation and time spent in the narrow or wide band of the ERM. Hence his groupings are slightly different; the seven original members of the narrow band ERM form the first, the wide band group, the UK, Italy and Spain, form the second, and finally, at the time he wrote, Greece and Portugal, with double digit inflation and unpegged exchange rates, form the third.

We propose a different method of grouping the members of the EU. In the context of the book the aim of grouping is to clearly define countries which have reached certain stages on the road to high convergence. With this in mind data for the Maastricht criteria are used as the raw data, and cluster analysis is used as the grouping tool. Cluster analysis compares members of a population on the basis of defined variables. It groups members according to how "close" the variables are to each other, using an arbitrary distance measure, for example Euclidean. If there are n members with m describing variables for each, the Euclidean distance, d, between two members is defined as

$$d = \sqrt{\sum_{i=1}^{m} (a_i - b_i)^2} \qquad (2.2)$$

where a and b are the corresponding values of each variable for each member. Of course there are numerous generalizations of the above (see Aldendorfer and Blashfield, 1984).

The algorithm begins with n clusters (i.e. each individual member forms a cluster), and defines an $n \times n$ distance matrix. The algorithm then searches the matrix for the nearest pair of clusters. These two clusters are merged, forming a new cluster, and the distance matrix is updated. This process is repeated $n - 1$ times, until all members are in one cluster. Since the process repeats until there are no more individuals, there is no "natural" number of groups. Instead one can limit the amount of groups and stop the algorithm when the desired amount of groups has been defined.

When a cluster has more than one element (i.e. sub-cluster) there are several methods of measuring the distance between clusters – single linkage (minimum distance, where the closest members in each cluster are used); complete linkage (maximum distance, where the farthest apart members are used); and average linkage (where the average linkage between each member of the two clusters is used). There are numerous refinements of these methods available.

It should be clear that cluster analysis is not the most rigorous of statistical methods. In fact, there is no statistical assumption made about the underlying population of cases. Therefore there is no right or wrong way to form groups through cluster analysis. However it is a useful tool for thinking in a structured way about the nature of the similarities between groups of similar members.

Since the data set to be used contains widely differing types of numbers for the four variables, for example, debt ratios of over 100% and inflation figures of less than 5%, the data were re-scaled, so as to give a common basis for measuring the deviation for each variable, and to stop any one variable dominating the others. Various clustering methods were used, with little variation in results.

Using annual data for 1994 and assuming three groups, clustering produces the results shown in Table 2.2.[1] Increasing the amount of groups to four leaves groups 2 and 3 undisturbed, but removes Belgium from group 1 to its own group. Further expansion to 5 groups merely moves Italy to its own group. The basic membership of the three groups therefore seems fairly robust.

Table 2.2   Cluster analysis output, 1994 data, three groups

Group 1	Group 2	Group 3
Belgium	Italy	Greece
Denmark	Portugal	
France	Spain	
Germany		
Ireland		
Netherlands		
UK		

The overriding message of this analysis is that the difference between Greece and the rest is relatively large for 1994 data. Within the other groups, Denmark, the Netherlands, Germany and Ireland are closely packed. France and the UK form their own group, but very close to the first. Belgium is on her own, but not terribly removed from the rest. Meanwhile, Portugal and Spain are very similar, Italy is closer to these two than the rest, whilst as a group these three are a reasonable distance from the core.

Why are these groupings important? The point of the exercise is to show in the simplest and broadest way that members of the EU are not currently producing similar macroeconomic performance, nor have they done in the last decade, as discussed above. This truism is important when one begins to consider both the transitional and operating arrangements envisaged for MU, the ultimate target for (most of) the member states. It is clear from the data that each member faces a different set of problems if it is to pass the Maastricht criteria test. On the one hand, Greece could not contemplate membership of the ERM at this point, due to inflation and massive debt; how, then, to overcome these problems and join? On the other hand, Italy, a member of the system for some time, finds itself facing a debt crisis of frightening proportions, whilst Portugal and Spain face persistent inflation differentials coupled with growing deficits. For these countries, the question is not so much how to form or run a monetary union, but how to qualify for one. For the rest of the members, their level of convergence as measured by the Maastricht criteria is enough for them to seriously consider questions about monetary union, not so much about passing the criteria tests (Belgium being the exception).

By splitting the members in this way we can focus on the issues for each. Of course there are overlaps, and each member has a unique set of circumstances to deal with. However there is enough commonality in their levels of convergence for the pertinent questions to have some meaning to each member of each group (see Bradley *et al.*, 1995, for a discussion of the similarities between the peripheral countries). The groupings are generally similar to Dornbusch's and Tsoukalis', and make intuitive sense.

Table 2.3 shows the data used for the cluster analysis whilst Table 2.4 subjects the data to the Maastricht criteria rules. Some interesting points are immediately apparent. The trend groupings seen in the cluster analysis is generally followed in the "Score out of 4" column (Table 2.4). Greece, Portugal, Spain or Italy cannot manage to score more than 1 point out of the possible 4. Every other member, including the new ones, scores more than 2, but very few score a perfect 4. A second fact appears very clearly; the predomination of passes in the inflation and interest rate columns are impressive, whilst the deficit and debt column tell a more depressing tale. It is clear, therefore, where the need for adjustment lies.

Table 2.3   Maastricht criteria variables, values for 1994

	CPI inflation rate	Interest rates[1]	Deficit	Debt[2]
Austria	2.9	6.8	−4.2	58.1
Belgium	2.4	7.8	−5.3	142
Denmark	2	7.9	−4.2	68.2
Finland	1.1	9	−4.6	70.9
France	1.7	7.6	−5.7	56
Germany	3	7	−2.7	53.2
Greece	10.9	26	−13.1	121
Ireland	2.3	8.1	−2.3	88.2
Italy	4.1	10.6	−9.7	123
Luxembourg	2.2	5.7[3]	1.1	
Netherlands	2.8	7	−3.8	78.8
Norway	1.4	7.5	−1.3	46.7
Portugal	5.2	13.5	−7.1	71.6
Spain	4.7	9.8	−6.8	64
UK	2.5	8.2	−6.9	51.8

Notes: 1. Long-term rates.
2. General government gross financial liabilities (does not correspond exactly with Maastricht measure of debt).
3. Short-term rate.
Sources: IMF (col. (1)); OECD (col. (2)); OECD (col. (3)); OECD (col. (4)); Barclays Bank (Luxembourg data in col. (2)).

Table 2.4   Maastricht criteria, pass–fail

	CPI inflation rate[1]	Interest rates[2]	Deficit[3]	Debt[4]	Score out of 4
Austria	Pass	Pass	Fail	Pass	3/4
Belgium	Pass	Pass	Fail	Fail	2/4
Denmark	Pass	Pass	Fail	Fail	2/4
Finland	Pass	Pass	Fail	Fail	2/4
France	Pass	Pass	Fail	Pass	3/4
Germany	Fail	Pass	Pass	Pass	3/4
Greece	Fail	Fail	Fail	Fail	0/4
Ireland	Pass	Pass	Pass	Fail	3/4
Italy	Fail	Fail	Fail	Fail	0/4
Luxembourg	Pass	Pass	Pass	Pass	4/4
Netherlands	Pass	Pass	Fail	Fail	2/4
Norway	Pass	Pass	Pass	Pass	4/4
Portugal	Fail	Fail	Fail	Fail	0/4
Spain	Fail	Pass	Fail	Fail	1/4
UK	Pass	Pass	Fail	Pass	3/4

Notes: 1. Pass if less than 2.9% based on $1/3(1.1 + 1.4 + 1.7) + 1.5$.
2. Pass if less than 10% based on $1/3(9 + 7.6 + 7.5) + 2$.
3. Pass if less than 3%.
4. Pass if less than 60%.

2.4   CONCLUSIONS

Chapter 2 has reviewed the general convergence trends in the EU since the formation of the ERM, and has shown the differing performances of the member states. Whilst all members have experienced some nominal convergence, there is a wide variation in performance. Fiscal measures have shown an upward trend, with some members faced with extremely large debts, raising the issue of stability. Thus, whilst the ERM does seem to have promoted convergence of monetary policies, it does not seem to have promoted fiscal stability. It would appear that whilst nominal convergence has proceeded, real convergence has not; *per capita* GDP measures still exhibit large differentials.

Using cluster analysis based on data for the Maastricht criteria, groupings were found for the EU-12 of 1994. The groupings are generally robust to the specification of the clustering and to increasing the amount of groups. This demonstrates that, as far as the Maastricht criteria variables go, different groups do exist, and that they face different issues and problems. Applying the Maastricht tests supports this evidence; some members fail on all counts, whilst in general a large number pass for inflation and interest rates, but fail for the fiscal measures. The scale of the fiscal problems for some members, and inflation differentials for others, indicates that the likelihood of being in the first selection for MU is small. The suggestion is therefore that the EU is made up of multiple tiers of members, and that therefore flexibility is required in terms of convergence policy for each, and the timing of membership of the various stages. If the EU does have outliers, they must be allowed to interact with Europe at their own pace.

The countries selected to represent each group are, for the core (Group 1), France and Germany; for the median (Group 2), Spain; and for the periphery (Group 3), Greece.

3 Issues in the Three Stages of Convergence

3.1 ISSUES IN THE BOOK

Chapter 2 presented evidence as to the multispeed nature of the European integration process. If one imagines convergence as a continuum between two arbitrary end points then the economies of Europe would be spread out along the continuum.

In the context of modern European convergence, the high convergence end point is represented by MU. To be eligible for MU a country must pass the criteria discussed in Section 1.5. Therefore the dimensions of the continuum are the Maastricht criteria. Since the economies considered in this book have all ratified the Treaty it is assumed that they are all committed to entering MU at some stage. There are then two general questions. First, what particular attributes should MU have? Second, how to achieve the Maastricht criteria and thus qualify for MU?

The evidence presented in Chapter 2 indicated a wide divergence amongst the members *vis-à-vis* the Maastricht criteria. This suggests that the proper approach is to break the questions up and address them to those countries or groups which have the most to gain from the answers. Essentially it is a question of who will face what, and when? It would seem unlikely that MU would be formed without France and Germany, less likely that Greece would be included at an early stage.

European monetary integration has generated an enormous literature. The main areas of research have centred on the suitability of Europe as a single currency area, the transition to and formation of MU, the functioning of the ERM, credibility, disinflation and the ERM, public finance issues, and the benefits and costs of fixed versus flexible exchange rates.

The research can be classified as in Table 3.1, where each stage on the road to MU is characterized by one of the groups discussed in Chapter 2.

The spread of literature over these topics is variable. In some cases, for example credibility and the cost of disinflation, the literature is very large, whilst in others the coverage is sparse or non-existent. The obvious interrelations between the three areas of research, fiscal and monetary policy and the wage–price sector indicate why the literature has tended to concentrate on individual topics for the three country groups. For example,

Table 3.1   Summary of the main research issues in the literature

	Core group (MU)	Median group (transition to MU)	Peripheral group (ERM and disinflation)
Fiscal policy	Discipline or active stabilization?	Disinflation and debt: role of the Maastricht criteria	Disinflation and debt: seigniorage losses
Monetary and exchange rate policy	Targets and indicators Timing of MU "Euro" policy credibility	What targets, tight or loose ERM credibility	Timing of ERM entry and parity choice
The wage–price sector	Effect of converging or single wage–price sector	Liberating and enhancing flexibility	Credibility

issues about credibility and disinflation for high inflation countries have been looked at without paying attention to the impact on public finance. On the other hand, studies which have examined the impact of disinflation on public finances have ignored credibility. Federal fiscal policy in MU is another example: the interactions between a common monetary policy and national fiscal policies need to be considered together in a multi-country framework, yet this has not been achieved. Any study which attempts to take any one of these issues into account, must, by necessity consider other related variables and policies at the same time.

The methodology adopted in this book allows this requirement to be fulfilled. It is dynamic, multi-country, and flexible enough for both the stylized facts and relevant interactions to be included.

Which MU?

European MU will entail the creation of either irrevocably fixed exchange rates or a single currency, and thus a single monetary policy set by a European central bank (ECB). The gains from European MU have been quantified by many; a good, if somewhat optimistic, example is the Commission's Report *One Market, One Money* (Commission of the European Communities, 1990). These gains accrue from two sides, a one-off gain from the elimination of foreign exchange transaction costs of the order of 0.25 to 0.20% of European GDP, and dynamic gains from the elimination of exchange risks of the order of 2% of European GDP. The latter gain is closely linked with the Single Market process and represents such effects as induced investment as the equilibrium capital stock expands. This is an appreciable saving, but many authors, for example Hughes Hallett and Vines (1993), have raised the issue of whether MU will cause losses which could be of a large enough magnitude to overwhelm these gains.

These worries stem from the fear that Europe is not an Optimal Currency Area (OCA). Therefore asymmetric shocks which impact on the union could, since the exchange rate and sovereign monetary policy have gone, increase the time required for adjustment, or increase the size of the required adjustment. The answer has been, since the time of Mundell (1961), McKinnon (1963), and especially Kenen (1969), that if labour markets are inflexible and migration low, fiscal policy must "take up the slack". Proposals for US-style federal fiscal systems have received varied attention in the literature, but have not appeared in the Maastricht Treaty (Branson, 1990). Indeed the Treaty, in a sense, goes the other way by placing upper limits on the amount of government debt outstanding and the size of deficits. The reasoning behind this is that fiscal freedom could place untoward pressure on the ECB to "bail out" governments with debt problems, therefore pressure must be brought to bear on offenders with high or unsustainable debt positions. Markets, it has been argued, cannot perform this limiting role, and may not be able to distinguish between government bonds with high default risk and those with low. Thus, a debt crisis in Italy, within a MU, could lead to unjustified crises in other member states (Eichengreen, 1993; Frenkel and Goldstein, 1991; Bovenberg *et al.*, 1991; McKinnon, 1990; Goodhart, 1992b).

As a result, Europe is facing the possibility of a common currency by the end of the decade, with low labour mobility, inflexible labour markets, and little consensus on how fiscal policy should be determined.

The question "which MU?" refers to the method by which fiscal, monetary and exchange rate policy should be set. The focus is on creating policy rules or regimes which minimise the cost of giving up intra-European exchange rates under a variety of shocks. It must also be borne in mind that decisions amongst the members of MU will have an impact on non-members. It is feasible that MU could bring less stability in macroeconomic variables, which would be transmitted to the peripheral or median groups. In this case being left out of MU, but being committed to enter at some stage, and thereby continuing membership of the ERM, would incur a cost.

The work centres around core fiscal policy. A variety of regimes are examined, being modelled in a stylized fashion. First, a stylization of the

Table 3.2   Utility function outcomes for different MUs

	Core			
Periphery	MU_1 P_1,C_1	MU_2 P_2,C_2	MU_{n-1} P_{n-1},C_{n-1}	MU_n P_n,C_n

projected *Maastricht regime* would impose strict upper limits on the levels of government deficits and debts. This would limit the possibility of activist fiscal policy. Second, an easier regime where some *output stabilizing fiscal policy* could be implemented. Finally a *federal fiscal policy scheme* is modelled. In this regime, a federal budget is created which receives a small amount of revenue from the members, from which it spends according to each member's individual requirements. These various regimes are shocked in order to compare their ability to overcome welfare losses as measured by an objective function. All simulations are compared to the non-activist Maastricht regime. We then have a method of determining benefits and costs by looking at the differences between welfare over time.

The relationship between the core's decision on the form of MU and its effect on the non-members can be summarised with the aid of Table 3.2. The core countries can decide which regime they wish to adopt, whilst the periphery country is passive in this decision, taking whichever regime is adopted by the core as the policy framework within which it must work.

P_1 refers to the Periphery's pay-off under strategy MU_1 by the Core, C_1 refers to the Core's. These pay-offs are determined by the objective functions that each country operates under. Table 3.2 is repeated for each shock in order to ascertain which regime performs best for each country under asymmetric and symmetric demand and supply shocks.

There are several essential aspects to modelling these issues if the results are to have any plausible meaning. First, the attempt to differentiate between the three countries in terms of their economic structures is important. Second, the implementation of the fiscal policy rules must capture the essence of the real policy options. Third, the modelling of monetary union itself raises important issues about the ECB's targets, which have not been properly examined in the literature.

Taking each point in turn, the approach of Levine (1993) and Hughes Hallett and Vines (1993) is to employ simple two-country simulation models with perfectly symmetrical economies and to then use dynamic optimization techniques to model fiscal policy. Whilst this approach has borne fruitful insights into the important role fiscal policy has to play within a MU, it is essential to examine the result when economies of different sizes and different response characteristics are examined. The *ex ante* expectation would be that the results would still hold, but that the differing sizes of the economies would lead to qualitatively different results due to the size of spillover effects from each country's fiscal policy, and the impact of each country on MU monetary policy.

On the second point, Hughes Hallett and Vines, and Levine, do not derive, or at least present, clear policy lessons for how fiscal policy should adjust, whilst Masson and Melitz (1990) use extremely simple policy rules selectively to target, for example, the current account in the case of France, and the inflation rate in the case of Germany. The latter study presents evidence that under certain conditions, i.e. differing objective functions and initial conditions for France and Germany, the retention of fiscal freedom is warranted, although when these different objectives clash externalities will emerge which could be substantially reduced through coordination. However, despite the elegance of the work, no clear policy prescription is given, nor are methods of coordination considered, a point the authors acknowledge. None of these studies examine the possibility of "coordination" through some sort of federal policy.

Two studies which do examine federal policy in a stabilization role appear in the *European Economy* supplement "Report and Studies on the Economics of Community Public Finance" (Commission of the European Communities, 1993), a timely examination of the issue after the concentration on monetary aspects in *One Market, One Money*. The first paper, by Italianer and van Heukelen (1993) suggests a possible scheme for a federal system, which offsets regional unemployment changes by a fixed amount of a central grant. They find that levels of stabilization seen in the USA[1] can be replicated with a budget which, based on historical data, would be around 0.2% of EU GDP. Whilst this is a concrete policy suggestion they are not able to examine either the financing of this scheme, or its dynamic effects. The second paper by Pisani-Ferry *et al.* (1993), illustrates the working of the federal system in France, Germany and the USA by building small calibrated simulation models of these countries. They find that the degree of centralised stabilization is less than previously thought, indicating that MU may not require a large-scale federal budget to remain viable. This paper's focus is to reassess existing federal states' stabilization properties in line with the traditional approach in the literature which has been to examine the experience of existing federal states, not to assess a European MU's needs. Instead, the implication from these two papers is that MU should somehow attempt to replicate existing federal systems. Whilst this may well be the case, there have been no attempts to apply these concepts to an empirical simulation model of a MU in order to assess which policies are stable and the amount of stabilization which is possible.

In summary, therefore, the literature has examined the issue of fiscal policy in MU on two fronts. First, the issue of fiscal flexibility within an MU and, second, the possibility of a federal fiscal policy and suggestions as to what form it should take. The shortcomings of the work to date have been simplifications of either the representation of the economies, the fiscal policies, or the inclusion of dynamic effects.

On the final point, empirical papers which compare MU with the ERM and floating regimes, for example, Masson and Symansky (1993), Annex E of *One Market, One Money*, Minford *et al.* (1991) and Whitley (1992), have assumed that the ECB will target some weighted average of the national economies' inflation rates which, if the consumer price index is used, is wrong. The appropriate measure is developed and used in the research.

Transition to MU

For the median group, membership of the ERM is taken as given. What is of more importance is completing the process of disinflation and convergence. Faced with high levels of unemployment, and in some cases growing public debts, the challenge is to find an appropriate fiscal and monetary policy mix. In order for this to occur successfully there are two important criteria. First, the cost of converging to core inflation levels cannot be allowed to worsen an already bad employment situation (particularly in Spain), second, it cannot be done at the cost of higher debts, since success in the inflation criterion would be worthless if it entailed failing the debt criterion.

Furthermore in a free capital Europe an important issue for these countries is that of maintaining the peg. But the widening of the ERM bands may offer an opportunity, in a possibly counterintuitive way, to achieve the criteria. By altering the monetary policy rule, reducing the weight given to the exchange rate target, the debt problem may be attenuated as interest rates decline.

The Delors approach to MU, enshrined in the Maastricht Treaty, is gradualist, with each successive stage building on the last. To this extent it followed the earlier Werner Report plans. This gradualist approach envisages ever-increasing levels of convergence before MU actually begins. The deadline date in the Treaty ensures that this process is bounded. The dangers involved in continuing *à la* Delors have been identified for some time, Padoa Schioppa summed it up well (see Section 1.4): the approach of slow, gradual reduction in macroeconomic divergences fails when faced with an adverse economic environment and mutually inconsistent "rules of the game".

The initial fears in the late 1980s about an ERM collapse have been proved correct. The question therefore remains, how to proceed to MU if the ever-tightening ERM approach is out of the question? The members themselves have chosen differing answers and routes – contrast the response of the UK and Italy with that of France – and the widely varying nature of the authorities' responses are clear.

The question is: do these differing responses endanger the convergence already achieved and that required or, put another way, do they promote divergence and threaten subsequent MU membership? On the other hand, it has been argued (see, for example, Eichengreen, 1993) that the most compelling reason for MU stems from political economy considerations due to the Single Market process. This argues that large swings in exchange rates in a Single Market going through transition could lead to pressure to abandon the Single Market. We would attach a rider to this. If the transition to MU is excessively painful or unstable then the commitment to MU may be abandoned, and thus, via Eichengreen's argument, the Single Market.

To formalize the argument, one can make the distinction between stabilization policies and convergence policies. Whilst the two are not mutually exclusive, under certain shocks and conditions, for example German re-unification, the two objectives can clash, resulting in pressure to abandon the convergence policy. Once convergence is viewed in this manner important issues relating to the authority's targets are raised. It would appear obvious that for a converging country the targets in the objective function would be the Maastricht criteria; however, these do not include output or unemployment. Therefore, objective functions which target convergence do not necessarily imply stabilization, as it is commonly understood. There is therefore the possibility for conflict between the two policy objectives of convergence and stabilization. Any policy mix which is put in place in order to achieve convergence must thus have two characteristics. First the convergence objectives must be attainable and clearly stated, and second the policy mix should define how to stabilize the economy on its convergence path, and indeed what are the stabilization targets. On the one hand the policy regime defines how convergence is to be achieved, but on the other it also defines how shocks to the system will be treated.

In order to implement this approach to policy selection we consider the case of a country inside the ERM which has achieved a certain amount of convergence, but which still has some way to go. The questions addressed centre around the "tightness" of the exchange rate target given the need for fiscal consolidation. Since the ERM bands have widened to 15% either side of the central parity rate the opportunity exists for ERM members to pursue other targets with monetary policy, or to reduce the weight attached to the exchange rate target.

Two regimes are considered which promote convergence and fiscal consolidation, but which have varying weights attached to stabilization. The first regime is labelled a "narrow band" ERM. In this regime the exchange rate target is the dominant target for monetary policy, with output and inflation taking a lesser role. The second regime is a "wide band" ERM, where the weight attached to the exchange rate target is reduced, whilst the weights attached to inflation and output remain unchanged. For both regimes the tax rate is adjusted to hit the Maastricht criteria debt target. The question is: which regime achieves the best mix of convergence and stabilization? The two regimes are compared on the basis of their ability to meet the Maastricht criteria and to stabilize output and inflation. Furthermore, the two regimes are subjected to shocks in order to further assess their stabilization and convergence properties.

The country used as the representative in the median group is Spain. The reasoning is three-fold. First, Spanish unemployment levels are high, second the government debt and deficit situation deteriorated during the last downturn and, third, inflation convergence is not complete. The first aspect, unemployment, could suggest that any option to pursue other monetary policy targets, namely output or unemployment, might be attractive to the Spanish authorities. The latter two refer to the Maastricht Criteria. The extent of the deterioration in public finances is such that Spain now misses the Maastricht criteria for these variables, whilst reference to Table 2.3 (p. 37) indicates that the inflation target has not been achieved either.

Whilst the literature has concentrated on issues such as transitional mechanisms to MU, convergence, debt sustainability, and the Maastricht criteria themselves, little has been done to integrate each of these elements into a general equilibrium environment. By using a numerical simulation approach we can treat the issues in a fully dynamic and encompassing environment.

This approach to convergence policy making gives a better insight into the most successful policy mix to be chosen in order to promote successful convergence, and thus MU. It is unique in the sense that it clearly differentiates between stabilization issues and convergence, which has not been the case in the literature so far.

The timing of ERM entry

Greece represents the peripheral country in the study. The Greek problems are high inflation, stubborn deficits and a soaring debt. Furthermore, Greece has not yet participated in the ERM. Greece fails the Maastricht criteria on every count, and thus to be considered for MU much needs to be done. The problem of combining a serious debt position with the contemplation of ERM entry has not been adequately dealt with in the literature. For Greece, the loss of seigniorage revenue, and the wider fiscal implications of reducing inflation whether inside or outside the ERM, is important. Possibly the most important question is not the timing of entry to the ERM in order to minimize output costs, but timing in order to avoid an unsustainable debt path. The issue of credibility is also addressed, as is the danger of overestimating the level of credibility when forming policy.

Little has been done to address the question of at what point during a disinflation a country should join the ERM. Discussion of such practical issues as the timing of disinflation and fiscal consolidation is not extensive. Such literature as there is presents two views. On the one hand advocates of early ERM entry propose that the anti-inflation credibility increases resulting from membership, coupled with some form of wage freeze, would be enough to reduce inflation to close to the ERM average swiftly; this is the "tying hands" hypothesis (Giavazzi and Pagano, 1988). Moreover, adherents of this view suggest that membership would compel the fiscal authorities to act responsibly which, given a high debt position, they have failed to do in the past. Membership of the ERM forces the responsible authorities to undertake the structural change required in fiscal policy setting, otherwise, in a free capital world, speculative attacks would force an ERM exit. Alogoskoufis (1993) is representative of this approach.

This sort of membership proposal can be characterised as "shock treatment"; it relies, for success, on the right sort of reputational effects taking place. Essentially, credibility must be extremely high for this to work. Otherwise interest rates would rise, not fall, exacerbating the debt problem, not solving it. Furthermore experience with wage freezes does not indicate that this would be a successful way of stopping wage inflation for good.

Papademos (1993) presents the counter view. In his world, inflation expectations do not adjust as fast under regime changes as in Alogoskoufis'. Papademos also points out that deficit restructuring has to take place before the drop in inflation, otherwise the revenue losses associated with the disinflation lead to a higher deficit. Papademos suggests that the proper way forward is to start the disinflation and stabilize debt *before* ERM membership. When inflation has reached some arbitrary differential from either the average or highest rate in the ERM, membership should commence.

The argument hinges on the response of the economy to the policy choice and the objective function of the policy maker. If inflation expectations are slow to adjust and the market perceives the exchange rate commitment to be weak then a transitory loss of output may result, and the debt ratio will increase. On the other hand, if the private sector believes that the inflationary process has been permanently changed, lower inflation expectations will result without an output loss. The critical determinant of which response is more likely is credibility.

There are two closely linked aspects to credibility in the ERM: the anti-inflation credibility of the government and the credibility of the exchange rate target. If the exchange rate target is seen as a signalling mechanism to wage bargainers, then an incredible target will not result in a more flexible labour market. There is a second and important aspect related to the sustainability of the exchange rate target, which could be viewed in terms of deviations from the fundamental equilibrium exchange rate (FEER), and internal equilibrium (as measured by the NAIRU, for example). A clearly misaligned exchange rate would result in internal disequilibrium, and thus put pressure on the exchange rate target through increased risk premia. If this is the case it is unlikely that the exchange rate target will be viewed as credible (in terms of longevity) by the private sector.

It is argued that joining a regime such as the ERM can help reduce the cost, in terms of output or employment, of disinflation. The theory is quite simple: costs are associated with disinflation due to downward wage rigidity. The literature explains rigidity in numerous ways, and the issue goes to the heart of the neo-Classical, Keynesian debate.

On the one hand wage rigidity could be explained by friction in the operation of the labour market due, for example, to contracts, information availability, union power and coordination failures. Another view explains the problem by viewing the wage bargaining process as a game between the authorities and unions, with inflation expectations causing the wage rigidity. If the authorities have a low reputation for inflation control, or an incentive to renege on a low inflation pledge, then the credibility of any inflation target is small, unions observe this and alter their inflation expectations as a result.[2] It is essentially an issue of the time inconsistency of policy: what may be optimal now may not, given the policy maker's preferences, be optimal later (Frenkel *et al.*, 1989). The way to avoid this excessive inflation equilibrium is to find a method of credibly committing the authorities to the announced anti-inflation policy, to create binding rules.

Numerous suggestions have been made to solve this reputational problem. Rogoff (1985) suggests that the appointment of a "conservative"[3] central banker may create the necessary credibility and hence low inflation expectations on the part of the private sector. However, once the banker has instigated the disinflation programme the temptation to renege and reflate is still present and can be achieved simply by replacing the conservative banker.

Another suggestion centres around the EMS. By committing themselves to the disinflationary external target, the argument runs, the authorities can solve the reputational problem. In the case of the asymmetric ERM, a credible commitment to the regime implies acceptance of the Bundesbank's monetary policy stance. Since it is generally accepted that the Bundesbank has the highest level of anti-inflation reputation in Europe, the ERM member gains the most by following its lead. The wage bargaining process takes into account the Bundesbank's reputation for not reneging and alters its inflation expectations accordingly. Applications of this game theoretic approach to the EMS are legion. Melitz (1988), Giavazzi and Pagano (1988), Giavazzi and Giovannini (1989), Weber (1992), Gros (1990), Begg and Wyplosz (1987), Andersen and Risager (1988), Horn and Persson (1988) present typical examples of the approach.

According to the game theoretic view, the sacrifice ratio involved in deflating can be reduced by joining the ERM instead of undertaking the disinflation outside the ERM. The difference between the two stems from the argument that joining an international exchange rate regime binds the authorities more tightly than a domestic policy initiative (see Begg and Wyplosz, 1987; De Grauwe, 1992). This premise is based on the level of reputation cost involved in reneging, said to be higher in the ERM due to factors such as the visibility of failure (a devaluation is more obvious than an unannounced increase in the inflation target), the fact that a devaluation of the exchange rate has wider implications than increased inflation, for example, the workings of the CAP[4], and the notion of ''saving face'' in an international environment.

There is little empirical evidence to support the claims of the theory. Collins (1988), Dornbusch (1989), and Giovannini (1990) all point out the lack of supportive evidence. Collins (1988) takes data from before and after the introduction of the ERM, and finds little evidence to support the claim that credibility effects played the main part in the disinflation of the 1980s. Anderton *et al.* (1992) examine European labour markets as a way of explaining the convergence that has occurred. They find evidence that there has been a downward shift in the ''wage inflation processes'' during the last decade. However, this is not a result of credibility, in their view, but rather structural changes caused by institutional reforms and the competitive nature of the product market. These changes are related to membership of the ERM but not fully explained by membership; they reject the hypothesis that disinflation costs were reduced due to credibility gains from ERM membership.

Furthermore as Collins (1988) and Dornbusch (1990) point out, the sacrifice ratio of some countries within the ERM was higher than that of some other countries outside the system. As Goodhart (1990) and De Grauwe (1992) suggest, replacing a domestic anti-inflation policy with the ERM does not necessarily ensure a change in credibility. Instead the credibility question shifts from the authority's anti-inflation policy to its exchange rate policy. Instead of the authorities having to gain credibility for an anti-inflation policy, they now have to build credibility for the exchange rate target.

It would appear, therefore, that the process by which inflation expectations are derived does not change simply by joining the ERM, credibility takes time to build. Kremers (1990), Dornbusch (1991) and Anderton *et al.* (1992) identify the crucial link between using the ERM as one tool in disinflation and other policies. If fiscal policy, for example, does not reflect the authority's commitment to the regime, credibility will not be built, as seen in Ireland, France and Italy in the early 1980s. The issue is very clouded, but it is generally agreed that the ERM mechanism during its second and third phases was an important aspect of members' anti-inflation policy. Whether it helped reduce the cost is another issue. The ERM does help in disinflation since it forces governments to adopt policies consistent with membership; it is through this disciplinary channel that credibility is built, governments must maintain the commitment for inflationary expectations to adjust.

An area which has received equal attention in the literature is the effect of disinflation on public finances in the context of MU. The fear is that the loss of seigniorage revenue from adopting a disinflationary[5] stance could lead to an explosive debt path and thus endanger both the disinflation and prospective MU membership. In general the approach has been to first quantify the importance of seigniorage and then approach the problem from the optimal public finance model.

In essence, the justification for an optimal inflation tax comes from any one, or all, of the following: the distortionary effect of direct taxes, rigidities in fiscal policy decision making, the existence of a small tax base, tax evasion, or a large "black" economy (Giavazzi, 1989). If these factors are important, the model suggests that money balances should be taxed up until the point where the marginal welfare cost of raising revenue through the inflation tax equals the marginal cost of raising revenue through other forms of taxation. Certainly in some of the Southern states the existence of tax evasion, a healthy "black" economy, and large shares of agriculture in GDP and self-employed in labour income, suggest that these economies have a non-zero optimal inflation rate.

But is seigniorage an important revenue source for governments in Europe as a whole and the Southern states in particular? Cohen and Wyplosz (1989) see it as a "second order effect", whilst Dornbusch (1988b), Giavazzi and Pagano (1988) and Drazen (1989) believe it to be of extreme importance and could stop some countries from joining an MU.

It is clear from the data that there is an asymmetry in the importance of seigniorage between the Northern and Southern states. The Southern states' revenue collection from this source is an order of magnitude greater than the North's (see Giavazzi, 1989; Cohen and Wyplosz, 1989; "One Market, One Money" for the relevant data).

This would indicate that when considering the Southern states seigniorage should be taken into account, whilst it is not important for the North. However, as Gros (1990) indicates, there is no reason to expect that discretionary policy would achieve the theoretical optimum inflation tax level. Gros constructs a measure of the potential gain to be had from ERM discipline and finds that many of the current members, and certainly countries such as Italy, would gain under ERM discipline.

Grilli (1989), using the same sort of model (closely related to that of Mankiw, 1987) confronts it with actual data. The model performs badly compared to its theoretical predictions. Grilli's paper is one of the few to link the dangers of combining a disinflationary policy with debt accumulation dynamics. During a phase when fiscal reforms are required the temptation "to resort to seigniorage and thus reintroduce capital controls or abandon the exchange rate parity, may become very strong". However he indicates the danger without actually examining it in a dynamic way.

Dornbusch (1988b) sums up: "the quest for disinflation has been pursued without recognition of the long-term budget consequences. To put it simply the public finance role of inflation was left out of sight" in all of Southern Europe.

Seigniorage represents only one aspect of public finance in a disinflationary environment. Disinflation, either inside or outside the ERM (given the evidence on credibility), requires high interest rates in the short term, placing more pressure on government debt repayments, reducing the growth rate of output, and raising the question of debt sustainability. This danger is easily demonstrated by examining a government budget constraint with inflation and growth

$$\Delta b = d + (r - y)b - \Delta m - pm \qquad (3.1)$$

where
Δb = change in total debt/GDP
r = interest rate
y = real growth
d = non-interest deficit/GDP
p = inflation rate
Δm = change in money/GDP

The first two terms on the right-hand side explain the growth of debt as the non-interest deficit and the difference between the interest rate and the growth of output. The third term captures that part of the deficit financed through money creation (seigniorage) and the final term captures the inflation tax.

This relationship highlights several important consequences related to disinflation and debt dynamics. First we can note that a higher interest rate will lead to faster debt accumulation through higher repayments on outstanding debt. Reduced output growth will limit the level of seigniorage available at each inflation rate (as the growth in demand for real money balances declines) and increase both the primary and interest payment parts of the deficit. Reduced inflation reduces the inflation tax, increasing the non-interest deficit. A permanent drop in inflation means that the disinflating country will experience permanent *ex ante* revenue losses, which must be compensated for by an increase in taxation or a reduction in expenditure.

Ergo: disinflation, if it entails high real interest rates and reduced growth, can easily lead to unsustainable debts, requiring either a reduction in government spending (which, in the short run, compounds the loss of growth), higher taxes (distortionary), the possibility of reneging on debt, or monetizing deficits and abandoning the stabilization (the risk of which would lead to higher risk premiums and therefore higher interest rates, further compounding the problem).

Nowhere in the literature have we been able to find a model that considers these aspects of disinflation together and dynamically; the output costs of disinflation, loss of the inflation tax, the costs of increased interest rates on public debt and the importance of credibility. The book remedies this shortcoming by combining these aspects in one model. The outcome is a set of results which clearly indicate the scale of adjustment required by Greece, and an indication of the dangers of Alogoskoufis' "shock treatment".

3.2 METHODOLOGY AND APPROACH

The issues discussed above are addressed using multi-country simulation models. This approach was chosen due to the complexity and dynamic aspects of the modelling required to capture the stylised facts of the processes involved. Analytical models would have meant a reduction in coverage, and a limited ability to consider the dynamic nature of the problems at hand.[6]

The orientation of the book is toward capturing the relevant stylized facts of both the groups of countries and the economic regimes in place, and to, in effect, experiment with a host of possible policy choices. Instead of using fully estimated models, the book relies on a novel modelling mix which takes aspects from the computable general equilibrium, econometric, and theoretical simulation modelling literature. This allows models with well understood theoretical properties, but which also have a close and intimate link with the data to be built. The models take into account the current economic situation and underlying differences in each of these countries. Expectations are forward looking in financial markets and adaptive in the goods and the labour market.

By its nature, therefore, the book required an approach which provides the necessary modelling coverage, coupled with the ability to easily, and quickly, repeat shocks under various different reaction rules. Optimal control methods could have been used, but as discussed in Appendix 1, they were felt not to match the spirit of the research. Instead plausible reaction functions have been used for monetary and fiscal policy. The success or failure of individual experiments are generally tested using an objective function which penalizes deviations of inflation and output from their targets. In some cases, for example Chapter 5 on Spain, policies are ranked by their ability to attain the Maastricht Criteria.

The models contain three countries each, France, Germany, and either Spain or Greece. Whilst, especially in the case of Greece, the small country framework could have been used, this was felt to be too limiting since the reaction of the core was seen as important. To have simply exogenized the core would have removed a crucial aspect of the simulations.

3.3   CONCLUSIONS

It is assumed that the member states are committed to forming a MU at some point in the future. Since distinct groups of countries can be identified based on the Maastricht Treaty criteria, the first question which arises is how these country groupings can achieve the criteria within a given time frame. The second question refers to those countries which will probably make up the first wave of MU members; essentially it is how to make it work successfully. The answers deal with appropriate fiscal and monetary policies.

It should be clear from the way the book is structured that it covers all points on the path to full convergence. At the *start* we have Greece: how should it go about this daunting process? *Half way* along the road we have Spain: how to continue the process successfully and at minimum cost? And near the *finish* we have Germany and France, who are faced with the question: what do we do now we are here? In the light of this we believe that the results are not only important to current members but to new and prospective members of the EU, who fall into all three categories.

For the core states the book is concerned with fiscal policy after MU is formed. Fiscal policy has received much attention, for example the role of a European federal coinsurance package, but this has not been examined in an empirical framework and hence no attempt has been made to quantify the size of expected gains. Of equal importance, given the likelihood of a multispeed MU, is the impact of the core's decision about what form MU takes on both stabilization and convergence for the non-members. The literature has not examined the impact of MU on non-members.

For the median group the questions centre around the issue of completing convergence whilst minimizing the costs incurred in terms of lost output, unemployment and public finances. This is approached via the opportunity the widened ERM bands offer to alter monetary policy targets. Whilst there is a body of literature concerned with the transition to MU, there is little which examines the appropriate monetary policy rule which enhances convergence in the presence of a debt constraint without imperiling stabilization. Whilst the suggestion was made some time ago that the ERM would have to move to wider bands after the removal of capital controls, the impact of this on convergence has not been examined.

For the periphery the issues are more to do with the timing of ERM entry in the context of debt control in a deflationary environment where seigniorage has previously been an important component of government finances. Once again this issue has received limited attention. The literature on credibility effects and the "tying of hands" is now well understood; unfortunately the paradigm does not appear to work well. Thus, to take credibility for granted when planning a disinflation programme which uses the ERM as a nominal anchor could be exceedingly dangerous. Furthermore, this literature has ignored the impact of disinflation on public finances.

The other side of the coin is that the literature on public finance and disinflation has concentrated on the seigniorage losses incurred during the disinflation without considering credibility, and has used the public finance model which has some implausible underpinnings. Neither approach is sufficient to give useful information about what policy rules are appropriate. Work which has considered these elements together – disinflation, the ERM and revenue losses – is not based on any theoretical or empirical underpinnings and comes to different conclusions. This book attempts to both clarify the issues which are important and give some practical policy guidance about ERM entry timing in the presence of a binding fiscal constraint. Since the issues examined for each group require either a multi-country framework or the inclusion of various interacting effects the analytical approach was discounted in favour of numerical simulation models. The models developed represent a hybrid between the purely theoretical, computable general equilibrium and empirical approaches, and are capable of capturing the important stylized facts of the countries modelled.

4 Timing of ERM Entry, Disinflation and Debt: Greece

4.1 INTRODUCTION

Chapter 4 discusses the problems a peripheral country, Greece, may expect to face in attempting to meet the Maastricht criteria and in joining the ERM. The policy choices available to avoid or minimize these problems are investigated and compared under differing assumptions about credibility. The analysis in this chapter could equally apply to a new EU member with similar problems to Greece which wishes to join the ERM.

The particular problems facing Greece are large deficits and debt levels and a substantial inflation differential with ERM members. The inflation rate, which has been well over the EU average for some time, indicates that the amount of output reduction required to achieve nominal convergence may be large if wages are sticky. Fixing the exchange rate will lead to an appreciating real exchange rate if inflation does not adjust. Falling output coupled with higher interest rates will result in higher deficits and larger debts. There is thus a vicious circle, where disinflation causes output losses, whilst output losses and disinflation result in larger deficits.

Furthermore, although there is some uncertainty regarding the implementation of the MU timetable envisaged in the Maastricht Treaty, there is a pressing problem in terms of time. According to the Maastricht timetable Stage III can occur at any time after 31 December 1996 and automatically in 1999, whilst the last date by which a country can be considered for membership in 1999 is July 1998. Hence, due to the criteria concerning exchange rates, Greece must be in the ERM by July 1996, and go on to avoid unilateral devaluations. Whilst this timetable looks increasingly unlikely, and the exchange rate criteria increasingly difficult to interpret, the chapter uses this scenario as a focus for the discussion. The analysis would apply equally well to any economy with these particular constraints, problems and targets. The fundamental point is that Greece can either join the ERM early or late in its stabilization programme.

Whilst the literature presented and discussed in Chapter 3 covers in some detail both the dynamic disinflation path of countries which join a system such as the ERM and the debt sustainability question, the literature has failed to relate the two issues and to give practical advice to policy makers contemplating such an entry. The model presented in Appendix 1 allows this to be rectified by including fiscal policy and the full interaction between inflation and the government's budget constraint.

What is the lesson that policy makers should take from the theoretical literature on credibility and seigniorage? Two views emerge, depending on how much credence is given to the theoretical points of view.

On the one hand advocates of early ERM entry propose that the anti-inflation credibility increase resulting from membership would be enough to reduce inflation to the ERM average swiftly; this is the "tying hands" hypothesis typified by Giavazzi and Pagano (1988) and Alogoskoufis (1993). However, there are numerous weaknesses in Giavazzi and Pagano's analysis, for example the ability of governments to instantaneously set the inflation rate through money growth (they do not make clear how this is achieved in the ERM, thereby falling into Whitley's trap, see Appendix 1, p. 222).

Papademos (1993) represents the counter view based on the empirical evidence which indicates that inflation expectations do not adjust any faster in the ERM. He also points out that deficit restructuring has to take place before inflation is reduced, otherwise the revenue losses associated with disinflation lead to a higher deficit. Papademos suggests that the proper way forward is to start the disinflation and stabilize debt *before* ERM membership. When inflation has reached some arbitrary differential from either the average or highest rate, the membership should commence.

The policy maker is therefore forced to choose between two conflicting views, neither of which has been presented in a convincing manner. Both Alogoskoufis and Papademos simply present discussions and opinions, whilst the credibility literature has been unable to incorporate sufficiently realistic assumptions into its partial analysis for the results to be totally convincing (see Begg, 1988; Goodhart, 1990).

This chapter elucidates the argument by drawing on the model introduced in Appendix 1 to study some policy options for Greece under different assumptions about credibility. We assume initially that ERM membership does not change credibility. In terms of the model, this means that inflation and exchange rate expectations follow the same process inside or outside the ERM. We first examine early ERM membership without a fiscal stabilization plan. This is used as an exercise to show what impact ERM membership has on the evolution of the debt: GDP ratio and the adjustment path of the economy to low inflation. This is clearly not a viable option for Greece, for the debt ratio becomes explosive. Next, we examine the option of joining early with a debt stabilization plan in operation. This indicates the degree of adjustment required in order for MU membership to be considered in the medium term.

If, for some reason, nothing is done to alter policy and Greece avoids the required stabilization, joining the ERM later, we illustrate how this increases the size and cost of the adjustment. This clearly demonstrates the need for action sooner rather than later, and leads us to the final option examined, which is to stabilize the debt ratio and deficit now, and to join the ERM later.

We then turn to the issue of how credibility affects the dynamic adjustment path. Although credibility is approached in the theoretical literature via game theory and optimal bargaining, the process can be proxied by changing either the speed of private sector expectations or, in the case of complete credibility, setting those expectations equal to the authority's announced targets. This is a static view of credibility which does not allow credibility to alter over the simulation horizon. However, this problem is common to both the theoretical work and the scant empirical attempts to model credibility. A promising avenue would appear to be the new literature on Bayesian learning (see Hall and Garratt, 1995), but unfortunately this is not far enough advanced to incorporate into the model at this stage.

The problem can be avoided by taking the extreme cases, full credibility and unchanged credibility. Once the impact of the extreme cases is understood it is possible to infer the effects of smaller changes in credibility. This is the approach adopted here. The effect of higher credibility is investigated in Section 4.7, by first increasing the speed of expectations adjustment and, second, by considering the cost of adjustment of the two policy choices (early or late membership) under high and low credibility. A decision framework is developed which allows the policy maker to estimate the expected cost of such policy choices based on their assumptions about credibility. A clear result emerges.

By combining the theoretical insights of the credibility literature with debt accumulation, the methodology adopted allows the interaction of these two processes to be examined dynamically under differing assumptions about inflation and exchange rate expectations which has not been achieved in the literature, either theoretically or with simulation models. Small-scale theoretical models are incapable of performing the analysis, whilst few large-scale econometric models exist for the peripheral countries (an exception is Garganas, 1991; however, this model is unsuitable for this sort of policy analysis). The outcome is a more complete view of the disinflation process and clearer policy prescriptions than have previously been available from partial equilibrium analyses alone.

Section 4.2 gives some background on the structure and recent events of the Greek economy. Section 4.3 outlines the policy problems and framework of analysis, whilst Section 4.4 is concerned with the cost of disinflation. Section 4.5 highlights the debt and deficit problems and considers the effect of a fiscal policy rule. Section 4.6 discusses ERM entry timing and fiscal policy. Sections 4.7 and 4.8 are concerned with the effects of credibility on the adjustment path, and Section 4.9 concludes.

4.2 BACKGROUND AND STRUCTURAL FEATURES

In order to indicate the size of the problem Greece faces and to examine past attempts at stabilization, this section examines the recent Greek economic experience and structure.

The strong growth of the 1960s and early 1970s masked the inherent weaknesses of Greece's economy, which became more obvious after the oil shocks and membership of the EC in 1981. In discussing the recent Greek economic experience therefore, it is possibly best to begin in 1979, when the ERM was formed, the second oil shock was occurring and the Greek economy was undergoing a nominal expansion.

Between 1979 and 1985 both fiscal and monetary policy were, on average, expansionary. Tariff barriers remained on imports whereas exports were free to enter the EC (this helps explain why Greece's GDP split between industries has remained mainly unchanged since the end of the 1960s; see Larre and Torres, 1991). After the oil shock of 1979 fiscal policy was loose, as is shown by the increase in the PSBR from 5.9% of GDP in 1979 to 14.7% in 1981; monetary policy accommodated this fiscal expansion, with M3 growth at 31% in 1981. Unit labour costs were also growing at a high rate, around 25% in 1981.

The 1981 general election brought a change in policy, with the fiscal stance tightening and the PSBR being reduced in 1982 and 1983. However monetary expansion decelerated at a modest pace, whilst labour costs kept rising at an average of 23% over the two years. The stabilization failed, and was short-lived. Adherents of the political business cycle view may point to the two elections over the next two years as a reason for the failure of the stabilization, since fiscal policy was once again expansionary, with the PSBR at 17.9% of GDP in 1985 (Papademos, 1990, 1993). Money growth was also high in 1985 and short-term real interest rates continued to be negative. These policies are reflected in the growth of internal and external debt over this period (debt rose from 28% of GDP in 1979 to 76% in 1985, whilst external debt went from 13% to 50% in the same period).

To see these policies in context one can compare them to the EC average. After 1982 most EC countries were undertaking successful stabilization policies in order to rid themselves of the inflationary effects of the last oil shock. Hence, unsurprisingly, large nominal divergences occurred between Greece and the EC average up until the crisis year of 1985. The inflation differential, measured by consumer prices, reached a maximum in 1986 at 17.6% (20.8% as compared to ERM members), the PSBR differential was 12.1% of GDP in 1985, and the current account deficit was 9.8% of GDP whilst EC countries were, generally, in surplus.

These nominal divergences were not compensated for by a large growth in real output, indeed GDP growth was broadly in line with EC growth. As Papademos (1990) points out, real economic convergence was achieved,[1] but at the low and unsatisfactory EC growth rate of the time. The failure of these expansionary policies to create growth can be blamed on inefficiencies in the productive sector of the Greek economy. Katseli (1989) characterizes the mode of economic and social organization in Greece as "State Corporatism" which involves "the State, traditional industries and the financial sector in a highly structured system of political relationships" leading to a pervasive dualism in the treatment of industries.

Katseli goes on to state that "official" industries with command economy characteristics have been selectively protected from competition and extensively subsidized (both directly and through very cheap capital loans). This is one explanation for the government's deficit problem, the availability of credit to these organizations without any consideration of their ability to repay. The inefficiencies have been exposed by the accession of Greece to the EC. In short, the supply side of the economy could not meet the policy stimulus to nominal aggregate demand, hence the inflationary consequences.

The rather obvious imbalances and misalignments in 1985 forced a two-year stabilization to be attempted, from the end of 1985 to 1987. The targets of policy were to reduce both inflation and the current account deficit, and to stabilize external debt. The policy package consisted of a 15% devaluation of the drachma, changes to the wage indexation scheme, from backward indexation to forward, based on official forecasts. This change was legally binding until the end of 1987 for both public and private firms. Measures were also introduced to curb private sector credit demand, and the preferential interest rates offered to certain industries were raised.

As a result of these policy changes inflation halved, the current account improved to a 2.6% deficit, and capital inflows increased markedly, easily offsetting the current account deficit. As a result the external position also improved, with external debt falling to 41.5% of GDP at the end of 1987. The PSBR fell to 13.2% of GDP, but did not reach its initial target, nor did private sector credit expansion meet its target. However the wage indexation scheme did have an effect, reducing real wages by 13% over the two-year period, and rapidly decelerating nominal wages. The drachma's devaluation was followed by a policy of targeting the real exchange rate, and the nominal depreciation of the drachma was slowed. These effects helped keep inflation down.

This period of relative austerity ended in 1987. Fiscal policy was again loosened, and incomes policies were relaxed; consequently the PSBR grew in 1988 by 3% of GDP and unit labour costs rose by 19.3% after averaging 12% through the two years of stabilization. Short-term lending rates had been gradually rising through 1986–7, but they now rose dramatically, with real lending rates to the private sector averaging 8.3% in 1988. The current account and inflation continued to improve through 1988, and this coupled with the fiscal laxity produced a growth rate of 4.3% for the year.

Growth slowed from 1988 onwards, again following the EC trend. Inflation and unit labour costs began to rise sharply in 1990 and have remained fairly high since. Unemployment has also risen, although employment has not fallen a large amount, reflecting changing participation rates. Public debt has grown at a fairly constant rate, reflecting continuing large structural deficits, higher real interest rates and stagnant growth.

1990 presented another crisis in terms of many macroeconomic variables, which in some ways surpassed the problems of 1985. Policy tightened in mid-1990 (with the arrival of a new government), stricter wage indexation levels were introduced in the spring of 1990; however, this could not stop inflation reaching 23% by December (according to the OECD's measure). Export market shares continued their trend loss, whilst import penetration continued, resulting in worsening trade conditions which were not offset by capital inflows, both from official EU transfers and privately.

Measures to reduce the PSBR were offset by a rise in public enterprise's deficits, and hence 1990 brought another increase in the PSBR. Monetary policy was also tightened at this time, resulting in very high real interest rates of over 10%, an appreciation of the drachma and the achievement of monetary targets for the first time in a decade. February 1991 brought the announcement of the Medium-term Adjustment Programme by the authorities. The projections were reductions in the PSBR to 12.5% in 1991 and 6.5% in 1992 through reductions in spending and increases in indirect taxes, social security contributions, privatization receipts and a stronger targeting of tax evasion. Monetary policy was also to remain tight. The rationale for the Programme was obvious, to stabilize the nominal and public finance variables to a degree which allows membership of the ERM and to guarantee continued EC transfers which help the balance of payments. Most of the Programme has been implemented, including privatization (although the weak financial position of these companies has held up wide scale sell-offs), and increases in taxation. However public debt levels have continued to rise. The drachma's depreciation was slowed, following the earlier period of continual inflation differential offsetting; this helped, along with tight monetary policy, to reduce inflation to 13.6% in July 1992 from around 20.5% in 1990.

The EC's large loan to Greece, which was granted in 1991, has half left to be disbursed; this was made conditional on certain economic objectives being met, a reduction in the current account deficit to 3% of GDP, the inflation rate to 8% and reductions in employment in the public sector. The second half of the loan has not been paid due to failures on the part of the New Democracy government to implement their Programme fully as of September 1992.

The October 1993 election brought a change of government as the Panhellenic Socialist Movement (PASOK) returned to power. The new government maintained its predecessor's austere economic policy outlook, but once again fiscal slippage occurred in 1994, and inflation increased. A revised Convergence Plan appeared in September 1994 with ambitious targets for the deficit and inflation. The EU has accepted the plan, but has indicated that supplementary measures will be required if the convergence targets are to be met (Barclays Bank, 1994). The disbursement of EU funds (around 5% of Greek annual GDP) is still tied to convergence performance. Whilst the deficit is projected to fall, the debt situation is less encouraging, with a continuing upward trend being forecast. Meanwhile inflationary pressures have abated as the output gap has remained negative and output growth sluggish. The government currently predicts entry to the ERM in mid-1996.

So, in summary, Greece over the last decade was characterized by double digit inflation levels, high PSBRs and debt levels, current account deficits and exchange controls, the drachma has been managed to produce constant competitiveness, and growth has been lower than the EC average over the period. The situation has improved, but there are still problems, especially the debt situation and continued inflation differentials with the core ERM members.

The challenge for Greece is substantial; the EC offers the opportunities for Greece to "catch-up" in real *per capita* GDP terms with its Northern partners; to take advantage of the opportunities requires continued movement toward MU with these partners. This, unfortunately, requires nominal convergence, something Greece has found singularly difficult to achieve over the last decade, although the 1986–7 stabilization shows what can be done, and large scale fiscal restructuring and consolidation.

4.3 THE SIMULATION FRAMEWORK

The stylized facts for Greece at the end of 1992 were high inflation, large government deficits and debt, a persistent current account deficit, and a purchasing power parity (PPP) exchange rate rule coupled with capital controls. This is taken as the status quo non-ERM regime. It is modelled via a PPP exchange rate rule and capital controls which insulate the Greek economy from price shocks and foreign interest rate movements whilst ensuring constant competitiveness. This regime accommodates inflationary pressures in the economy, imported inflation is the same as domestic inflation, and the real money supply is kept constant.

Monetary policy outside the ERM is a money supply rule which targets the real money stock, through nominal money growth as shown

$$M = M_{t-1}\,(1 + cpi) \tag{4.1}$$

Hence nominal money growth is set at the level of inflation. The nominal money supply, wealth, and output determine the interest rate in this setting via a rearranged equation (A1.44). If Greece joins the ERM the exchange rate is fixed by adjusting the interest rate in line with the exchange rate equation. The interest rate is set by the following equation

$$r = 1 + rG - ee/eb - \gamma CB/Y \tag{4.2}$$

(4.2) states that the Greek interest rate equals the German one, *plus* a risk premium, captured by the real current account balance as a percentage of output,[2] *less* the ratio of the expected exchange rate, *ee*, and the target rate, *eb*. If rational expectations are assumed, then the government is just as good at predicting the next period's exchange rate as the private sector, and if there is an expected depreciation they can counteract this by increasing interest rates now. Since the interest rate is set by the external commitment, the rate of nominal money growth is no longer determined by the inflation rate relationship shown above, but is dependent on changes in the interest rate.

In the status quo setting the stance of fiscal policy remains unchanged. However, for the simulations where fiscal policy is adjusted a reaction function is used which targets the real debt level,

$$SRT = SRT_{t-1} + \alpha_1(D_t - D_T) + \alpha_2(D_t/D_{t-1} - 1) \tag{4.3}$$

where D_T is the debt target, D is the actual debt ratio and SRT is the tax rate (values for α_1 and α_2 are given in Appendix 2 and are derived in a similar fashion as the monetary policy reaction functions discussed in Appendix 1).

In summary, there are two basic monetary regimes, either the ERM or not, and two forms of fiscal policy rules, unchanged or debt targets. If Greece decides to enter the ERM, two options as regards timing are explored, immediately or later. A similar option exists for the required fiscal consolidation. The simulations start in the third quarter of 1993, which constitutes early ERM membership. Late membership corresponds to entry in mid-1996. The interest is to ascertain first, when Greece is better off joining, secondly, what fiscal policies must be implemented for membership to be a success, and thirdly, the impact of credibility on these decisions.

The results begin by exploring the impact of early membership with an unchanged fiscal policy stance. The fiscal policy rule discussed above is then implemented, before the question of policy timing is considered. Finally, the question of credibility is examined in the light of the results on optimal policy implementation timings.

4.4 ERM WITH UNCHANGED FISCAL POLICY

This section examines the impact on output, inflation and the fiscal variables if Greece opts for early ERM membership without instigating a fiscal correction. The interest is to illustrate the size of the required adjustment and the necessity of combining appropriate fiscal policy with the change in monetary regime. The early starting date corresponds to the third quarter of 1993.

Since Greece has a higher inflation rate than the rest of the EU, convergence implies a tight monetary policy with higher interest rates at least for a short period of time. This would lead to a disinflation period with transient losses in output and competitiveness, a rising budget deficit and increasing public debt. As can be seen from Figure 4.4, there is an initial increase in the interest rate upon entry followed by a decline before final equilibrium is reached at a much lower rate. This increase in the interest rate aids the disinflation process.

The increase in the interest rate, coupled with the inflation differential leads to an appreciation of the real exchange rate, as can be seen from Figure 4.1, which shows the loss of competitiveness of Greece with respect to Germany (a rise indicating a loss of competitiveness).

From the time of entry onwards the real exchange rate appreciates quite significantly in a short space of time. The reason for this is that Greek inflation is above its partners', and thus, since the exchange rate is now fixed, the relative price levels between the countries grow further apart. However, this is a dynamic process whereby the real appreciation feeds back into

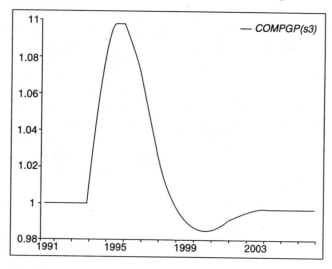

Figure 4.1   Greece, competitiveness, 1991–2003

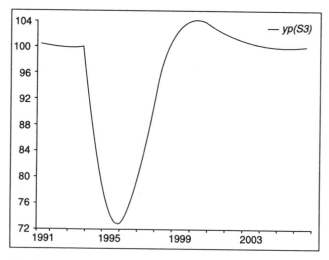

Figure 4.2   Greece, output, 1991–2003

demand through the current account. Exports drop and imports rise, leading to a reduction in output (Figure 4.2). This reduction is increased due to tight monetary policy and falling inflation expectations which increase the real interest rate.

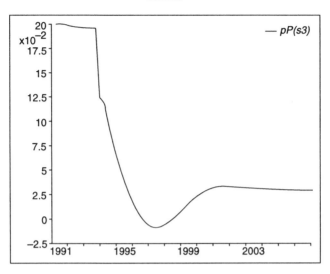

Figure 4.3   Greece, inflation, 1991–2003

The resulting recession reduces inflation. Imported inflation is also brought down, since the exchange rate no longer depreciates in the way it did prior to ERM entry.

The reduction in inflation (Figure 4.3), reduces the real appreciation of the exchange rate, and, eventually, as inflation drops *below* the competitors', the real appreciation is reversed. The process continues until equilibrium is reached, where inflation is the same as the partner country's, which, in turn, is equal to the *world* inflation rate. At this stage, the real exchange rate is constant at PPP and output has recovered to its potential level. The fall in inflation raises the real interest rate considerably, which helps to force output down, further reducing inflation (see Figure 4.4). This process stabilizes as inflation falls below the competitors' allowing a recovery in net exports, which begins to bring output out of recession.

In summary, the disinflation process results in nominal convergence with equalization of inflation rates and interest rates (taking into account risk premia). So, in these terms the adjustment consists of a temporary loss of output, followed by a recovery, coupled with a lower level of inflation, and a stable exchange rate. The long-run equilibrium position is neo-Classical in that output returns to potential, whilst inflation expectations have adjusted to the external nominal anchor, world inflation.

The drawback of the disinflation process based upon tight monetary policy alone is in terms of public finances. Greece starts the disinflation process with

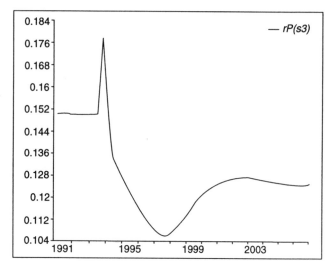

Figure 4.4   Greece, interest rate, 1991–2003

a relatively high government deficit. The effect of ERM membership and its attendant loss of output, reduction in inflation and higher short-term interest rates leads, respectively, to a loss of tax revenue, loss of inflation tax revenue, and higher interest payments on outstanding debt. These all serve to increase the government deficit (Figure 4.5), and hence debt (Figure 4.6).

The deficit jumps relatively quickly after membership, an effect which can be related to the rapid drop in the inflation tax. From there on the variation is dominated by fluctuations in output, settling down to a long-run deficit considerably higher than the original level. Debt follows an analogous form, rising from the initial level and settling at a level well over 100% of GDP as the adjustment finishes, and well above the Maastricht criteria level.

Figure 4.7 shows clearly the worsening of the current account as the real exchange rate appreciates, with exports being reduced and imports increasing. This is reversed as the exchange rate stabilizes. However, in the long run we have a persistent deficit which mirrors the government deficit.

This section has indicated the basic disinflation process in this sort of model. Nominal convergence does take place, but results in a short-term loss of output, and increased unemployment. It is interesting to note that for equilibrium to occur (if the exchange rate is not devalued) domestic inflation

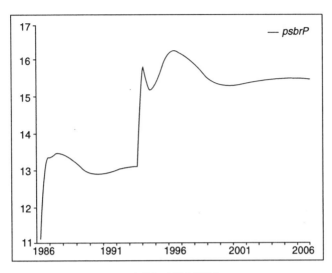

Figure 4.5 Greece, government deficit, 1986–2006

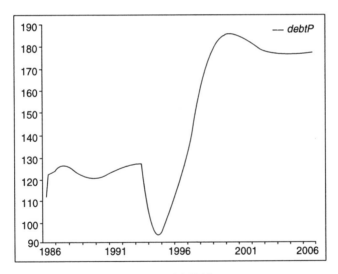

Figure 4.6 Greece, government debt, 1986–2006

must fall below the competitors' for some time. The obvious downside of this policy mix is the dangerously large increase in debt. Section 4.5 repeats the exercise, but this time combines ERM membership with the simultaneous adoption of the fiscal policy rule shown in Section 4.3.

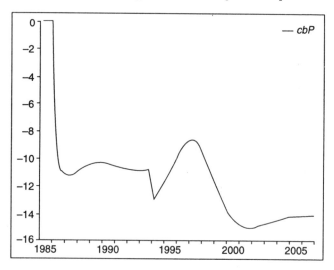

Figure 4.7   Greece, current balance, 1986–2005

4.5   ERM WITH TIGHT FISCAL POLICY

The debt problem stems from three sources, as mentioned above. The first is the reduction in tax revenue collected during the output loss after ERM entry. The second is the loss of inflation tax due to reduced inflation. The third comes from the increase in interest payments due to higher interest rates initially, and later due to higher debt levels.

What is, therefore, the appropriate fiscal policy? The government has two instruments after joining the ERM to tackle the debt problem: cut spending, or increase taxation. Using the tax rate based fiscal policy rule of Section 4.3, the authorities can stabilize the debt level close to the target (Figure 4.8).

This is achieved by increasing the effective tax rate considerably (see Figure 4.9). Greece's tax revenue problem is not a result of low tax *rates*, but rather a small tax *base*, due to avoidance and the economy's structure. It has been argued in the literature that it is optimal for such a country to have a non-zero inflation rate in order to collect revenue from money creation (Giavazzi, 1989). However, ERM entry reduces inflation, and consequently the inflation tax. This revenue needs to be replaced, hence the increase in the tax rate.

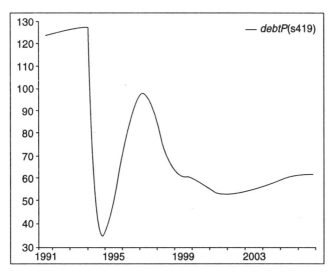

Figure 4.8   Greece, government debt with tax rule, 1991–2003

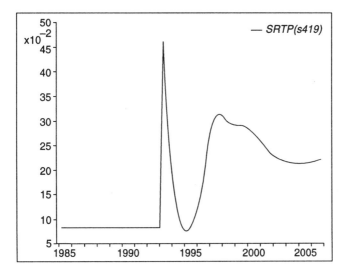

Figure 4.9   Greece, effective tax rate, 1985–2005

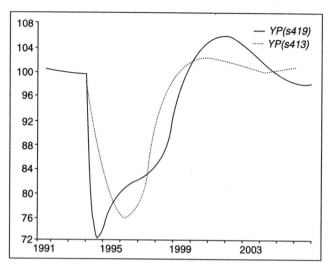

Figure 4.10   Greece, output with tax rule, 1991–2003
Solid line is with debt stabilization.
Dotted line is without debt stabilization.

The effect of increasing taxes to stabilize the deficit is to increase the depth of the recession (Figure 4.10). However this leads to an even greater fall in inflation than in the fiscally ''neutral'' case, which allows competitiveness to increase, since inflation remains below the partners' for longer. We see an improvement in output, and a small boom before the return to potential output occurs.

The government deficit moves into surplus during the adjustment, and the greater loss of output, coupled with the gains in price competitiveness, help to reduce imports and increase exports by enough to move the balance of payments into surplus. In fact, by ''interfering'' with the adjustment through fiscal policy, the government reduces inflation by *more* than required, leading to an increase in competitiveness with other ERM members which is sustained in the long term. In the long run, debt is stable at close to its target level, and the government budget is very nearly balanced. The current account, after recovering from a large deficit followed by a small surplus, is also close to balance. These effects take some time to work through, with the full adjustment not finished by the end of the simulation period. However, the results are clearly stable. It appears that the problem of joining the ERM and keeping public finances stable can be solved. The price is a larger loss of output than would otherwise be the case. Since this is perhaps an unpalatable result in the short run, Section 4.6 indicates the impact of delaying the adjustment further.

4.6   JOINING LATE OR EARLY

In considering the time of entry, we can distinguish two choices: first, Greece can join now, as is the case in the examples discussed above or, secondly, Greece can wait until the last possible moment for consideration for MU in 1999. This date corresponds to July 1996. The difference between the two dates in terms of how they affect entry conditions and the dynamic path of adjustment is discussed below.

The major difference stems from what happens to the debt level in Greece between now and July 1996. Figure 4.11 depicts Greek debt if fiscal policies remain unchanged. It is clear that the debt level is considerably worse in 1996 than 1993; hence, if fiscal policy remains loose the debt situation continues to deteriorate. This impacts on the cost of disinflation in the ERM by requiring an increase in taxes or decrease in government spending to stabilize the debt, which exacerbates the severity of the recession. Therefore, joining later, if debt has worsened in the interim, leads to relatively tighter fiscal policy.

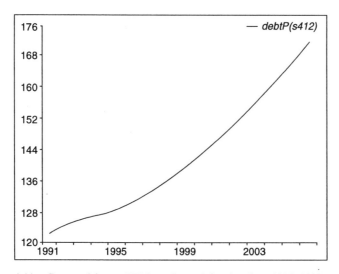

Figure 4.11   Greece, debt, no ERM, unchanged fiscal policy, 1991–2003

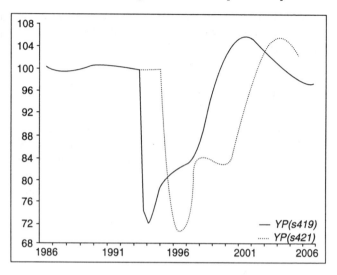

Figure 4.12   Greece, output, early and late ERM, tax rule, 1986–2006

Figures 4.12 and 4.13 highlight this by showing the effect of tighter fiscal policy on the adjustment path of output for the two cases of early and late membership. Obviously, as we see in Figure 4.12, to reduce debt to close to the Maastricht criteria level of 60% of GDP requires a relatively more severe recession if Greece were to join late. As Figure 4.13 shows, the target can be reached, but the costs are large.

It would appear, therefore, that if current fiscal policies are pursued the cost of disinflation and debt stabilization will increase in the future. The logical conclusion of this analysis is that joining early appears to be optimal, but this misses a simple yet crucial point. The authorities who make the decision about the timing of entry are also the ones who control fiscal policy. If they can stabilize the debt then the question of entry timing is not so clear cut in terms of costs and benefits. What matters is the realization that the deficit will worsen after entry into the ERM regardless of timing, and that this must be stabilized before MU membership can be considered. Therefore we turn to the possibility of stabilizing the debt now and joining later.

Figures 4.14 and 4.15 show the outcomes for output and debt if Greece starts to stabilize its debt now, and waits until 1996 to join the ERM. The stabilization causes a recession almost immediately, due to increased tax rates. However this brings debt down rather quickly, allowing taxes to be eased just before ERM membership occurs in 1996. An important side-effect

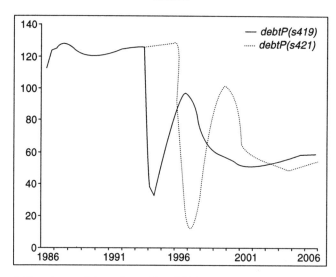

Figure 4.13 Greece, debt, early and late ERM, tax rule, 1986–2006
Solid line is early ERM.
Dotted line is late ERM.

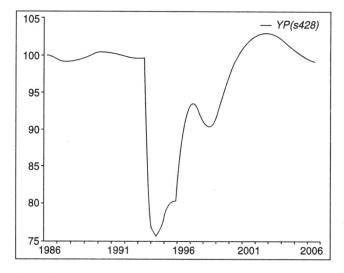

Figure 4.14 Greece, output, early debt stabilization, late ERM, 1986–2006

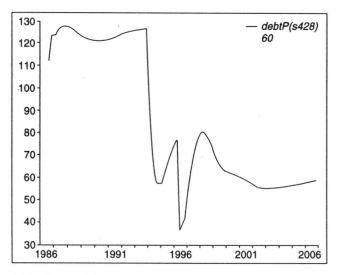

Figure 4.15   Greece, debt, early debt stabilization, late ERM, 1986–2006

of the debt stabilization is a decrease in the inflation rate (Figure 4.16), so that when Greece joins the ERM part of the disinflation process has already occurred. Hence after joining the ERM the competitiveness loss is not as great as it was in earlier examples, indeed there is an increase in competitiveness in the medium to long run.

This is clearly a more palatable policy mix, since in effect monetary policy cushions some of the impact of tighter fiscal policy on output (Section 4.8 shows objective function results which support this). However, the issue of credibility has been ignored so far, and I turn to this in Section 4.8, where the impact of increased credibility on the early ERM unchanged fiscal policy case is shown.

4.7   CREDIBILITY

Credibility enters the argument through two channels, expectations of inflation and exchange rates. In the analysis so far we have assumed that inflation expectations are based on the past actual inflation rate, with fairly sluggish adjustments. The credibility argument enters by changing the speed of adjustment of inflationary any expectations. Inflationary expectations are seen as the outcome of a game between the private sector and the authorities

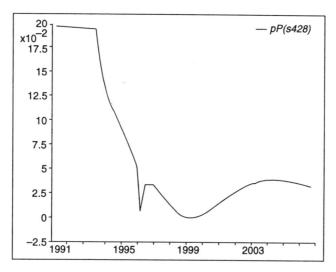

Figure 4.16   Greece, inflation, early debt stabilization, late ERM, 1991–2003

responsible for policy. Joining the ERM is meant to enhance the anti-inflationary reputation of the authorities, by attaching their monetary policy to the reputable Bundesbank (see Giavazzi and Pagano, 1988). This may well be the case, but many studies have failed to find any strong evidence in favour of this contention, for example Collins (1988). Possibly the reputation of the commitment to *membership itself*, or to defending the parity and the avoidance of devaluation, is what is being questioned by private agents, and it may take time for this commitment to be believed.

The same argument applies to the exchange rate target in the ERM. If the target is fully credible then agents believe that the government will defend the parity completely. If this is the case the risk premium disappears, and exchange rate expectations are exactly equal to the exchange rate target. Implementing these changes affects the outcome in two distinct ways: first, if inflation adjusts faster the adjustment speed for output is increased, that is, the recession is shallower and shorter (see Figure 4.17); at second, if the exchange rate is fully credible interest rates do not rise immediately, but *drop* toward the core's rates plus the risk premium (see Figure 4.18).

The sum of these two effects is a shorter and shallower recession. Thus, if reputation is built faster and the ERM target is believed, Alogoskoufis' thesis is supported. However, Section 4.9 shows there is a danger if full credibility occurs whilst monetary policy is exclusively targeting the exchange rate and not targeting inflation and output.

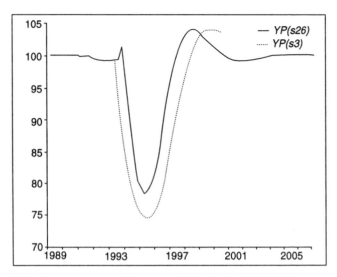

Figure 4.17   Greece, output, different credibility levels, 1989–2005

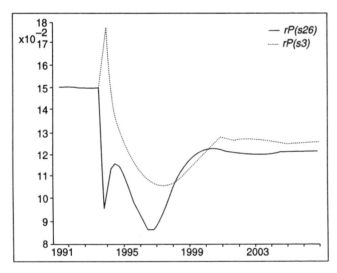

Figure 4.18   Greece, interest, different credibility levels, 1991–2003
                 Solid line is high credibility.
                 Dotted line is low credibility.

4.8 CREDIBILITY, DISINFLATION POLICY AND ENTRY TIMING

From the discussion in Sections 4.6 and 4.7 two main points emerge: first, the question of debt stabilization is of great importance to the disinflation path, and second, the importance of credibility to the economy's adjustment path. Based on the evidence in the literature about the time taken to build credibility, this chapter has argued that the best approach is to stabilize the debt ratio first, and join the ERM later since the combined cost of attempting both stabilisations at the same time is large.

It is difficult to choose which entry policy is the best in an ad hoc way, so an objective function is used to compare policy choices in a more consistent and systematic manner. The objective function is

$$UYP = \Sigma[(cpiP - cpiG)^2 + y^2] \qquad (4.4)$$

where *cpiP* is the Greek inflation rate, *cpiG* is the German inflation rate, *y* is the percentage difference of output from potential. This is an unweighted utility measure, both variables have equal importance, and while this may not be appropriate it is simpler than imposing preferences between the two (see Anderton *et al.*, 1992 for some discussion on these points). The higher the value of this function the higher the cost over the period in question.

Table 4.1   Objective function results

Early ERM, Early Debt Stabilization	8011
Late ERM, Late Debt Stabilization	8158
Late ERM, Early Debt Stabilization	5668

Table 4.1 provides a taxonomy of the various regimes in terms of the speed at which inflation is reduced in relation to the cost of disinflation. Since the objective function penalizes outcomes of inflation and output from their corresponding target values, the optimal regime is the one with the lowest cost. Thus, Table 4.1 shows that the best strategy is late ERM coupled with early debt stabilization.

Once the recognition is made that debt stabilization must occur, the policy choice which remains is how to couple this with ERM entry and disinflation. The options for this decision could be characterized as ''gradualist'' or ''cold turkey'' (i.e. early or late), and based on the assumption of no change in the formation of inflation expectations or credibility, the best policy choice is to take the ''gradualist'' route and join later.

Table 4.2   Objective function costs for different policies and credibility

		Private sector thinks policy is:	
		Credible	*Incredible*
Government thinks policy is:	Credible ("cold turkey")	U_{CC}	U_{CI}
	Incredible ("gradualist")	U_{IC}	U_{II}

However, if full credibility was attached to a disinflation policy which used the ERM as its main support, the pain of this adjustment could be reduced or, indeed, avoided, as indicated by the results in Section 4.7. The danger is that the authorities may assume, *ex ante*, that their policy will be credible, only to find out, *ex post*, that it is not. As Egebo and Englander (1992) point out, "it may be risky to count on economic agents acting in anticipation of lower inflation as a component of a disinflation programme".

Following a game theoretic approach, assume that there are two groups of agents in the economy, the government, and the private sector. There are four extreme cases which can occur *vis-à-vis* credibility in this framework. The private sector can view a policy as being highly credible, or having low credibility. The government must form a view about the private sector's perception of the policy's credibility, and form policy based on this assumption. The combination of views results in differing states for the economy, and thus different objective function results. This is shown in Table 4.2.

For Greece, if the authorities believe they have high credibility we assume they would opt for the "cold turkey" policy option and join the ERM now, whereas if they believe their credibility is low they would choose the "gradualist" approach. The pay-off for each policy will depend on the actual credibility of the authorities as perceived by wage bargainers and the financial markets.

The economy can therefore be in one of two fundamental states at any one time, as described by the private sector's view of the government's credibility. It is for the policy maker to decide which state the economy is in and to form policy accordingly. *A priori*, one might expect the cost of disinflation to be highest when the authorities assume that they are credible when they are not, and lowest when they are credible and assume that they are. It is unclear in the general case how the other combinations would rank.

Table 4.3   Actual objective function costs for different policies and credibility

		Private sector thinks policy is:	
		Credible	Incredible
Government thinks policy is:	Credible ("cold turkey")	38.8	100
	Incredible ("gradualist")	19.5	41.5

In this framework the policy maker's decision is complicated by having to form a forecast of both his and his policy's credibility. He must decide which state the economy is most likely to be in and therefore which strategy would minimize the *expected* cost. The policy maker is thus faced with a world of policy setting under uncertainty about credibility or the amount of inertia in the economic system.

The two states of the economy, and the two policy choices, were implemented in the model. Both policy regimes employ the same fiscal policy rule which stabilizes the debt ratio. The gradualist strategy adjusts interest rates in line with an inflation and output target. The inflation target is the German inflation rate. When the inflation differential between Greece and Germany is 2%, Greece joins the ERM. The "cold turkey" strategy is to join the ERM immediately.

Credibility is modelled in a stylized fashion. Under low credibility the adjustment of inflation expectations continues under an adaptive expectations scheme, whilst the risk premium is attached to the exchange rate. Under full credibility inflation expectations are exactly equal to the target rate, German inflation, in every period, whilst the risk premium disappears from the exchange rate and exchange rate expectations are equal to the exchange rate target. The objective function results for the four combinations are shown in Table 4.3 as an index of the "cold turkey"/incredible result.

The worst combination, as expected, occurs for immediate ERM entry and low credibility, the best, for late ERM entry and high credibility. The other two policy options are close together, and essentially indistinguishable in terms of cost. It may be surprising that the "cold turkey"/credible option is so much worse than the "gradualist"/credible, but this is explained by the reaction of interest rates to high credibility. If expectations of devaluation are zero, and the risk premium disappears, then Greek interest rates immediatly drop to the German level, a very large fall in nominal rates. Even though

Table 4.4   Expected disinflation costs

P (Credibility) (%)	0	20	40	60	80	100
"Cold turkey"	100	87.8	75.5	63.3	51	38.8
"Gradualist"	41.5	37.1	32.7	28.3	23.9	19.5

inflation expectations also fall to the German level, so that real interest rates are equalized between the two countries, the fall in Greek real interest rates is around 6%. This results in a short term increase in output, and higher actual inflation. Hence, if the interest rate is driven by the exchange rate target only, and not internal targets, full credibility actually leads to a larger output and inflation cost in the short term.

If the policy maker attaches a probability to the existence of credibility an expected disinflation cost can be determined for each policy regime based on the projected probable state of the economy. The expected costs for each regime under differing probabilities of full credibility are shown in Table 4.4.

In this case the "gradualist" policy dominates "cold turkey" regardless of the level of credibility, and thus the policy maker's choice is straightforward. However this is a specific result for a specific country and policy objective. In the general case it is possible that the objective function results would be such that at a certain probability of credibility the two policy regimes would switch in terms of which gives the minimum expected cost. There would therefore be a credibility probability point, analogous to a break-even point, beyond which the "cold turkey" regime would dominate.

Figure 4.19 depicts the variation of the expected cost of a policy as the probability of full credibility varies, where the cases are ranked in the following order (where (1) is lowest cost combination, (4) highest):

(1)   "Cold turkey"/ Credible
(2)   "Gradual"/ Credible
(3)   "Gradual"/ Incredible
(4)   "Cold turkey"/ Incredible.

The policy maker now has a clear decision rule, if he believes the probability of credibility is greater than $P(2)$ then choose the "cold turkey" option, if less the "gradualist" option. For Greece the expected cost indicates that the decision to follow the "gradualist" path will result in the least cost

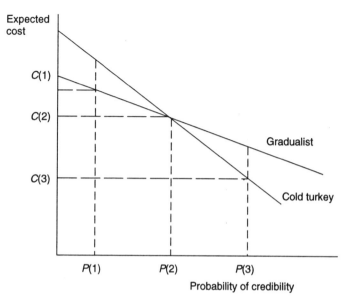

Figure 4.19   Greece, expected cost of policy versus probability of credibility

disinflation path regardless of the level of credibility. This result is supported by evidence in Chadha *et al.* (1992) who, using the Multimod model of the IMF, find that policies which are pre-announced and slowly phased in reduce the output cost associated with disinflation. Furthermore, the findings in the literature about the time required for credibility to be built presents a further forceful argument against planning policy on the assumption that credibility will be instantly gained. Viewed in this light Alogoskoufis' entry proposal appears risky; instead, Papademos' suggestion would appear to offer the least cost adjustment path.

4.9   CONCLUSIONS

Chapter 4 has discussed the problems Greece may expect to face in attempting to meet the Maastricht criteria, and the policy choices available to avoid or minimize these problems. Utilizing a three-country simulation modelling approach, the dynamic path of Greek disinflation was examined. The three countries modelled are Greece, France and Germany. The ERM regime is modelled with the Bundesbank setting monetary policy for Europe by following an objective function based on German variables. Section 4.8

provides a detailed discussion of the analytical framework and the policy issues of concern.

Taking into account the dynamic interaction between disinflation, recession and public sector debt, we have investigated the timing of entry and fiscal policy rules which allow Greece to successfully enter the ERM with the least cost as measured by an objective function. In summary, there are two distinct choices for Greece: join the ERM immediately, or later. The chapter tries to ascertain first when Greece is better off joining, secondly what fiscal policies must be implemented for membership to be a success, and thirdly what impact credibility has on the adjustment path.

Since Greece has a higher inflation rate than the rest of the Community, convergence implies, with unchanged fiscal policies, a tight monetary policy with higher interest rates at least for a short period of time. This would lead to a disinflation period with transient losses in output and competitiveness, a rising budget deficit and soaring public debt. The disinflation process results in nominal convergence with equalization of inflation rates and interest rates (taking into account risk premia). So, in these terms the adjustment consists of a temporary loss of output, followed by a recovery, coupled with a lower level of inflation, and a stable exchange rate. However, with unchanged fiscal policy this disinflation process produces increased budget deficits and explosive public debt.

To deal with these undesirable effects on budget deficits and public debt, fiscal policy also needs to be tightened. That is, the optimal policy mix of the disinflation process is tight monetary policy with higher interest rates, and tight fiscal policy with increased taxation and/or spending cuts. Using a fiscal policy rule, the authorities can stabilize the debt level close to its target, but at the cost of a deeper recession. Inflation is reduced more, while there is a small gain in competitiveness. Debt is stabilized near to its target level, and the budget is almost balanced. The current account, after recovering from a large deficit followed by a small surplus, is also close to balance.

The issue of whether Greece should join the ERM early or late hinges on the realization that the budget deficit and public debt would worsen after entry into the ERM. It is therefore tempting to conclude that by joining early Greece is better off because it deals with both problems simultaneously. However, the cost of such an approach is a much deeper and longer recession. Thus, the solution to the optimal timing for entry and stabilizing the debt is to deal with the latter first and the former second. By stabilizing the debt first the recession is both shallower and shorter and inflation is reduced. By joining late, after the debt stabilization is tackled, part of the disinflation process has already occurred and the subsequent recession is smaller.

The chapter also suggests a coherent method by which such a policy decision could be made. Since the policy maker is faced with uncertainty about both the model and the state of the economy, decision making without analysis of the possible states of the economy is dangerous. Instead, by clearly stating the assumptions used to model each of the economy's states and allowing the policy maker to attach probabilities to the existence of each state, it is possible to derive the expected cost of a policy decision over the possible states of the economy.

For Greece, the states of the economy which are examined are high and low credibility for the government and its disinflation policy. Further states could also be investigated, for example the degree of inertia in or speed of adjustment of the wage–price sector. The government faces a choice between a "cold turkey" or "gradualist" approach to disinflation and ERM membership, which corresponds to its belief about its credibility. Each policy was examined under high and low credibility and objective function results were calculated. For Greece, the results clearly demonstrate the dominance of the "gradualist" approach, regardless of the level of credibility. For either policy, improving credibility reduces the adjustment cost, but the "gradualist" policy, in line with evidence in the literature, dominates the "cold turkey". This is explained by the difference in the speed of response between the real economy and exchange rate and inflation rate expectations. Under perfect credibility interest rates and expected inflation converge to German rates immediately, involving a large fall in Greek real interest rates, creating a shock to the real economy, which adjusts at the same rate under either high or unchanged credibility. Thus, lower nominal inertia can increase the cost of adjustment if real inertia is present, and monetary policy is targeted wholly at an external constraint.

For the general case, however, the approach is useful since it helps clarify the basis under which policy decisions are made by forcing a clear description and account of the influences which are important to the outcome. This is a "robust" approach to policy making. The target is not to select a policy which minimizes an objective function for a single set of assumptions, but instead to find the policy which minimizes the *expected* cost over a range of assumptions about key variables, the effects of which are not easily quantified, for example, the level of credibility. By taking extreme values for credibility the upper and lower bounds of cost for a policy are identified, and decisions about the most likely scenario are left to the policy maker.

Of course assumptions about the likelihood of credibility emerging could change over time, and this sort of analysis should be updated and repeated. The evolution of the expected cost should be examined over time as credibility is built. Thus the optimum policy may change over time, raising the issue of time inconsistency. However, as credibility emerges the probability attached to this emergence by the policy maker would increase, resulting in the adoption of policies which are consistent with higher credibility. Thus as credibility is gained policies change to accommodate this after the fact, leading to a virtuous circle.

The policy recommendations are therefore to implement fiscal and monetary tightening now and to join the ERM when the inflation differential reaches some pre-announced level. This is the gradualist approach as advocated by Papademos. However, there are problems with this approach; a new government, or indeed the current government, could renege on the policy, leading, via the credibility and cost of commitment arguments discussed in Chapter 1, to higher inflation than under the ERM. A solution might be central bank independence coupled with clear policy rules and the removal of capital controls. Greece has done some, but not all, of these things. A further problem with the recommendation that the debt and deficit situation must be stabilized does not begin to address the complex problems of revenue collection and spending commitments which successive Greek governments have faced. Whilst the gradualist approach has nothing concrete to offer in terms of specific suggestions as to how to tackle these problems the analysis does point to the least cost and, according to Section 4.8, least risk convergence path.

The numerous results produced in this chapter could only have been achieved through the modelling approach adopted. The flexible approach of these medium-sized simulation models allows experiments to be conducted quickly and easily under different assumptions, whilst including the relevant interactions in a logical manner. They are thus more convincing than either the discussion of the Alogoskoufis–Papademos type or the partial analysis of the credibility and public finance literature. Even if the model or results are not accepted, at the very least they provide a more structured forum for discussion and experimentation.

5 The ERM and the Maastricht Criteria: Spain

5.1 INTRODUCTION

If the accession of current or new EU members to the ERM is seen as widening, then Chapter 5 deals with an issue in deepening. It considers the transition of a median country to the core group, and thus MU selection, via ERM membership. In order to qualify for MU a country must satisfy the constraints laid out in the Maastricht Treaty, as discussed in Chapter 1. For the current EU member states this requires varying amounts of nominal convergence coupled with fiscal consolidation, as shown in Chapter 2.

The Treaty does not rank the criteria in any order of relative importance, a member must satisfy all (although there is some leeway on the interpretation of the fiscal requirements). What the Treaty does not give a target for is output or unemployment. As long as the criteria are met, a country's unemployment position, for example, does not affect membership.

Eichengreen (1993) and others have argued that the most compelling reason for MU comes from political economy considerations linked to the Single Market process. They argue that large swings in exchange rates during the transition to a Single Market could lead to pressure to abandon the integration process. Following this argument through leads to a logical extension. If the transition to MU is excessively painful or unstable then the commitment to MU may be abandoned, and thus, via Eichengreen's argument, commitment to the Single Market process.

To formalize the argument, one can make the distinction between stabilization policies and convergence policies. Most policy studies attempt to define policy mixes which minimize an objective function. Normally, the objective function is made up of absolute or squared deviations of variables, for example inflation or output, from their base or target values. Positive and negative deviations are equally costly in this framework. The targets can either be exogenous, for example potential output, or derived from some "base" set.

Convergence raises an important question in this context. What are the targets? It would appear obvious that for a converging country the targets would be the Maastricht criteria; however, these do not include output or unemployment. Therefore, policies which target convergence exclusively do not support direct stabilization of output, whereas stabilization is normally seen as an integral part of policy. Any policy mix put in place in order to achieve convergence must therefore have two characteristics. First the convergence objectives must be attainable and clearly stated, and second, the policy mix should define how to stabilize the economy around its convergence path. On the one hand the policy regime defines how convergence is to be achieved, but on the other it also defines how shocks to the system are to be treated.

Whilst the literature has concentrated on issues such as transitional mechanisms to MU, convergence, debt sustainability, and the Maastricht criteria themselves, little has been done to integrate each of these elements into a general equilibrium framework or to combine these issues with stabilization. This chapter remedies this by integrating the Maastricht targets into a dynamic general equilibrium model with a fully specified demand and supply side. Furthermore, the treatment of the ERM regime and its effects on members' monetary policy is carefully constructed to capture the stylized facts. Small theoretical models are incapable of convincingly capturing the multiple targets of government policy attendant on convergence, and whilst large-scale models can do this, the problems discussed in Appendix 1 limit their attractiveness for such policy analysis. The model used in this chapter is both simple enough to be tractable and transparent, whilst offering the ability to convincingly model the ERM and the objectives of the domestic country and Germany.

The widening of the ERM bands to 15% presents an opportunity for ERM members to pursue other targets with monetary policy, or to reduce the weight attached to the exchange rate target, without breaking the exchange rate criteria. This chapter therefore considers two regimes which promote convergence and fiscal consolidation, but which have varying weights attached to stabilization. The first regime is labelled a "narrow band" ERM, corresponding to 2.25% bands, the second a "wide band" ERM, corresponding to 15% bands. For both regimes the tax rate is adjusted to hit the Maastricht criteria debt target.

The questions are: does the wide band ERM compromise convergence, and if not which regime offers the best mix of convergence and stabilization? The two regimes are compared on the basis of their ability to hit the Maastricht criteria. They are also subjected to shocks in order to compare their robustness and ability to stabilize output and inflation. In essence, the regime which minimizes the cost of convergence both with and without shocks is chosen as the dominant regime.

This approach to the issue of convergence gives a better insight into which mix of policy targets is likely to promote successful convergence and thus

MU. It is unique in the sense that it clearly differentiates between stabilization issues and convergence, which has not been the case in the literature. Furthermore, by using a numerical simulation approach the issues are treated in a fully dynamic environment.

In order to implement this approach to policy selection this chapter considers the case of a country inside the ERM which has achieved a certain amount of convergence, but which still has some way to go. The country used as the representative of this group is Spain. The reasoning is three-fold. First, Spanish unemployment levels are very high, second the government debt and deficit situation deteriorated during the last downturn, and third, inflation convergence is not complete.

The first reason, unemployment, is that any option to pursue other monetary policy targets, namely output or unemployment, might be attractive to the Spanish authorities. The latter two refer to the Maastricht criteria. The extent of the deterioration in public finances is such that Spain now misses the Maastricht criteria for these variables, whilst reference to Table 2.4 indicates that the inflation target has not been achieved either.

Therefore we can identify two temptations and two dangers. The temptations are to target growth in order to reduce unemployment and increase government revenues, thereby assuaging the deficit problem. The danger is that any perceived change in policy stance could trigger speculative crises in the foreign exchange market and inflationary pressures from wages.

The chapter is organized as follows. Section 5.2 presents some background on Spain's recent economic performance and some stylized facts about Spain's economic institutions. Section 5.3 considers the modelling framework and policy rules which were used. Section 5.4 presents the results. First a policy mix which targets the debt level and the tight ERM band is examined, then the ability to exercise more freedom is considered by switching to the loose ERM rule. The chapter examines the impact of four shocks on the two regimes. A conclusion follows.

5.2 BACKGROUND AND STRUCTURAL FEATURES

Spain became a full member of the EC in January 1986, and since then has experienced a sustained increase in trade with Europe, due in large part to the reductions in tariffs placed on Spanish exports by member states[1] and the later reduction in import tariffs placed on EC goods, a fact which explains the relatively slower import penetration of EC goods in Spain (see Figure 5.1).

An equally important effect of this opening up of the Spanish economy has been the influx of foreign direct investment into profitable sectors. This has

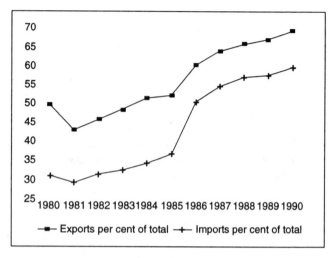

Figure 5.1   Spain, exports and imports with the EC as a per cent of total, 1980–90
Source: Galy *et al.* (1993)

helped fuel the tremendous growth rates which were the dominant feature of
the Spanish economy during the 1980s. As a result of this investment boom,
trend productivity growth increased markedly in the early 1980s, but since
1985 productivity increases have been very poor in most sectors, although in
those industries where foreign investment has been high, productivity growth
has been twice the national average.

The extremely high growth rate of the 1980s coupled with the level of
public sector dis-saving led to large current account deficits. This partly
reflected imports of capital equipment, and as such, was less of a constraint
than otherwise. Underscoring the current account balance deterioration is the
loss of competitiveness which Spain has experienced since the early 1980
(see Table 5.1). This can be explained by turning to the labour market and the
dynamics of price determination. Spain seems to be an inflation-prone
country, a fact that stems from the structure and inefficiency of its productive
sector. During the 1980s service sector wage inflation was up to 2% higher
than in the tradables sector, a wide margin by international standards. This
differential cannot be fully explained by an equilibrium ''catch-up'' process
(Larre and Torres, 1991).

Lack of competition in the service sector, due to oligopolistic structures,
cartels and large public sector utility monopolies, has meant that domestic
inflation has been difficult to reduce. Whilst the manufacturing sector appears

Table 5.1   Sectoral GDP deflators (average annual increase, %)

	Weight(1989)	*1974–82*	*1983–6*	*1987–9*
Agriculture	5.6	13.3	8.3	4.1
Industry	30.1	16.6	12.2	3.8
Building	8.1	21.6	9.5	12.9
Services	56.2	19.3	10.2	7.3

Sources: IMF, Galy *et al.* (1994)

to be quite sensitive to international competition, as compared to the service sector, its wage setting still seems to be relatively sticky. Profit margins were high enough before the main brunt of disinflation occurred to initially take most of the impact.

Structural rigidities in the labour market are partly to blame. Systems like the *Ordenanzas Laborales*, which ensures strict job separation, excessive long-term employee protection and lay-off costs, coupled with high labour immobility and the semi-centralized wage-bargaining process, do not enhance wage flexibility. In an attempt to introduce more flexibility a short-term contract scheme has been introduced. The system has reduced the costs involved in terminating labour, and the contracts are renewed bi-annually, improving flexibility. Since the system was introduced most newly created jobs have been through this scheme (see Table 5.2). However the jobs that existed before this time are exempt from the system, and the costs of laying off workers with permanent contracts are extremely high. This has reduced the willingness of employers to expand employment under long-term contracts which would allow skill levels to be increased. The

Table 5.2   Workers with temporary contracts (% of total employees)

1987	*1988*	*1989*	*1990*	*1991*	*1992*
18	23	27	30	32	34

Source: OECD *Economic Survey Country Report* (1993)

"equilibrium" is a system where some workers enjoy relative immunity from economic conditions whilst the rest are more exposed.

During the 1980s Spain posted remarkable growth rates, mostly from buoyant private consumption and high investment expenditure, a significant proportion of which was financed from external sources. Per capita GDP growth, between 1985 and 1990, was the highest in the OECD area, whilst employment creation was exceptional.[2] Private capital flows, both direct and portfolio, more than offset any current account deficit during the period.

The period was not without its problems, though. Observed productivity increases occurred mostly in those industries which had experienced foreign direct investment (FDI). Other industries, where average company sizes are small, experienced foreign competition for the first time. Companies in the tradables sector were forced to cut profit margins, with wage moderation following. The non-traded sector has not experienced such levels of wage moderation; structural rigidities still hinder the speed of adjustment, and hence cause pain in the process.

Since the late 1980s the government has been targeting a reduction in inflation, through relatively tight demand policies and high interest rates. Inflation convergence with Europe was occurring before the ERM membership in 1989, with the peseta not offsetting inflation differentials. ERM membership, in July 1989, followed a period of debate which highlighted worries about the peseta's ability to hold its own in the regime, consideration of the benefits versus costs of a fixed exchange rate, and concern about exchange rate stability at the expense of interest rate stability (see Vinals, 1990). In the end the perceived benefits of a stable exchange rate, considering the trade and capital flow levels with Europe, won the day.

Inflation convergence seems to be back on track; however, the non-traded sector may pose a problem, especially since it makes up a large proportion of output. The sluggishness of adjustment in this sector may well increase the pain of full inflation convergence. The convergence which has taken place has stemmed from the traded sector and from reductions in what were large profit margins. Fundamental changes in the labour market have not occurred, and to rid the economy of the last part of the inflation differential may be difficult.

Long-term interest rate convergence is possibly not such a problem. The elimination of capital controls means that Spanish long rates are much more market determined within the European context. However, on the downside, any sustained increase in government debt would tend to push up long rates, as would the expectation of currency depreciation within the new 15% ERM bands.

The last downturn, caused, as elsewhere, by the need for private sector balance sheet adjustment and a tightening of government policy, has worsened government finances. The Maastricht target ratios of 3% deficit and 60% debt ratios have been breached, whereas this was not considered to be a problem in the past, see Galy *et al.* (1993). At current rates of output growth, inflation and interest rates, the planned structural fiscal changes may not be enough.

The debt and deficit problems could be tackled through fiscal policy, which will increase national savings and hence improve the current account. In this case, monetary policy is the only tool left to target unemployment, apart from direct changes to employment laws. However, a looser monetary policy could have undesirable side effects. First, any easing implies a risk of devaluation in the ERM. This may impact further on the credibility problems highlighted during the currency crises of 1992 and 1993. Private short-term capital inflows have slowed since the beginning of the decade, and any exchange rate uncertainty would tend to enhance this effect. Second, easing monetary policy could ignite inflationary pressures in the non-traded sector at least, leading to further deterioration of the real exchange rate, and possible missing of the Maastricht inflation criteria.

5.3   THE SIMULATION FRAMEWORK

Spanish monetary policy is modelled via a mixed rule which targets the inflation differential between Spain and the core ERM average, output, and the exchange rate with a rule of the form

$$r = rb + \alpha_1(cpiS - (cpiG + cpiF)/2) + \alpha_2(YS - YS_{pot}) + \alpha_3(e/e_T - 1)^3 \quad (5.1)$$

where r is the Spanish short-term interest rate, rb is the base interest rate, $cpiG$, $cpiF$ and $cpiS$ are the German, French and Spanish consumer price inflation rates respectively, YS is Spanish output, and YS_{pot} is potential output, e is the Spanish–German exchange rate and e_T is the exchange rate target.

In the narrow band ERM case α_3 is much larger than both α_2 and α_1, and so the Spanish authorities are assumed to be highly committed to the exchange rate target as compared to the other two targets. Furthermore α_2 is greater than α_1 so that the Spanish are also assumed to care about inflation convergence more than output. In the wide band ERM case, α_2 and α_1 remain unchanged, whilst α_3 is reduced by a factor of 5. Table 5.3 shows the weights used in the two regimes.

Table 5.3   Parameter weights in Spanish monetary rule

	Narrow ERM	Wide ERM
α_1	0.9	0.9
α_2	0.5	0.5
α_3	50000	10000

The OECD projections for the Spanish fiscal policy stance for 1994 and 1995, which reveal a fiscal consolidation of the order of 1.3% of GDP for the structural balance per year, are fed into the model. This is done by allocating half of the adjustment to spending and half to tax rates in each year. However as a supplement to this a fiscal policy rule is available which concerns the debt level

$$TS = TS_{t-1} + \alpha_4(\text{debt}/60 - 1) + \alpha_5(\text{debt}/\text{debt}_{t-1} - 1) \qquad (5.2)$$

where *TS* represents Spanish taxes, debt is the Spanish debt: GDP ratio, and 60 represents the Maastricht debt criteria. This is assumed to be available from 1996 onwards, that is after the planned initial tightening has occurred. The values attached to α_4 and α_5 are 0.01 and 0.3 throughout the simulation period.

The wage–price sector of the Spanish model is set up in order to capture important stylized facts. These facts include the different treatment of temporary and permanent workers, the different responses of the manufacturing and services sectors, and the downward stickiness of service sector wage inflation.

The Spanish labour market is based on a combination of two unemployment equations to reflect the dual nature of the labour market. The treatment of workers with temporary contracts differs from those with long-term contracts in that the former are cheaper to lay off, and hence their employment levels respond much faster to output differences than do permanent contract holders. This asymmetry is accounted for by having two equations to describe Spanish unemployment rates. The unemployment rate is determined by the natural rate of unemployment, the difference of output from its potential and its rate of change, in order to capture hysteresis effects. The two employment sectors react differently to output changes, with temporary workers' employment rates being more responsive. The total Spanish unemployment rate is made up of a weighted average of the two employment markets' rates, with the weight reflecting the current distribution of temporary and permanent employees. At the moment around 34% of employees have temporary contracts.

The recent Spanish disinflation has revealed the asymmetric nature of wage formation in the manufacturing and services sectors. Service sector wage inflation has responded more sluggishly than in manufacturing, reflecting the differing levels of domestic and international competition between the two sectors. We therefore make service wage inflation respond more slowly to changes in unemployment. Furthermore, if unemployment is below the natural rate, wages respond faster than they do if unemployment is above the natural rate, in other words service sector wages are downwardly sluggish. Both sectors' wage inflation rates are dependent on the unemployment rate relative to the natural rate and to expected consumer price inflation over the next period. There is also some degree of wage indexation in the service sector. Expected consumer price inflation follows an adaptive adjustment path.

Consumer prices are determined by a weighted average of total import prices and producer prices in manufacturing and services. The relative weights on the latter reflect their contribution to GDP, around 64% to services and the rest to manufacturing.

The measures of convergence and stabilization used are the root cumulative squared deviation (*RCSD*) from its target path for variables expressed in per cent, inflation and the interest rate, and the root cumulative squared percentage deviation (RCS%D) from its target for output.[3] The measures are expressed formally below. For simulation *J* the RCS%D for output, *Y*, over *T* periods of the simulation is

$$RCS\%D_J(Y_T) = \sqrt{\Sigma_{t=1}^{T}\left[100\left(\frac{Y_t - Y_t^B}{Y_t^B}\right)^2\right]} \qquad (5.3)$$

where Y_t^B is the baseline value in each period t. Similarly for inflation and interest rates in simulation *J* at time *T*

$$RCSD_J(cpi_T) = \sqrt{\Sigma_{t=1}^{T}[100(cpi_t - cpi_t^B)^2]} \qquad (5.4)$$

These measures are taken shown for one, five and ten years after the shock. For stabilization the targets of output and inflation are zero inflation and potential output. For convergence, the targets are the French and German average inflation and interest rates.

5.4   SIMULATION RESULTS

The first set of results are with the narrow band ERM and the planned fiscal tightening for 1994 and 1995 only. This allows consideration of whether the planned policy is tight enough to meet the Maastricht criteria and its effect on the evolution of unemployment. The two policy regimes are then compared without shocks in order to consider the convergence paths generated by each, and to compare these paths both in terms of the Maastricht criteria and their stabilization properties. Results for shocks to these regimes are then considered. The purpose of this final exercise is to determine if the wide band ERM regime is stable in terms of convergence, and if it is, whether it outperforms the narrow band ERM in terms of its stabilization properties.

Unchanged fiscal policies, narrow band ERM

The model was run over the period 1994 to 2010 without any changes in the assumptions about the conduct of monetary policy and with two consecutive years of fiscal tightening. This "unchanged policies" simulation should not be taken as a forecast of the future path of the Spanish economy, since we have made no assumptions about how fiscal policy will evolve, and nor has the peseta's depreciation been taken into account. Furthermore, the model is not being used as a forecasting tool, thus this "base" case is meant to indicate the general path, and pace, of nominal convergence and debt.

With this policy mix nominal convergence is achieved via two routes: monetary policy and the trade account. Allowing only small fluctuations in the exchange rate with EU members leads, if there is an inflation differential, to an appreciation of the real exchange rate and a worsening trade balance. Furthermore, since the inflation differential is a target of monetary policy, interest rates remain high. Finally, the increase in tax rates and decrease in government spending in the first two years of the simulation have a negative effect on the inflation rate.

The result of these effects is to reduce output and inflation, the latter through the wage–price spiral (see Figures 5.2–5.3). Over time, as producer price inflation declines the decrease in competitiveness begins to be reversed, output recovers and interest rates begin to fall. Inflation convergence proceeds; however, as Karakitsos *et al.* (1993), and Driffill and Miller (1992) found, and as discussed in more detail in Chapter 4, in order for equilibrium to occur competitiveness must either return to or achieve its equilibrium value, and this requires a lower inflation rate than a country's competitors' for some time. This is indeed the case for Spain in this model, as shown in Figure 5.4.

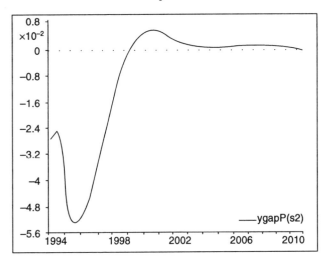

Figure 5.2   Spain, output gap, unchanged policies, 1994–2010

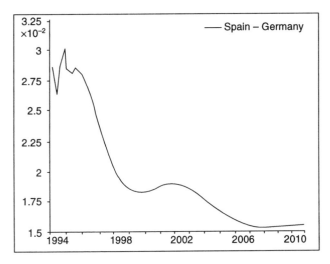

Figure 5.3   Spain, interest rates, unchanged, policies, 1994–2010

In the medium term output recovers, slightly overshooting its long-run value, interest rates continue to decline and inflation approaches the EU average. The convergence of interest rates does not proceed at the same speed or to the same extent as for inflation, reflecting the evolution of the risk

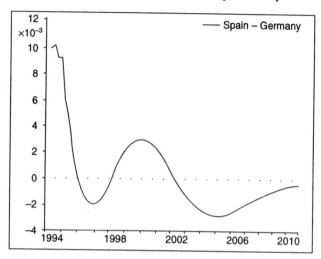

Figure 5.4   Spain, inflation rate, unchanged policies, 1994–2010

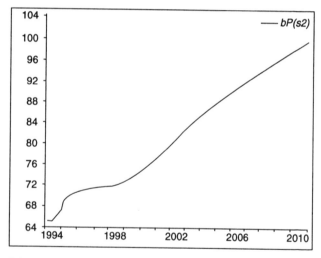

Figure 5.5   Spain, debt ratio, unchanged policies, 1994–2010

premium term. The risk premium, whilst declining, remains positive throughout the period, explaining the positive differential between Spanish and German rates. The reason for this risk premium response is two fold.

As Figures 5.5 and 5.6 show, although the changes to spending and taxation do bring the government deficit down, they do not stabilize the debt: GDP

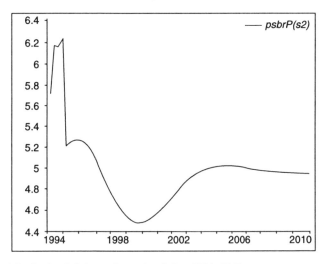

Figure 5.6   Spain, deficit, unchanged policies, 1994–2010

ratio, which continues to grow throughout the simulation period. This would tend to increase the risk premium, as agents discount the possibility of a change in monetary policy to inflate away the value of the debt, or to ''go for growth'' via a depreciation. On the other hand inflation convergence and the recovery in employment tend to reduce the risk premium. The trade-off between the two channels is a slow reduction in the risk premium over the period.

In summary then, with this hypothesized policy mix, Spain does achieve inflation convergence and some interest rate convergence, but does not achieve the Maastricht criteria for public debt and the government deficit.

Let us assume, therefore, that Spain must further tighten its fiscal policy stance in order to achieve the Maastricht targets. We next consider how the two monetary policy regimes discussed above perform in this context.

Active fiscal policy, narrow and wide ERM bands

In considering the unchanged policies result above, it is obvious that the projected fiscal tightening is not going to be enough to meet the Maastricht criteria. More needs to be done on this front. We therefore introduce a fiscal policy rule from 1996 onwards in order to examine its ability to reduce debt levels to the required level and its effect on unemployment and output. This is necessary whether MU is a target or not, if the debt ratio is important to policy makers.

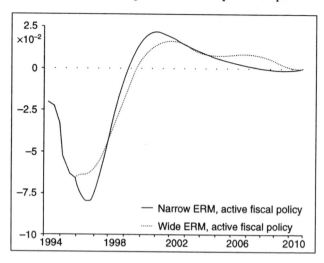

Figure 5.7   Spain, output gap, 1994–2010

This is where the opportunity offered by the wider ERM bands comes into play. We therefore run two sets of simulations, the first representing the narrow band ERM, the second the wide band ERM. It should be noted of course that the advent of the wide band ERM does not imply that the authorities will necessarily use it. There is therefore a clear policy choice: remain within the old bands, or use the new found freedom of the wide bands. Taking each regime in turn, this section examines the ability of the two regimes to produce the required convergence without creating further stabilization problems.

In both regimes the immediate effect of the fiscal rule is to increase tax rates. However the extent of the increase in taxation and the effect on output differs between the two regimes (see Figure 5.7). In the narrow band ERM case interest rates do not decline in response to the negative effect of the tax shock; furthermore, the exchange rate does not change. The result is a decline in output as compared to the "unchanged policies" rule just discussed. The debt: GDP ratio increases initially, leading to further increases in the tax rate and a further decline in output. This tax rate adjustment is shown in the deficit measure (Figure 5.12, p. 103). Under the narrow band the deficit falls faster, since tax rates increase by more.

For the wide band version interest rates fall slightly, but the main result of loosening the exchange rate target is a depreciation of the currency. These two effects taken together are enough to increase output as compared to the base case. The increase in the debt ratio is smaller as compared to the narrow ERM case, leading to a smaller increase in the tax rate, and thus a slower reduction in the deficit. The result is that the wide ERM regime stabilizes output more effectively than the narrow ERM regime during the process of fiscal consolidation. On the downside, the rate of reduction of the inflation rate is smaller, but the path is smoother, and in terms of convergence to and deviations from the EU average the rule performs better.

In the medium term the faster fall in inflation for the narrow band ERM rule produces a faster output recovery than the wide rule, through the current account and the interest rate. Furthermore the faster output recovery, and fall in interest rates, lead to a larger fall in debt in the medium term than for the wide ERM policy.

The medium to long run shows similar properties for both rules. Debt is steadily declining toward the Maastricht target value, the deficit is well inside the target level, and the output gap is essentially closed, as is the inflation differential. The big difference between the active fiscal policy simulations and the non-active simulations, apart from the obvious debt response, is the interest rate. Figure 5.8 depicts how the interest rate differs for the two regimes, compared to the "unchanged policies" base. In both cases, the interest differential is reduced by much more, reflecting the successful fiscal adjustment. In both the wide and narrow ERM regimes nominal interest convergence is enough to meet the Maastricht limit.

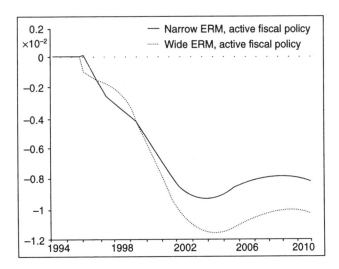

Figure 5.8   Spain, interest rate, difference from base, 1994–2010

Thus, the real difference between the two regimes is in the way monetary policy responds during the fiscal adjustment. The nominal convergence paths are not much affected, and in fact the wider ERM rule is more successful at keeping inflation closer to the EU average than the narrow ERM rule,

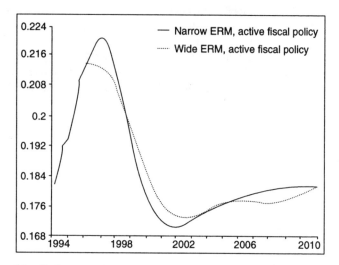

Figure 5.9   Spain, unemployment rate, 1994–2010

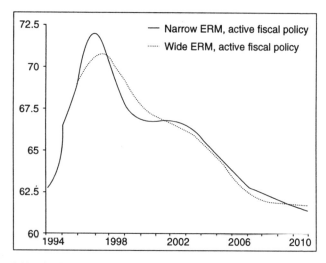

Figure 5.10   Spain, debt: GDP ratio, 1994–2010

although the latter rule does bring inflation down by more initially. The initial difference in interest rates is very small, but this, coupled with the exchange rates's depreciation, is enough to stabilize output faster. Therefore the wide-ERM rule is more successful at counteracting the further deflationary

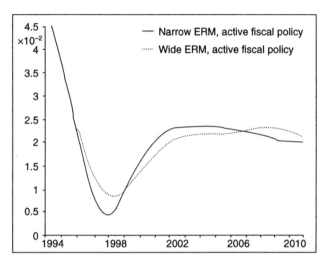

Figure 5.11   Spain, inflation rate, 1994–2010

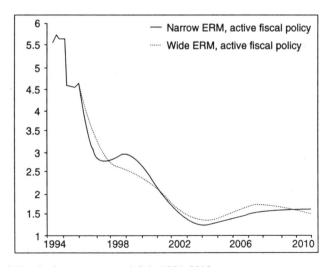

Figure 5.12   Spain, government deficit, 1994–2010

impetus of the fiscal adjustment, without materially affecting the convergence path. It certainly does not lead to a divergence.

However, the timing of the monetary easing would appear to be important. Since the economy is still in recession at the time of the policy switch, inflationary pressure remains low. Moreover the policy mix is important; maintaining a "tight" ERM stance whilst instigating a tighter fiscal policy stance does not improve convergence by any more than moving to a "looser" ERM instead.

These results are borne out by the data shown in Tables 5.4 and 5.5. Table 5.4 shows the "stabilization" performance of the two regimes in terms of output and inflation, whilst Table 5.5 shows the convergence performance. Table 5.4 shows the root cumulative squared deviation of inflation from zero, and the root cumulative squared percentage deviation of output from potential. Table 5.5 shows the root cumulative squared deviation of inflation and interest rates from the French and German average, and the debt and government deficit. The deviation measures are expressed with the wide ERM as an index of the narrow ERM regime.

In terms of stabilization, Table 5.4 shows that the "wide" ERM regime offers a sustained benefit as compared to the narrow for the output gap. However on the inflation front the ranking is reversed. This reflects the smaller initial fall in inflation under the "wide" regime, and since the "target" is zero inflation the "narrow" regime wins out. The contrast with Table 5.5 is clear for the inflation figure. The "wide" ERM outscores the "narrow" by a wide margin. This is perhaps unsurprising, since the inflation target which appears in the monetary policy rule is the inflation differential with the French–German average. By reducing the weight given to the exchange rate, what rule increases the relative weight given to the inflation differential? This explains the increased ability to promote inflation convergence. It also indicates that a strict exchange rate target in the presence of an endogenous risk premium can hinder the process of inflation convergence, if the risk premium is affected by variables other than inflation differentials.

In essence, if the risk premium is responding to, for example, debt or unemployment, then interest rates will also respond to these variables due to the exchange rate target. However, it the weight attached to that target is reduced, the response of interest rates to these variables is also reduced. If one of the other targets of monetary policy is the inflation differential or, put differently, inflation convergence, then this target now receives a higher priority. What this means in practice is that inflation convergence does not depend on tight pegging of the exchange rate, instead it can be achieved by an explicit inflation convergence target. On the interest rate convergence

Table 5.4   Stabilization performance of the two Regimes – no shocks

Year	Inflation		Output	
	Narrow	Wide	Narrow	Wide
1	100	102.4	100	91.4
5	100	101.9	100	92.6
10	100	100.2	100	92.6

Table 5.5   Convergence performance of the two Regimes – no shocks

Year	Narrow ERM				Wide ERM			
	Inflation diff.	Interest rate diff.	Debt	Deficit	Inflation diff.	Interest rate diff.	Debt	Deficit
1	100	100	70.5	3.9	89.4	98.7	70.3	3.9
5	100	100	69.1	1.4	80.4	100.5	69	1.5
10	100	100	64.3	1.3	82.1	96.3	64.2	1.3

front the two rules are fairly similar, whilst the difference between the two rules for debts and deficits is negligible.

The result of changing the priority attached to the exchange rate target is to increase the role monetary policy attaches to both output stabilization and inflation convergence (see Tables 5.4 and 5.5). These simulations suggest that the two are not mutually exclusive, and that if a tight fiscal policy is also being implemented this rule is beneficial. We next examine the two monetary policy regimes under various shocks to determine whether this result is robust.

Shocks

This part of the chapter considers the effects of five exogenous shocks on the adjustment paths of the two policy combinations discussed above. The aim is to first find if the two policies are stable under a range of shocks, and secondly to indicate the comparative ability of the two to stabilize the economy. Specifically, we examine a positive and permanent world trade shock, a permanent increase in German government spending, a 800 increase in German inflation expectations, a 800 increase in Spanish inflation expectations, and a permanent increase in the price of oil.

As for the unshocked results, the regimes are compared both on their stabilization and convergence performances. The first objective is measured via the rule's ability to limit the deviation of output and inflation around their unshocked values for each regime. The latter is measured via the root cumulative squared deviation of inflation and interest rates from the French and German average and the debt and deficit ratios.

German government spending

This shock represents a permanent increase in German government spending of 1% of German GDP. This is an asymmetric shock to Spanish demand, further complicated by the assumed asymmetric nature of the ERM. Spain is too small to substantially affect the German interest rate decisions. The impact for Germany is an increase in interest rates as German output and inflation rise. In both the narrow and wide ERM this translates into an increase in Spanish and French interest rates. The result is a negative spillover to Spanish output in the short-term, as shown in Figure 5.13.

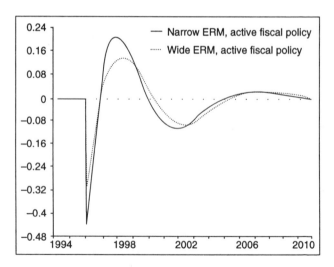

Figure 5.13 Spain, output, difference from base, German spending shock, 1994–2010

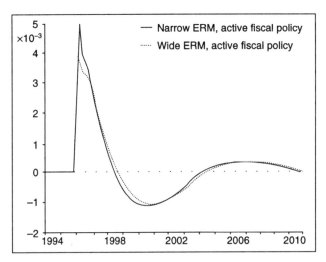

Figure 5.14   Spain, interest rate, difference from base, German spending shock, 1994–2010

However, the extent of the increase in Spanish interest rates is affected by the regime in place. As Figure 5.14 shows, Spanish interest rates rise by less under the wide ERM than under the narrow. This is reflected in a smaller decrease in output the deficit under the wide ERM regime. Therefore inflation and unemployment do not vary by as much from their base values, nor does the debt ratio. This enhanced stability is reflected in the objective function data presented in Tables 5.6 and 5.7, where the stabilization and convergence properties of the regimes are shown.

Table 5.6   Stabilization performance of the two Regimes – German spending shock

Year	Inflation		Output	
	Narrow	*Wide*	*Narrow*	*Wide*
1	100	70.8	100	70.1
5	100	77.2	100	71.6
10	100	79	100	73.9

Table 5.7 Convergence performance of the two Regimes – German spending shock

Year	Narrow ERM				Wide ERM			
	Inflation diff.	Interest rate diff.	Debt	Deficit	Inflation diff.	Interest rate diff.	Debt	Deficit
1	100	100	70.4	3.9	18.2	92.8	70.3	3.9
5	100	100	69.1	1.4	28.7	100.8	69	1.5
10	100	100	64.2	1.3	36	93.3	64.2	1.3

It is clear from Table 5.6 that the wide regime insulates the Spanish economy from the shock more effectively than the narrow regime. Thus, in terms of stabilization, the wide ERM is more successful for asymmetric shocks stemming from the ERM leader. However, is this success bought at the price of divergence? Table 5.7 would indicate that this is not the case, indeed it suggests the opposite. The debt and deficit ratios are largely unaffected by the regime choice since the fiscal policy rule ensures that tax

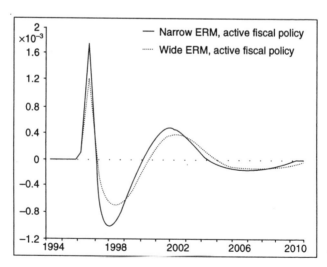

Figure 5.15 Spain, unemployment, difference from base, German spending shock, 1994–2010

rates adjust to approach or hit the target regardless of the targets of monetary policy. For inflation, the data suggests that the wide ERM rule outperforms the narrow by a larger amount than in the unshocked case, whilst the extent of the improvement is not as marked for interest rates.

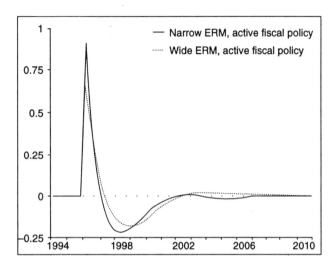

Figure 5.16 Spain, debt, difference from base, German spending shock, 1994–2010

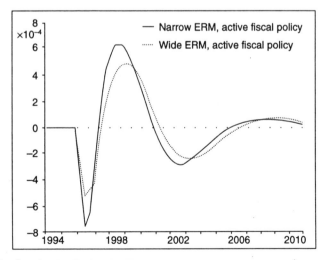

Figure 5.17 Spain, inflation, difference from base, German spending shock, 1994–2010

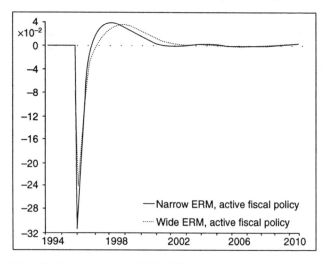

Figure 5.18   Spain, government deficit, difference from base, German spending shock, 1994–2010

World trade

A positive and permanent world trade shock of 1% was applied to the two regimes in order to compare the responses for a symmetric demand shock, and to examine the impact compared to the asymmetric German demand shock. The shock impacts through the trade balance, increasing Spanish exports to the rest of the world. Furthermore France and Germany also experience increased export demand and thus increased output, leading to a further increase in total Spanish export demand. The result, under both monetary policy rules is an increase in Spanish output in the short term peaking at just over 1% in both cases in the year after the shock (see Figure 5.19).

As would be expected from the similar output response the other variables of interest – inflation, interest rates, debt and the deficit – also follow very similar dynamic paths under both regimes. However, Figures 5.20–5.23 do show some small differences in response. Output peaks at a slightly higher value under the narrow band ERM, leading to larger increase in inflation. This is explained by the interest rate response, shown in Figure 5.20. The wider ERM bands allow Spanish interest rates to adjust more fully in line with domestic developments than the narrow ERM, and thus rates rise by more under the wide band system. Overall, though, the differences are minor, indicating that for symmetric demand shocks the narrow band ERM produces broadly appropriate interest rate responses.

This can be explained by the symmetric nature of the shock. Since all European economies are hit by the shock, they all experience a similar increase in demand. Differences between countries stem from their export shares with the rest of the world and their openness. Thus, the interest rate

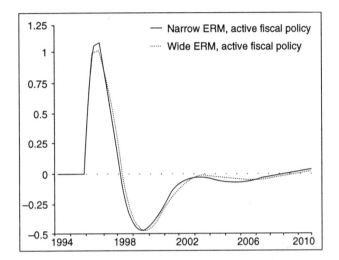

Figure 5.19   Spain, output, difference from base, world trade shock, 1994–2010

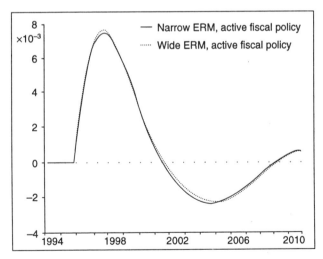

Figure 5.20   Spain, interest rate, difference from base, world trade shock, 1994–2010

response of the Bundesbank would be similar to that of the Spanish central bank under the wide band regime. This is not the case for the German demand shock. In the asymmetric demand case the response of Spanish interest rates under the narrow ERM is larger than it is under the wide ERM, creating a larger disturbance to the economy.

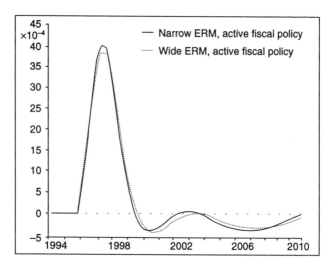

Figure 5.21   Spain, inflation, difference from base, world trade shock, 1994–2010

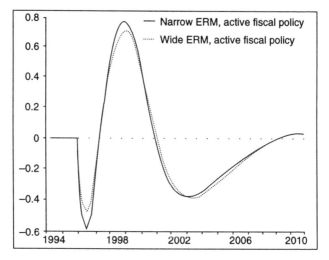

Figure 5.22   Spain, debt, difference from base, world trade shock, 1994–2010

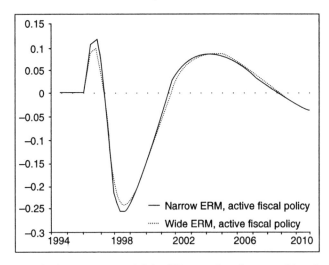

Figure 5.23 Spain, government deficit, difference from base, world trade shock, 1994–2010

Table 5.8 compares the regimes in terms of their stabilizing properties. In keeping with the discussion, the gains from a wide band ERM are less clear here than they were for the German demand shock. Furthermore Table 5.9 shows that the inflation convergence performance for the two regimes is much closer than for the asymmetric demand shock. Once again, we find that the interest rate performance is rather similar as is that of the fiscal measures.

Table 5.8 Stabilization performance of the two regimes – world trade shock

Year	Inflation		Output	
	Narrow	*Wide*	*Narrow*	*Wide*
1	100	94.5	100	94.7
5	100	99	100	96.9
10	100	99	100	97.2

Table 5.9   Convergence performance of the two regimes – world trade shock

Year	Narrow ERM				Wide ERM			
	Inflation diff.	*Interest rate diff.*	*Debt*	*Deficit*	*Inflation diff.*	*Interest rate diff.*	*Debt*	*Deficit*
1	100	100	70.6	4.6	4	98.5	70	4.8
5	100	100	69	1.4	42	102.1	68.9	1.5
10	100	100	64.1	1.3	51.1	94.7	64	1.4

German inflation expectations

German inflation expectations were increased by 4% in annual terms for one quarter. Since inflation expectations are assumed to be adaptive, the shock persists for some time. This represents an asymmetric inflationary shock for Europe, with German interest rates rising immediately as wage claims are increased. Due to the nature of the Bundesbank's response function German rates are increased aggressively and quickly resulting, via the ERM, to upward pressure on Spanish rates under both interest rate policy schemes.

The risk premium also acts to increase Spanish rates through the German inflation term, leading to a higher risk premium and further pressure on the peseta and thus Spanish interest rates. The result is an increase in Spanish interest rates, and reduction in Spanish output. Moreover, the fall in Spanish output worsens the debt: GDP ratio and results in higher taxes in both regimes, exacerbating the initial output loss. The Bundesbank's response rids the German economy of the increased inflation within the first year, allowing Spanish interest rates and tax rates to fall quickly. The economy overshoots its equilibrium position due to a mix of competitiveness gains from the large drop in inflation and the reduction in tax and interest rates.

Under the narrow ERM regime the Spanish interest rate response is more than enough to clear any inflation impetus from the system. The large response is due not only to the Bundesbank's aggressive policy, but to the ratchet effect of the risk premium. Substituting the policy with the wide ERM results in markedly less volatility for the Spanish economy. Output neither falls nor overshoots by as much, inflation and unemployment mirror this, whilst the fiscal variables are also more stable.

Table 5.10 Stabilization performance of the two regimes – German inflation shock

Year	Inflation		Output	
	Narrow	Wide	Narrow	Wide
1	100	63.9	100	69.4
5	100	65.8	100	68.3
10	100	68.2	100	69

Table 5.11 Convergence performance of the two regimes – German inflation shock

Year	Narrow ERM				Wide ERM			
	Inflation diff.	Interest rate diff.	Debt	Deficit	Inflation diff.	Interest rate diff.	Debt	Deficit
1	100	100	68.8	3.9	28.3	72.6	69.4	3.9
5	100	100	68.4	1.5	30.8	90.8	68.6	1.5
10	100	100	64.2	1.2	34.9	87.7	64.3	1.2

The wide ERM Spanish response, whilst keeping with the ERM boundaries, focuses more closely on domestic variables than it does under the narrow ERM. The result is more stability, since the Spanish response does not need to be as aggressive as the narrow band regime produces. Tables 5.10 and 5.11 confirm this. The wide band ERM produces a substantially better performance than the narrow both in terms of convergence and stability. Thus if the shock is of German origin, and whether it is from the demand or the supply side Spain would be better off with a wide band ERM. Again, this does not endanger the convergence process, but actually enhances it by reducing the impact of the risk premium on domestic interest rates.

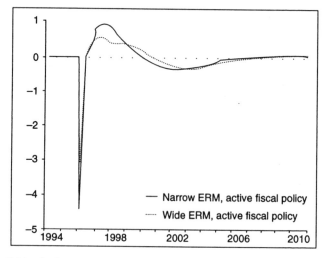

Figure 5.24   Spain, output, difference from base, German inflation expectations shock, 1994–2010

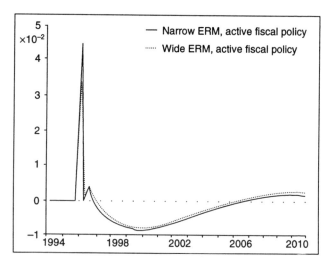

Figure 5.25   Spain, interest rates, difference from base, German inflation expectations shock, 1994–2010

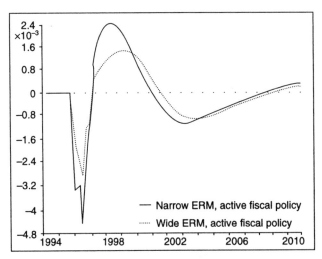

Figure 5.26 Spain, inflation rate, difference from base, German inflation expectations shock, 1994–2010

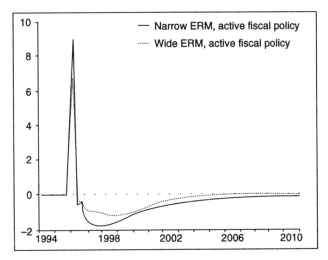

Figure 5.27 Spain, debt, difference from base, German inflation expectations shock, 1994–2010

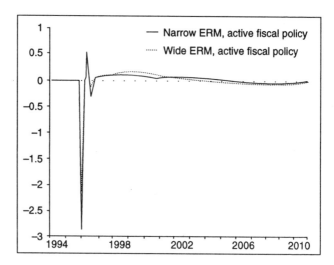

Figure 5.28   Spain, government deficit, difference from base, German inflation expectations shock, 1994–2010

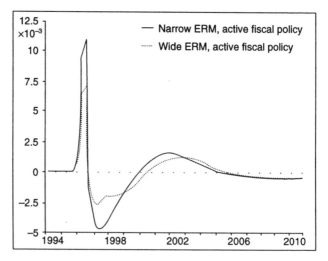

Figure 5.29   Spain, unemployment, difference from base, German inflation expectations shock, 1994–2010

Spanish inflation expectations

As a counterpoint to the German inflationary shock, this shock repeats the process, but this time applies the shock to Spanish inflation expectations.

The short-term response under both regimes is almost identical for this shock. Under the wide band ERM interest rates rise to offset the inflation differential with the rest of the ERM, and whilst under the narrow ERM the priority given to this target is relatively less, the term also appears in the risk premium. Therefore although the exchange rate target is more important for the narrow band the inflation differential affects the exchange rate and thus interest rates.

Since the short-term monetary policy response is similar it is unsurprising to find that the rest of the economy also responds in a similar fashion in the short term for both regimes. However, the subsequent interest rate path is illuminating. Since the wide band ERM puts less emphasis on the exchange rate and thus the risk premium, interest rates fall more quickly in response to the drop in output under this regime. Under the narrow band regime interest rates remain higher for longer, slowing the recovery of output (Figures 5.31 and 5.32). This faster drop in interest rates reduces the deficit and results in a relatively smaller increase in debt when compared to the narrow band ERM.

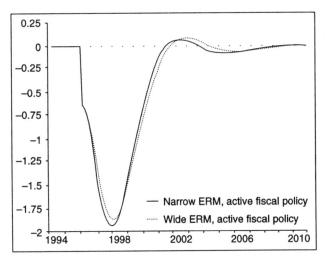

Figure 5.30   Spain, output, difference from base, Spanish inflation expectations shock, 1994–2010

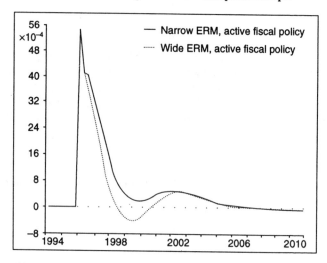

Figure 5.31 Spain, interest rates, difference from base, Spanish inflation expectations shock, 1994–2010

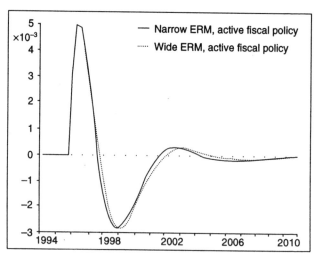

Figure 5.32 Spain, inflation rate, difference from base, Spanish inflation expectations shock, 1994–2010

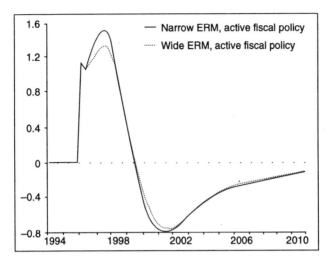

Figure 5.33 Spain, debt, difference from base, Spanish inflation expectations shock, 1994–2010

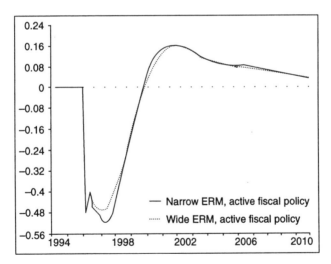

Figure 5.34 Spain, government deficit, difference from base, Spanish inflation expectations shock, 1994–2010

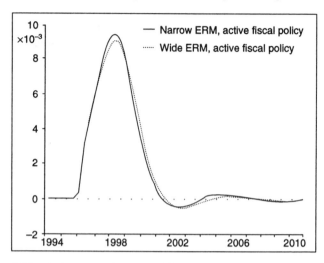

Figure 5.35   Spain, unemployment, difference from base, Spanish inflation expectations shock, 1994–2010

In the medium and long term the two regimes produce very similar responses, indicating once again, that it is in the transition after a shock that the differences in policy setting count. However, as shown in Tables 5.12 and 5.13 the absolute differences between the regimes are not great for stabilization. The convergence measures also show little absolute advantage for the wide band ERM regime.

Table 5.12   Stabilization performance of the two regimes – Spanish inflation shock

Year	Inflation		Output	
	Narrow	Wide	Narrow	Wide
1	100	100.4	100	95.8
5	100	101.4	100	99.1
10	100	101.7	100	99.1

Table 5.13   Convergence performance of the two regimes – Spanish inflation shock

Year	Narrow ERM				Wide ERM			
	Inflation diff.	Interest rate diff.	Debt	Deficit	Inflation diff.	Interest rate diff.	Debt	Deficit
1	100	100	72	3.4	205.3	95.4	71.6	3.4
5	100	100	68.3	1.6	78.4	96	68.3	1.6
10	100	100	64	1.3	85.4	90.6	64	1.4

Oil prices

The final shock considered is a permanent increase in the oil price index of 2.5%. Since the index jumps from its base value to the new value between two quarters, this translates into an annualized increase in imported raw materials prices of 10.4% in the first quarter of 1996. The initial impact is a large increase in imported inflation throughout Europe. However output responses differ between German and Spain, as shown in Figure 5.37.

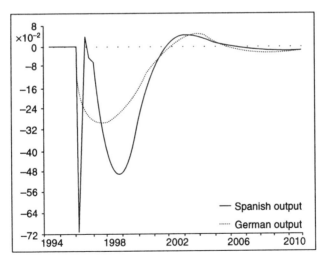

Figure 5.36   Spanish and German output, difference from base, oil shock, 1994–2010

Spanish interest rates rise by much more than German rates after the shock, as shown in Figure 5.37, which is explained by the exchange rate commitment and the risk premium, Figure 5.45. This occurs under both regimes, and results in an immediate and large fall in Spanish output.

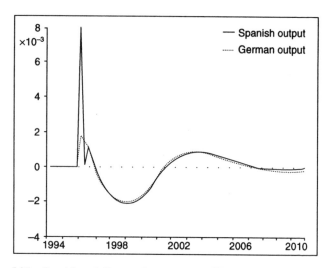

Figure 5.37   Spanish and German interest rates, difference from base, oil shock, 1994–2010

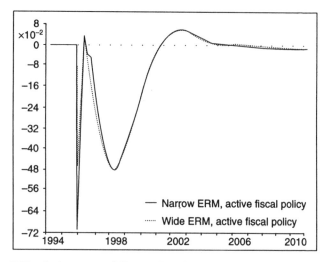

Figure 5.38   Spain, output, difference from base, oil shock, 1994–2010

However, as the increase in imported inflation is only temporary, this impetus to domestic price inflation disappears after the first quarter, and thus inflation drops very quickly from its peak, Figure 5.43, a process enhanced by the output loss. This allows interest rates to decline and the economy as a whole to move into an adjustment period which is more like that in Germany.

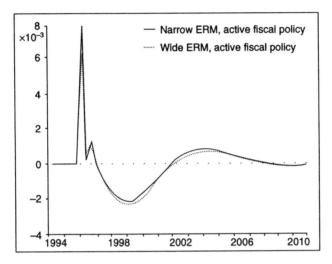

Figure 5.39   Spain, interest rate, difference from base, oil price shock, 1994–2010

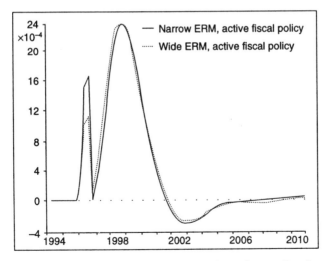

Figure 5.40   Spain, unemployment, difference from base, oil price shock, 1994–2010

After the initial volatility, caused by a mix of the risk premium and the exchange rate target, has worn off output remains negative for some time. This is explained by two main channels. First, as Figure 5.44 shows, domestic inflation remains higher than its base level in both regimes for

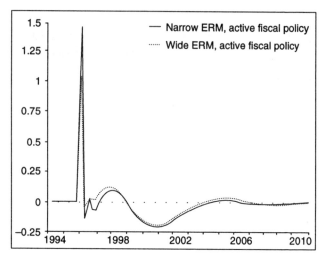

Figure 5.41   Spain, debt, difference from base, oil price shock, 1994–2010

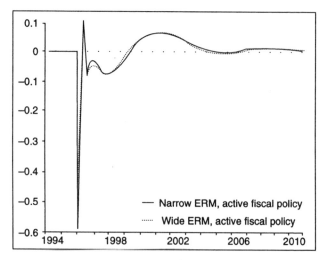

Figure 5.42   Spain, government deficit, difference from base, oil price shock, 1994–2010

longer than the rest of the world's resulting in lost competitiveness. Second, the increase in the inflation tax is greater than the increase in other personal income in the medium term, leading to a fall in disposable income for the private sector.

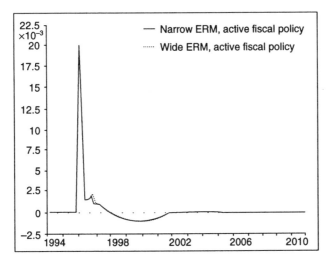

Figure 5.43 Spain, inflation rate, difference from base, oil price shock, 1994–2010

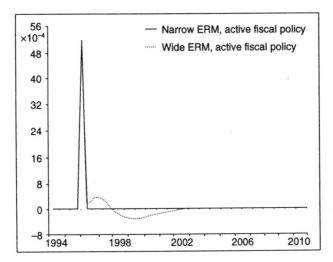

Figure 5.44 Spanish and ROW inflation rates, difference from base, 1994–2010

Since the exchange rate target causes short-term volatility, reducing the priority given to this target reduces this volatility. This is borne out in the comparative simulations, for example, Figures 5.39 and 5.40. The short-term impact on output and interest rates is reduced under the wide band ERM regime.

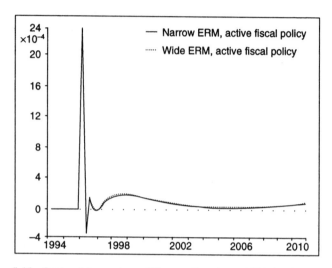

Figure 5.45   Spain, risk premium, difference from base, 1994–2010

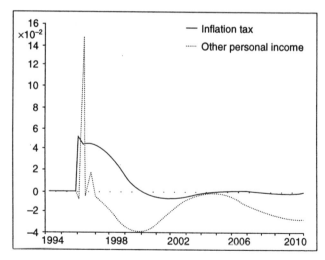

Figure 5.46   Spain, inflation tax and other personal income, narrow ERM, difference from base, 1994–2010

Table 5.14 Stabilization performance of the two regimes – oil price shock

Year	Inflation		Output	
	Narrow	Wide	Narrow	Wide
1	100	100.6	100	81.7
5	100	100.5	100	96.6
10	100	100.6	100	95.9

Table 5.14 indicates the level of improvement for output stabilization under the wide ERM regime. The inflation stabilization performance is not very different between the regimes, but this can be explained, in the short run, by the dominance of the imported inflation increase as compared to the response of wages. The shock to import prices swamps the effect of changes in wage claims, there is very little policy can do to offset the increase in prices in the direct aftermath of the shock in a fixed exchange rate regime. On the convergence front (see Table 5.15), the wide ERM outperforms the narrow for inflation and interest rates, whilst, once again, the comparative results for the fiscal variables are very similar.

Table 5.15 Convergence performance of the two regimes – oil price shock

Year	Narrow ERM				Wide ERM			
	Inflation diff.	Interest rate diff.	Debt	Deficit	Inflation diff.	Interest rate diff.	Debt	Deficit
1	100	100	71.3	2.3	70.6	85.6	71.1	2.5
5	100	100	65.2	2.4	75.5	93.6	65.5	2.4
10	100	100	63.2	1.6	90.6	90.5	63.1	1.7

5.5   CONCLUSIONS

Chapter 5 has concentrated on the convergence path of a "median" country as defined in Chapter 1. Taking Spain as a representative of this group, the essential problems are inflation and interest rate differentials, a worsening fiscal situation, and high unemployment. Spain was chosen to highlight the basic difference between policies which stabilize and policies which promote convergence in the context of the Maastricht criteria. Whilst the two policy objectives may be complementary, they could also be mutually exclusive depending on initial conditions, the economy's structure and shocks hitting the system over time.

Since Maastricht concentrates on the first two problem areas described for Spain, and ignores the latter, the scope for conflict is clear. If the reason for MU, and thus convergence, arises from fears that floating European currencies would ultimately destroy the Single Market and the CAP, then the method by which MU is achieved is also of importance, since if the transitional arrangements are too severe MU may never be reached, except by a handful of EU members.

This chapter has therefore examined two monetary policy alternatives for Spain. First, Spain can remain within the "narrow" band ERM, modelled by applying a relatively high weight to the exchange rate target in the monetary policy rule. Second, Spain can opt for a "wide" band ERM, modelled by reducing the weight attached to the exchange rate target. Fiscal policy follows a rule which targets the debt ratio, and is unchanged between the two regimes.

The regimes are compared on the basis of "stabilization" and "convergence" performance. In standard policy work policies are normally ranked according to their ability to achieve small variations in the target variables from some base path. As Simms (1993) points out some judgement must be made about the desirability of the base path itself. European convergence offers an interesting twist on this normal approach. The "base" path is determined by the convergence policies, a relatively straightforward idea, but the stabilization issue is not quite so straightforward.

The issue is: what to stabilize? Since the convergence targets do not include output, stabilization could be defined as policies which prevent deviations of the converging variables from their base trajectories. On the other hand, traditionally, and sensibly, output or unemployment are normally essential stabilization variables. The approach taken here is to produce a "stabil-ization" measure for each regime based on output and inflation, and a set of "convergence" measures.

The first measure is the root cumulative squared deviation of inflation and output from zero and potential respectively. The second group is the RCSD of Spanish inflation and interest rates from the French and German averages, and the government deficit and debt ratio.

The two regimes were first compared without shocks. The wide band ERM regime produced a clear benefit for output stabilization (Table 5.4). However, inflation does not drop by as much in the short run in this regime as compared to the narrow ERM. Since the inflation stabilization measure is based on differences from zero, the wide ERM does worse than the narrow. But when the convergence measure is examined (Table 5.5), it is clear that on the inflation front the wide band ERM actually improves convergence. For the narrow ERM regime, inflation falls below the EU average by more and for longer than it does for the wide band regime, which accounts for the improvement.

This result is due to two influences. First, by reducing the priority attached to the exchange rate target the authorities can react more responsively to the inflation differential component of the interest rate reaction function than they could under the tight ERM. Secondly the risk premium is affected by variables other than the inflation differential, thus this further diminishes the net effect of the inflation differential on interest rates under the narrow ERM. For the interest rate the improvement in convergence is more less clear, whilst under both regimes the fiscal rule ensures that the differences in the fiscal measures are marginal.

The are several insights and lessons to be drawn from these basic results. First, on a general level, the wide ERM produces higher amounts of convergence to core EU averages for the nominal targets than does the narrow. Furthermore, it does this with less pain in terms of output variability. An important insight comes from the result for inflation and relates to the choice of inflation target. If a country is undergoing a convergence process then it would seem logical that the inflation *target* should be that given by the Maastricht criteria. If the *measure* of inflation performance is then the inflation differential from the lowest inflation countries, the wide band ERM outperforms the narrow.

However, the authorities then have a moving target for inflation and, importantly, this target may not be desirable. If the ultimate stabilization target is zero inflation, or stable prices, then the higher the core EU inflation average, the higher the inflation target, and the greater the cost in terms of price stabilization. What this means in practice is that the inflation target needs to be carefully stated: is it to simply follow the lowest European rate, or to define an independent and low target rate?

This argument is secondary in the sense that the long-run inflation rate in a European fixed exchange rate system will be given according to some combination of the rate of inflation of import prices and the rate of depreciation or appreciation of the ERM area with the rest of the world.

Therefore the long-run inflation rate for Spain, in the model, is given. It is the dynamic path to that equilibrium which will be affected by the decision. Moreover, in terms of choosing between the two regimes, the choice of the inflation target itself is irrelevant. Whatever the target is, the wide ERM regime will be more capable of hitting it than the narrow.

In the case considered in this chapter, where it is assumed the Spanish authorities are committed to the convergence process, and that therefore their targets are those given by Maastricht, the wide band ERM promotes more convergence whilst stabilizing output. Thus, if the authorities change nothing else in their policy setting, except the weight attached to the exchange rate target, output stability will be promoted without the risk of divergence. The wide band regime therefore produces the more satisfactory "base" from which to work.

In order to compare the regimes under shocks, the stabilization measures were changed. For these results, the deviation of inflation and output from their base values were considered. The ranking seen for the unshocked experiments were preserved to varying degrees over the shocks considered. Whenever a shock hits the system, the increased ability of the wide band ERM to stabilize output and inflation produced consistently lower costs for the stabilization measures than did the narrow band system. Furthermore, the ranking was also maintained for the convergence measures. The greatest savings were made for asymmetric shocks stemming from Germany, but even for symmetric shocks, such as world trade and oil prices, savings were made.

The conclusion is therefore that a narrow band ERM, with a risk premium dependent on relative inflation rates, the unemployment rate, debt levels and the current account, performs worse in terms of both stabilization and convergence. If economies undergoing a disinflationary convergence programme can use wider bands for their exchange rate pegs they should do so, as long as the alternative continues to be a clearly stated inflation convergence target. It must be borne in mind that the other two targets of monetary policy, output and inflation, were not changed, nor was the relative importance of the two as reflected in the reaction function parameters.

The move to 15% ERM bands should not be seen as a step back from continued monetary integration, but rather as an opportunity for those countries still converging to proceed with less cost and volatility, and thus increase the likelihood of the system enduring. This result may seem surprising, but it stems from assumptions about the operating practices of the ERM, German hegemony, the treatment of risk premia, and the Maastricht targets. The interaction of these processes and variables is complicated, and as far as we are aware this model is unique in integrating these elements for a country such as Spain.

6 Fiscal Policy Regimes in a Monetary Union

6.1 INTRODUCTION

The question of fiscal policy setting in the projected European MU has received widespread attention in the literature. The Maastricht Treaty clarified the intended form, but left much unsaid. In response, calls have been made for further analysis of both the appropriate objectives and operation of fiscal policy in such a regime. Chapter 6 examines the issue by comparing various fiscal regimes under MU by their ability to stabilize output and inflation for the individual members and the EU as a whole. The chapter also examines an area which has not received attention: the effect of the core's choice on those left out.

The projected basis for fiscal policy formulation in MU as set out in Maastricht is strict limits on debt and deficit ratios. This arises as a direct result of the Delors Report (1989), which pointed out the danger inherent in allowing weak fiscal members to continue to run large deficits. The fear is that markets cannot apply the required discipline to stop the growth of deficits. A crisis in one market may spread to another, leading to general pressure for the ECB to "bail out" the member in trouble, and reducing the anti-inflationary credibility of the Bank. Thus, the Treaty expressly forbids the ECB from acting as any EU government's central bank. There are to be no "bail outs". In order to assure fiscal solvency the Treaty demands that MU member states adhere to the criteria values after MU is formed. If not, punitive actions can be taken, up to fining the member by an "appropriate" amount. The overall stance is to restrict fiscal policy freedom. There is no mention in the Treaty of either how fiscal policy should be coordinated, or the possibility of a federal fiscal system.

This is in contrast to the evidence from the optimal currency area literature which indicates clearly (see Kenen, 1969) that fiscal policy has an enhanced role to play in a currency union. However, this view has been criticized as naive in the light of increased understanding of the government solvency constraint. The ability of governments to use fiscal policy as an active stabilization tool has been reduced, and is reduced in direct proportion to the level of debt. Therefore, if fiscal policy is paralyzed by the solvency constraint and monetary policy unable to cushion local shocks, what recourse is there in a currency union for active fiscal stabilization policy? If the members are reasonably alike and the shocks which hit the members are predominantly symmetric, then the problem may not be acute. However, if the members' economies are unalike and they are hit by asymmetric shocks then the issue is extremely important. One option may be some form of federal fiscal policy, or coinsurance scheme.

The likelihood of some form of federal fiscal regime for coinsurance or active stabilization being required has long been recognized in the literature, for example Goodhart (1992b, 1994), Wyplosz (1991), Giovannini (1991), and Eichengreen (1993), as has the need for more, not less, fiscal freedom and coordination, for example Dornbusch (1991), Hughes Hallett and Vines (1993), and Masson and Melitz (1990). However, with the exception of Masson and Melitz and Hughes Hallett and Vines, none of these papers or articles has examined the quantitative gains to be had from using fiscal policy in a more active manner than the Maastricht Treaty would seem to allow.

In an attempt to remedy this, this chapter presents results from a three-country simulation model of France, Germany and Spain for a variety of fiscal policy arrangements under a variety of symmetric and asymmetric shocks. The latter country is included so that consideration can be given to the effects of the different fiscal policy regimes on the countries left out of MU.

The regimes are examined and explained in more detail in Section 6.2, but some description is given here. In all regimes government spending and tax rates adjust to ensure that on average, over the simulation period, the debt: GDP target ratio is met. This excludes the possibility of unstable debt paths, and thus bypasses the moral hazard problem associated with excessive deficits and debts. In some of the regimes, however, this target is partially relaxed, allowing spending and taxation to respond to the deviation of output from its potential. Put another way, these rules examine the impact of partially relaxing the Maastricht fiscal rules. It is to be expected that these rules would allow debt ratios to go beyond the 60% reference values for some time, but they do not allow this to persist.

Two sets of regimes are considered. First, two non-federal schemes are compared with and without shocks. Second, four federal schemes are investigated. The two non-federal schemes are:

(I) Debt target.
(II) Debt and output targets.

Regime (I) is a "tight" fiscal policy regime, where there is no attempt to stabilize output via government spending; instead tax rates and government spending are adjusted each quarter to insure that the debt to GDP target is, on average, met. Regime (II) allows government spending and tax rates in the two MU members to partially adjust in the light of their respective output deviations from potential; however, weight is still given to the debt: GDP ratio. The four federal schemes have a common basis but different assumptions about how the funds are disbursed, and the stance of national fiscal policies. The four schemes are:

(III) Regime (I) + redistributive federal budget, transfer payments.
(IV) Regime (II) + redistributive federal budget, transfer payments.
 (V) Regime (I) + redistributive federal budget, government spending.
(VI) Regime (II) + redistributive federal budget, government spending.

In all of these regimes a fixed proportion of the members' GDPs is passed to the federal authority, which is not permitted to either issue debt or levy taxes. The distribution of the tax revenue accruing to the authority is based on a formula which measures a member's output deviation from its "normal" share of the MU total output. This ensures that if there is a MU-wide recession there is no redistribution. On the other hand if one country experiences a recession, its share in MU GDP falls, and it receives a correspondingly higher amount of spending from the fiscal authorities. The fiscal budget is limited in size, and the federal authority cannot voluntarily increase that size through bond issue, in other words the budget is automatically balanced.

The differences between the two regimes is in the stance of national fiscal policies and the method of disbursement of the redistributed resources. In Regimes (III) and (V) the national governments do not target the output level, but exclusively pursue the debt ratio target with both government spending and tax rates, as in Regime (I). In Regimes (IV) and (VI) some attempt is made at the national level to stabilize output, as in Regime (II). The two disbursement methods are taken from suggestions in Goodhart and Smith (1993), either transfers to the private sector, or government spending. The former affects disposable income, the latter output directly. By comparing the two some indication of the relative effectiveness can be determined.

The regimes are compared and examined via deterministic simulations under differing demand and supply shocks. The results allow a quantitative measurement of the gains from allowing flexible fiscal policy in an MU made up of non-identical members, and the gains available from implementing a federal budget system with or without flexible national policies.

As discussed in Chapter 3, past empirical efforts have all suffered from some weakness *vis-à-vis* the issue raised in this chapter. The fundamentally multi-country nature of federal policy and the interaction of fiscal and monetary policy severely limits the applicability of analytical approaches. Aoki's sums and differences method could be of some help, save for one problem: it assumes that states are symmetric and identical in size. Hughes Hallett and Vines (1993) and Lossani and Tirelli (1993) adopt these assumptions in their simulation models, but as shown in this chapter the size differential between France and Germany has important influences on MU interest rates and thus the fiscal policy response. Therefore it is appropriate to take into account both the different structures and sizes of the economies considered. This is achieved by models such as Multimod and Quest, yet these modelling groups have concentrated on comparing MU with the ERM and floating, largely ignoring fiscal policy issues. Work which has emerged in the fiscal policy area using these models has not examined output and inflation stabilization or federal regimes. The model developed in Appendix 1 is not only capable of modelling the fiscal issues but also the size and structure issue. As such, the model and its application represents a step forward over what has gone before.

The chapter is organized as follows. Section 6.2 presents the simulation framework and modelling of fiscal policy in the various regimes. Section 6.3 presents the results. The results are split into two. First, the need for fiscal flexibility is examined under MU. Regimes (I) and (II) are compared both with and without shocks. Second, the federal fiscal policy schemes are examined and compared to their non-federal counterparts in order to determine if any benefits accrue from adopting such schemes. Finally, Section 6.4 concludes.

6.2   THE SIMULATION FRAMEWORK

The regimes are implemented in a three-country model comprising France, Germany and Spain. The inclusion of the latter country is to allow the impact of the various core policies on a probable non-MU member to be examined.

Monetary policy in the MU is set according to the equation discussed on p. 223 of Appendix 1, and we assume a fixed MU exchange rate with the rest of the world, whilst Spain and the rest of the ERM continue to set their monetary policies with the exchange rate commitment as their primary target; the ERM continues to function.

The fiscal policy rules rely on four basic equations. The first two relate to an individual member's tax rate and government spending level, the second two to the federal fiscal policy equations.

The members set their government spending and tax rates with two targets in mind, as shown in equations (6.1) and (6.2).

$$G = G_{t-1} + (\alpha(\eta \, Y_{\text{gap}}) + (1-\alpha)(\nu(B-B_T) + \rho(B/B_{t-1}-1)))100 \quad (6.1)$$

$$Tax = Tax_{t-1} + \alpha(\eta \, Y_{\text{gap}}) + (1 - \alpha)(\nu(B - B_T) + \rho(B/B_{t-1} - 1)) \quad (6.2)$$

The targets are the output gap and the debt:GDP ratio. An integral control rule is used for the latter target since this provided more stable adjustment.[1] Depending on the value given to the weight a the authorities can either target the output gap or the debt ratio, or some weighted average of the two. For the regimes where no national stabilization is undertaken a takes the value zero, indicating that the authorities adjust both spending and tax rates in order to achieve the target debt ratio, B_T, over time. The parameters ρ and ν are set such that the elasticities of tax rates and spending to the level and rate of change of the debt ratio are the same across the countries modelled.

Having described the national policy schemes we now turn to the federal, which are superimposed on the national policy options. Goodhart and Smith (1993) highlight three issues in the design of a federal policy. First, what indicator of activity should be employed; second, how transfers are utilized; and third, how the system should be financed.

Italianer and van Heukelen's (1993) choice of indicator is the difference between changes in each country's unemployment rate and the MU average as the determinant of the amount of redistribution. However, this approach has certain problems. The change in the unemployment rate could be caused by changes in the natural rate, not demand conditions. Moreover, if each member has a different relationship between output and unemployment this would affect the distribution in an inequitable fashion. Put another way, if the Okun relationship between output and unemployment is different in each country, than a given change in output experienced by all members, would result in different unemployment changes. Transfers would then result between members, even though they may all be in an identical recession as measured by the output gap.

Goodhart and Smith (1993) reject the unemployment measure, but indicate the problem of lags in output measures. Since stabilization needs to occur swiftly after a shock, this presents something of a problem. However, it is a problem associated with almost all measures of activity. On the indicator front they therefore suggest that demand measures such as telephone installations, or electricity demand, may be useful. For this book, output is used as the indicator, although it is fully accepted that there are potential problems with this choice.

There are numerous options for the second question, either a direct federal unemployment benefit system or intergovernmental transfers. The latter option allows governments to decide how the transfers should be utilized: government spending, reduced taxation, transfers to the private sector, or unemployment benefits. Goodhart and Smith advocate a *per capita* transfer system where grants are equally disbursed to the whole population. Once again, their reasoning has to do with the speed of response. Fiscal spending or revenue decision making is too slow, they argue, for it to offer any useful stabilization role when speed of reaction is of the essence. The assumption in this book is that statistical lags are unimportant, that the government is therefore fully aware of changes in economic activity as they occur, and that their objective is to stabilize output quickly. Two suggestions for the disbursement of the grant are therefore considered, one where demand is directly affected via either federal or national government spending, and one where disposable income is affected via a direct grant.

The final problem relates to the financing of the federal scheme. On the one hand a full federal budget could be envisaged, much as in existing federal states, with the ability to levy taxes and issue debt. However, the current likelihood of such a large-scale centralization of fiscal power in Europe is low. Another option, therefore, is a much less ambitious budgetary scheme, where transfers from national governments are passed to some central authority, which reallocates these resources based on the indicators discussed above, but which is budget neutral. The latter option is adopted in this chapter.

A fixed percentage of the national outputs is passed to the federal authority, which allocates spending based on the output performance of the members. The amount is set at 1% of national GDP, broadly in line with the current central EU budget. Furthermore, the authority completely reallocates the full amount received every period and excludes the possibility of the federal authorities levying taxes or issuing bonds.

This policy is explicitly stabilizing in its approach, unlike the normal definition of "redistribution" in a federal context. Normally this term is used to refer to policies which target regions with, for example, low *per capita* GDP, which can lead to permanent transfers, such as the Mezzogiorno region of Italy. The policy rule is called "redistributive" to indicate that it is by definition budget neutral, there can be no federal deficit or surplus, the federal authority merely receives funds which it then reallocates.

The process of reallocation requires some attention. The rule is based on a simple principle. If the MU area as a whole is in equilibrium, then whatever a country pays into the federal budget it receives back. Furthermore, if the MU as a whole experiences a recession of equal magnitude in each member country, there is no redistribution. It is only when *relative* output variations occur that redistribution takes place. This is the proper way to proceed if the point of a federal system is to reduce the cost involved in giving up the exchange rate (see Wyplosz, 1991), and if this cost is highest for asymmetric shocks.

The redistribution formula used ensures that these features are incorporated. In spirit it is close to that developed by Italianer and van Heukelen (1993), but differs in that they use changes in the unemployment rate, whilst we use output shares. If MU output is made up of the individual members' outputs such that

$$YMU = YF + YG \qquad (6.3)$$

then potential MU output is given by the individual members' potential outputs, as shown in (6.4)

$$YMU_{pot} = YF_{pot} + YG_{pot} \qquad (6.4)$$

If we first consider a zero growth[2] environment, then in equilibrium the French and German shares of actual *YMU* will be equal to their shares in potential *YMU*, and no redistribution should take place. If, however, the share of actual French output drops below its potential whilst the German share does not, then some redistribution is called for.

But we can look at this another way: if the French share of actual *YMU* drops below its potential, this means that the German share must rise above its potential, since by definition the two shares must equal 1. An example may help to illustrate this; suppose French and German output are both 100, therefore *MU* output is 200, and the shares are 0.5 each, assume also that this is an equilibrium position so that potential outputs are the same as actual. Now suppose French output drops to 98, the relative shares now change to 0.505 for Germany and 0.495 for France, whilst the potential ratios remain the same.

This is the essence of the redistribution formula: if a country finds itself at potential output, but its partners are below potential, then the first country has a larger share of *MU* output, and therefore contributes more to the *MU* pot than it receives. This facet of the rule can be seen in positive and negative terms. In positive terms it would be a clear indication by the member states that they were committed to *European* interests, not just national interests, and that their good fortune should be shared with the rest. Also, the cause of the shock would be important in this instance; for example, a decline in German imports from France could cause the switch in ratios described above, and in this case it could be argued that some of Germany's gains should be transferred to cover France's losses during the transition, if it is a permanent shock or, if it is transitory, over the period during which its effects last. On the other hand, the argument that one country should have part of its good fortune "stolen" to help the temporarily less well off could clearly lead to problems in the continued implementation of the plan. However, these arguments are at the heart of the federal fiscal policy question, and the fact that they arise here proves that the rule captures some of the essence.

The formula therefore uses the relationship between actual and potential output shares as its basis. If the total revenue available to the federal authority is *REVS*, then it is split according to (6.5):

$$GEF = REVS(YF_{pot}/YE_{pot} + \zeta(YF_{pot}/YE_{pot} - YF/YE)) \qquad (6.5)$$
$$GEG = REVS(YG_{pot}/YE_{pot} + \zeta(YG_{pot}/YE_{pot} - YG/YE))$$

therefore, in equilibrium *REVS* is shared out according to the potential shares of France and Germany in total *MU* output. This ensures that the portions of *REVS* given by the national authorities is returned to them. If both economies experience an equal decline in output as compared to potential then their respective shares would not change and, accordingly, the distribution would remain unchanged: they would continue to get exactly what they put in.

At first sight it could be supposed that this policy scheme would fail if France and Germany had different growth rates; the ratios would continually decline or increase. Consider the case where France grows at 2.5% per annum, and Germany at 3%. In this case the German share would continually grow, whilst the French would asymptotically decline; thus, it could be expected that even in equilibrium France would receive a declining amount of *REVS*. Whilst this is true it must be remembered that the French allocation to *REVS* would also be declining in line with its reduction in the make up of *MU* GDP. Thus, as long as equilibrium implies equal growth rates of actual and potential output, the rule still performs its basic task: to only change the distribution of tax revenues when a country's output falls below its potential output level, whilst all others remain at their potential.

Six shocks are discussed, representing a mix of symmetric and asymmetric demand and supply-shocks. These allow a comprehensive examination of the characteristics of each of the regimes. The supply-side shocks are an increase in the price of oil, and temporary shocks to inflation expectations in France and Germany. On the demand side there are two asymmetric shocks and one symmetric shock, as a result of a permanent increase in world demand and permanent decreases in French imports from Germany and German imports from France.

The ability of the fiscal policy regimes to stabilize the economies after a shock is measured by the deviation of output and inflation from their unshocked baseline paths, whilst the unshocked simulations are measured via deviations from ultimate target values. The deviations are measured as the root cumulative squared deviation (*RCSD*) of inflation from its baseline path or target, and for output, the root cumulative squared percentage deviation (*RCS%D*) from its baseline path or target. These are the same measures introduced in Chapter 5. The measures are shown for one, five and ten years after the shock.

6.3 RESULTS

Due to the number of regimes considered, and the quantity of shocks applied to each, an exhaustive discussion of the effect of each shock on each regime would be unnecessarily tedious. Instead, the results are presented in two parts. First, the need for a stabilizing role for fiscal policy is examined by comparing Regimes (I) and (II). Second, the benefits and costs of the various federal options are considered.

The need for stabilizing fiscal policy

Table 6.1 shows the *RCSD* and *RCS%D* of inflation and output from an arbitrary set of targets for Regime (II), the mixed target national fiscal policy. For output the target is potential output, and for inflation the deviation from

Table 6.1   Regimes (I) and (II), unshocked, deviations from target

Regime	Output			Inflation		
	Year 1	*Year 5*	*Year 10*	*Year 1*	*Year 5*	*Year 10*
			France			
II	73.4	80.5	78.5	65.6	79.6	70.5
			Germany			
II	56.8	78.3	82.1	98.3	88.6	92.3
			Spain			
II	101.6	97.4	96.8	103.1	96.6	95.8
			MU			
II	61.5	73.7	75.6	68.3	78	75.1

2% per annum.[3] Table 6.1 shows the *RCSD* values for Regime (II) as an index of Regime (I): if the index value is less than 100, Regime (II) is better at minimizing the deviation of output or inflation from their target values than Regime (I) and vice versa.

For all the countries examined, the inclusion of the output gap in the core countries' fiscal policy reaction function reduces the cumulative deviation of both output and inflation from target over the period as a whole. The explanation of this improvement comes from the initial conditions in France and Germany when the MU is formed. Both countries have government deficits which are too large to produce stationary debt ratios (the debt target in each country is set at its starting value). Thus, tax rates rise and government spending falls in both countries. Furthermore, German inflation is above the rest of the world's, France's and the ECB's target rate when the MU is formed. The combined effect of these two initial conditions is to force a recession in France and Germany, the latter's recession being deeper due to the adverse inflation differential and falling competitiveness.

Under Regime (I) German competitiveness losses and tighter fiscal policy lead to a relatively fast reduction in inflation, but a relatively large output loss (Figures 6.1 and 6.3). Inflation falls below the long-run equilibrium inflation rate, creating a short-term cycle in output and inflation before equilibrium is reached. When Regime (II) is introduced the depth of the recession is reduced and the speed of inflation adjustment is slowed. Fiscal policy does

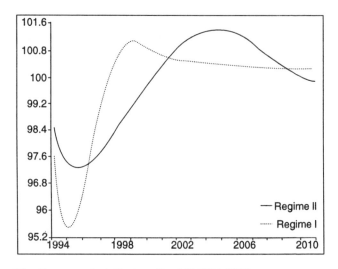

Figure 6.1   German output, Regimes I and II, 1994–2010

not tighten by as much in the short run, actually easing during the deepest
phase of output loss. As inflation falls, output begins to recover, but since the
depth of the recession has been reduced the required inflation adjustment
takes longer to occur, and so output remains below potential for longer.

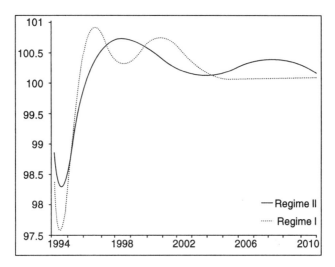

Figure 6.2   French output, Regimes I and II, 1994–2010

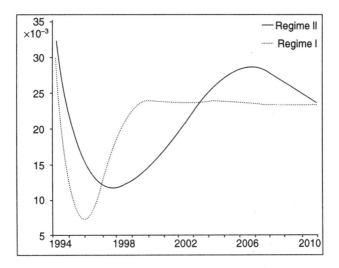

Figure 6.3   German inflation, Regimes I and II, 1994–2010

The cost of Regime (II) is a larger deficit and debt ratio (Figure 6.5), increased by up to 14% of GDP in the medium term in Germany. As output recovery takes hold, fiscal policy is tightened in order to stabilize the debt ratio. This reduces the size of output's recovery as compared to Regime (I)

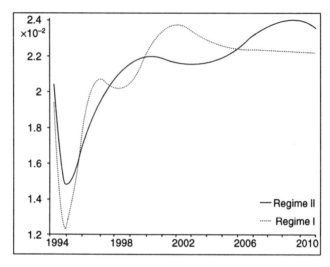

Figure 6.4   French inflation, Regimes I and II, 1994–2010

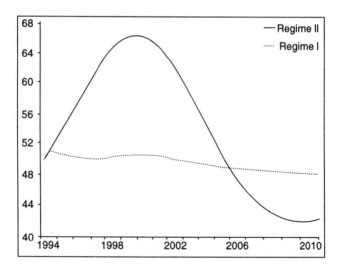

Figure 6.5   German debt, Regimes I and II, 1994–2010

but, once again, lengthens the adjustment period. By the end of the simulation output and inflation are at equilibrium in both Regimes, Regime (I) successfully hits the debt target, whilst the debt ratio is slightly below its target value in Regime (II), implying that some adjustment remains to be achieved. The impact of Regime (II) on Germany, in this unshocked version, is to smooth the disinflation path and to reduce the depth of the recession; it also implies a larger debt ratio which persists for some time, and a longer adjustment period.

Since the French initial conditions are different, the dynamic adjustment path also differs from Germany's. In Regime (I) France experiences a very mild recession (Figure 6.2), since its inflation rate is lower than Germany's and closer to the long-run equilibrium value (Figure 6.4). However, since the deficit needs to be reduced fiscal policy is tightened, and this, along with reduced exports to Germany, results in a short-term loss of output. As output falls inflation is reduced, improving France's competitive position and launching the French recovery via reduced imports and increased exports.

Employing Regime (II) in France smooths the adjustment path of output and inflation. The initial drop in output is reduced since the weight given to the debt ratio is less, and so fiscal policy does not tighten by as much as in Regime (I). The result is that the deficit does not fall by as much, or as fast, leading to a higher debt ratio in the medium-term (Figure 6.6). However, the size of the increase in debt is much smaller than Germany's, reflecting the

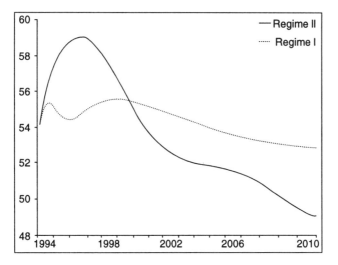

Figure 6.6   French debt, Regimes I and II, 1994–2010

smaller loss of French output and thus, the relatively smaller difference in fiscal policy between the two Regimes.

As output recovers and the debt ratio increases French fiscal policy grows progressively tighter in an attempt to return debt to its target value. By the end of the period debt is very close to target in Regime (I), whereas in Regime (II) it has undershot the target ratio, suggesting, as for Germany, that some adjustment still needs to occur.

Considering the MU variables reveals that the stabilizing effect of Regime (II) on output for the region as a whole is quite large, with the maximum drop in output reduced from around 3.5% to around 2% of potential (Figure 6.8). However, this improvement in output performance is at the expense of inflation performance (Figure 6.9). Inflation starts from a higher initial point and remains higher for the first three years of the simulation period. Subsequently the inflation rate is lower in Regime (II) than (I), reflecting the extended nature of the German response. The reduced output loss and higher inflation are reflected in the MU's interest rate which in the short-term remains higher in Regime (II) than (I) (Figure 6.7). In Regime (I) MU rates are cut in line with the fall in German output and inflation since Germany's size ensures that it dominates French variables in the ECB's reaction function. In Regime (II) since the fall in output and inflation is reduced, interest rates remain higher for longer in the short term, with a maximum difference of the order of 2% in the first year. Higher interest rates mean

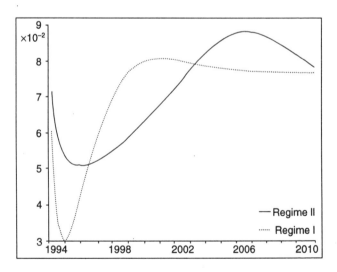

Figure 6.7   MU interest rates, Regimes I and II, 1994–2010

larger interest payments on the members' national debts, which tend to offset the positive impact of improved output on their deficits.

The qualitative differences between the Regimes for Spain is very similar to that for France and Germany, although the difference between the

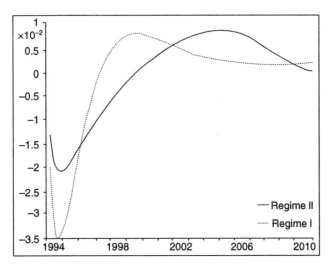

Figure 6.8   MU output gap, Regimes I and II, 1994–2010

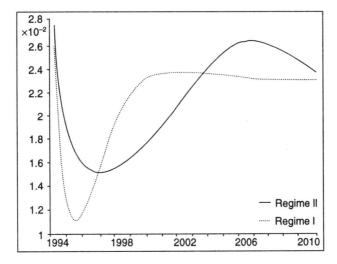

Figure 6.9   MU inflation rate, Regimes I and II, 1994–2010

two Regimes is small for Spanish variables. Since MU interest rates are higher in the short term under Regime (II) Spanish rates are also higher, by up to 1.8% in the second year, which results in a marginally larger drop in output initially. The relatively small difference in output between Regime (I) and (II) is explained via the trade-off between domestic demand variables

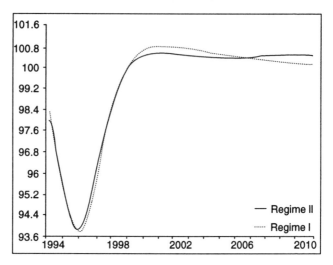

Figure 6.10   Spanish output, Regimes I and II, 1994–2010

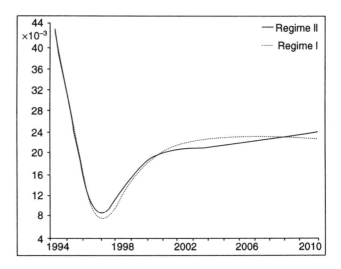

Figure 6.11   Spanish inflation, Regimes I and II, 1994–2010

and the trade account. Since both German and French output fall by less, Spanish exports also fall by less. Moreover, lower domestic demand reduces imports by more than in Regime (I). Therefore, although interest rates are higher, reducing consumption and investment and increasing the tax rate, the improvement in the trade account partially offsets this, resulting in only a small initial difference in output between the two Regimes. After the initial adjustment, output performance is improved in Regime (II), the maximum output loss during Spain's disinflation is reduced, although the size of the difference is small. Inflation reflects this; the difference between the two Regimes is tiny in the short run, whilst the subsequent path is smoother.

How to assess these results is not clear. The choice is between faster adjustment and higher variance in key macroeconomic variables, or slower adjustment with longer periods in recession or boom. Since these adjustments must take place, the choice is over which dynamic path should be adopted. Using the objective functions discussed in Section 6.2, Regime (II) is the clear winner, indicating that the sum of the areas beneath, for example, the output curves are smaller for Regime (II), even though this regime may cause the economy to stay in one state for longer. There is a clear trade-off between improved output scores and inflation. Germany is the best example. Since German inflation is too high and this type of model suggests that some output loss is necessary to reduce inflation, reducing the size of that output loss reduces the fall in inflation. Regime (II) also prolongs the length of the adjustment period. Output remains below (or above) potential for longer, albeit with a smaller difference from potential.

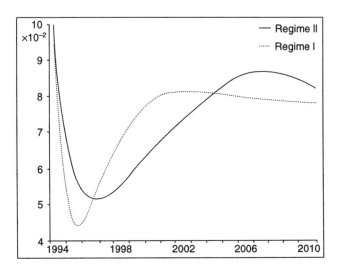

Figure 6.12   Spanish interest rates, Regimes I and II, 1994–2010

Shocks

Applying the shocks discussed in Section 6.2 provides more information about the characteristics of the two regimes, and reveals some dangers inherent in Regime (II) when it is mixed with a centralized monetary policy.

We examine the two regimes' responses to the demand and price shocks (see Tables 6.2–6.5). First, we discuss the results for the demand shocks and highlight some interesting aspects of MU interest rate response caused by the relative sizes of France and Germany. In general Regime (II) dominates Regime (I) for both inflation and output. We then present the results for the price or supply-side shocks. A different story emerges. As was indicated in the unshocked experiments, inflation adjustment presents a difficulty for Regime (II), and this is brought to the fore for the price shocks.

The Regimes are compared by their ability to stabilize output and inflation around their respective unshocked paths. Once again Regime (II) has its objective function measures presented as an index of Regime (I). Therefore, if Regime (II) is less successful at returning output or inflation to their baseline values, it will have an index number above 100.

However, if Regime (II) does return an index value over 100, this does not imply that the Regime is worse than Regime (I) when the targets are those

Table 6.2   France: results with shocks

Regime	Output			Inflation		
	Year 1	*Year 5*	*Year 10*	*Year 1*	*Year 5*	*Year 10*
			Oil price			
II	77.3	92.8	100	100.2	100.3	100.9
			German inflation expectations			
II	77.1	56.1	67.2	71.9	71.1	89.2
			French inflation expectations			
II	74.1	94.1	101.3	106.1	112.7	131.6
			World trade			
II	75.9	75.3	84.1	75.6	91.8	93
			German imports from France			
II	62.4	56.4	60	61.3	65.8	69.2
			French imports from Germany			
II	63.2	60.4	68.2	63.3	77	80.8

Table 6.3   Germany: results with shocks

Regime	Output			Inflation		
	Year 1	Year 5	Year 10	Year 1	Year 5	Year 10
	Oil price					
II	58	82.2	91.8	100.9	101	101.7
	German inflation expectations					
II	57.7	83.2	88.9	132.5	111.6	140.6
	French inflation expectations					
II	56.1	63.3	77.3	53.1	68.6	87.9
	World trade					
II	59.2	60.1	61.3	60.7	78.4	82.3
	German imports from France					
II	53.9	49.1	52.7	55.6	58.8	64
	French imports from Germany					
II	53.4	49.5	55.3	53.3	59.9	66.1

Table 6.4   Spain: results with shocks

Regime	Output			Inflation		
	Year 1	Year 5	Year 10	Year 1	Year 5	Year 10
	Oil price					
II	148.6	90	91.3	98.5	98.1	98.3
	German inflation expectations					
II	136.9	116.6	114.7	139	101.3	93.7
	French inflation expectations					
II	144	143.6	147.8	127.8	179.1	207.9
	World trade					
II	100	94.4	92.8	95.4	92	91.4
	German imports from France					
II	35	16.8	18	43.5	18.7	20.6
	French imports from Germany					
II	32.5	13.8	17.6	41	18.3	21.3

Table 6.5 MU: results with shocks

Regime	Output			Inflation		
	Year 1	Year 5	Year 10	Year 1	Year 5	Year 10
	Oil price					
II	64.2	89.4	97.2	100.6	100.8	101.4
	German inflation expectations					
II	62	83.2	92.1	144.6	125.5	174.4
	French inflation expectations					
II	66.6	96.2	100.5	144.9	157.6	162.9
	World trade					
II	65.7	71.6	72.8	65.8	74.8	86.9
	German imports from France					
II	29.4	25.1	43.1	41.6	41.5	52.7
	French imports from Germany					
II	24.5	27.6	42.4	42.2	32.3	48.8

used for the unshocked comparisons examined in the previous section. It is possible for a Regime to return a worse value in terms of deviation from the unshocked path and to in fact be more successful at stabilizing the economy around its ultimate targets. This should be borne in mind when examining the results tables.

Demand shocks The world trade shock produces a positive impact on French and German output in both Regimes, increasing inflation and the MU interest rate. Over time as the increase in inflation and interest rates impact on competitiveness and domestic demand, output begins to decline. Fiscal policy provides the channel which differentiates between the Regimes. In Regime (I) tax rates actually fall, whilst government spending increases since the debt ratio declines in the wake of the shock. Thus, fiscal policy acts as an extra spur to output in Regime (I), leading to a greater output increase in the short run than would be the case if fiscal policy remained unchanged. In contrast, Regime (II) responds with a decline in government spending and an increase in the tax rate as output increases. This dampens the shock to demand and reduces the increase in output. Inflation follows similar paths to output in the two regimes and in the two countries. The debt ratio drops in both countries under both regimes, but by far more in Regime (II) as a consequence of the fiscal tightening.

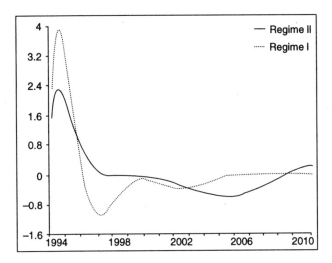

Figure 6.13   German output, world trade shock, 1994–2010

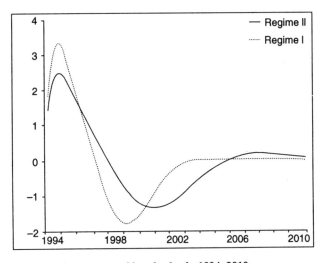

Figure 6.14   French output, world trade shock, 1994–2010

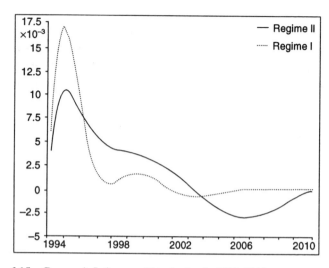

Figure 6.15   German inflation, world trade shock, 1994–2010

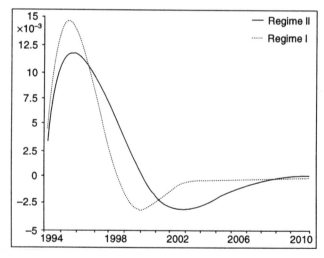

Figure 6.16   French inflation, world trade shock, 1994–2010

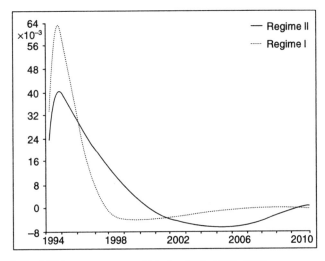

Figure 6.17   MU interest rates, world trade shock, 1994–2010

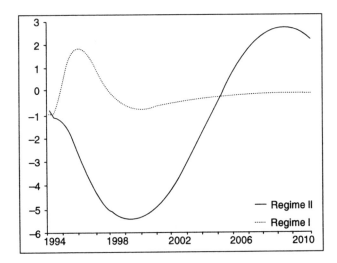

Figure 6.18   German debt, world trade shock, 1994–2010

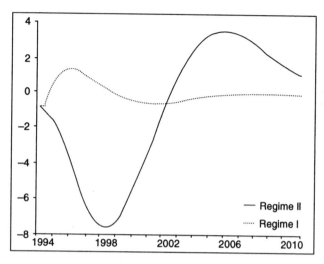

Figure 6.19   French debt, world trade shock, 1994–2010

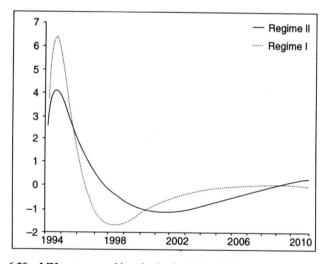

Figure 6.20   MU output, world trade shock, 1994–2010

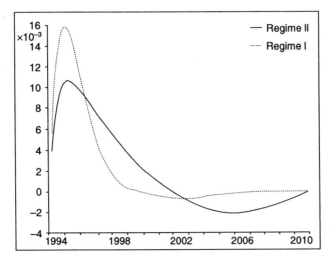

Figure 6.21   MU inflation rate, world trade shock, 1994–2010

As a consequence of the improved output stability under Regime (II) for the individual members, the MU the aggregate output response is also more stable, with the difference between the two output peaks being in the region of 3% of MU GDP, whilst for MU inflation the difference between the peaks is around 0.8%. As a consequence of this, the MU interest rate rises by less in Regime (II) than in Regime (I).

The interest rate response of the core countries under the two regimes impacts on Spain via the ERM commitment. Interest rates rise in Spain by less in Regime (II) than (I) in line with the core's interest rate, yet Spanish output rises by around the same amount under both Regimes in the direct aftermath of the shock. A relatively higher interest rate increase under Regime (I) does stop consumption and investment from increasing as much as they do under Regime (II), so that domestic absorption increases by less in Regime (I) than (II). However, since the core's demand increases by more under Regime (I) than (II) exports from Spain to the core are also up, by enough to partially offset the impact of higher interest rates. Furthermore, since core output goes up by less under Regime (II), whereas Spanish output increases by nearly the same amount, the comparative inflation paths of the core and Spain also differ under the two Regimes. In Regime (II) Spanish inflation increases by more than the core countries', which limits the increase in Spanish exports. Thus, the impact of the two Regimes on Spain in the short term is to alter the composition of GDP. Regime (I) increases exports at the expense of domestic investment and consumption, whilst Regime (II) leaves exports basically unchanged but allows consumption and investment to take a larger stake.

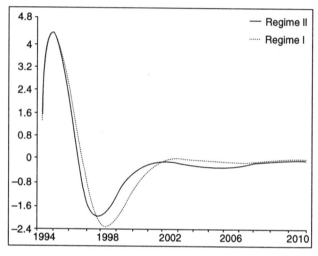

Figure 6.22   Spanish output, world trade shock, 1994–2010

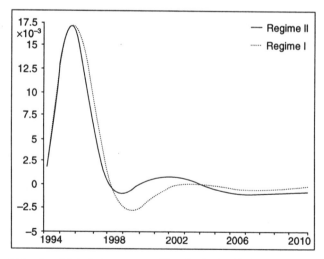

Figure 6.23   Spanish inflation rate, world trade shock, 1994–2010

Regime (II) also deals well with the asymmetric import demand shocks. Since both shocks produce opposite effects on German and French output, for instance the French import shock increases French output whilst reducing German output, the net effect on MU output and inflation is small, depending on the relative sizes of the two countries and the relative importance of trade with each other. This limits the usefulness of MU interest rate policy since the net effect on MU variables will be smaller than those on the individual member's, and thus interest rates will not be as affected by the shock. Furthermore, in this sort of shock one country would want to reduce interest rates whilst the other would want to increase rates. In Regime (I) the adjustment mechanism is through prices, whereas Regime (II) adds changes in fiscal policy to the adjustment path. The question is: which of the two mechanisms is the most effective in terms of the objective function?

The shock to German imports increases German output in both Regimes. Regime (II) limits the increase since German government spending drops whilst taxes rise, Regime (I) produces the opposite fiscal policy response since debt falls, spending rises and the tax rate is reduced, exacerbating the shock to German output and inflation. For France Regime (I) tightens fiscal policy as output declines, deepening the recession, Regime (II) eases policy and thus lessens the impact to demand and prices. Therefore for a negative shock the authorities ease the loss of output by allowing debt to increase, whereas for a positive shock the authorities tighten policy and arrest the increase in debt.

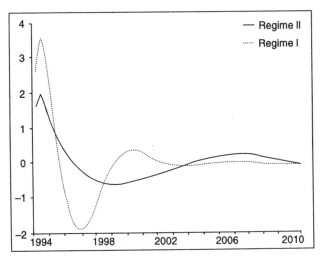

Figure 6.24   German output, German import shock, 1994–2010

The shock to French exports to Germany is never reversed, French exports to Germany remain permanently lower; however, the negative shock to prices improves French competitiveness and leads to a permanent increase in exports to the other countries in the model; in the long run total exports return

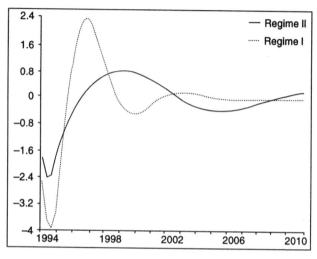

Figure 6.25   French output, German import shock, 1994–2010

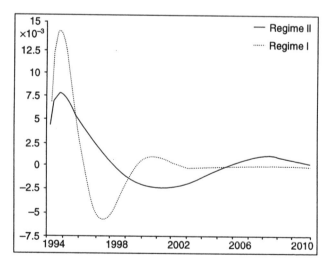

Figure 6.26   German inflation, German import shock, 1994–2010

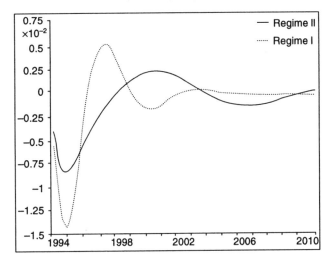

Figure 6.27   French inflation, German import shock, 1994–2010

to their base values. A similar result occurs for Germany for the French import shock. By reducing the size of the shock, and thus the impact on prices, Regime (II) slows down the process of adjustment in the trade sector, total exports do recover in France for the German shock and in Germany after the French shock, but equilibrium takes longer to achieve.

The results for the French import shock are very similar to those for the German, except for the effect on MU variables. The German shock increases MU output compared to the unshocked value, whilst the French shock reduces MU output. This is explained by the larger size of the German economy. Therefore, for the French shock the decrease in German output dominates the increase in French output and similarly for the German shock the German increase dominates the French loss (Figures 6.28 and 6.29). This dominance manifests itself in the response of the MU's interest rate (Figures 6.30 and 6.31). For the French shock it drops, whereas for the German it rises. By introducing Regime (II) and limiting the impact on national outputs MU aggregate output is also stabilized, as is inflation. The result is a much smaller change in MU interest rates.

For Spain the impacts of the two shocks differ, but the variance of output and inflation is lowered with the use of Regime (II). Since the shock to German imports increases MU interest rates, this translates into a rise in Spanish real interest rates and a reduction in consumption and investment. On the other hand, exports to Germany represent a larger component of total

Spanish exports, and the positive shock to German output increases Spanish exports. However the net effect on Spanish output is negative. For the French shock, the opposite is the case. Although German output and imports decline, reducing Spanish exports, the MU interest rate falls, a positive stimulus to

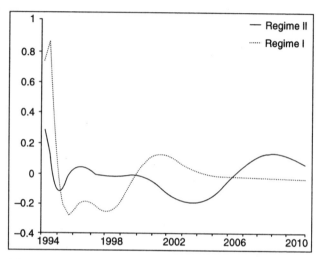

Figure 6.28   MU output, German import shock, 1994–2010

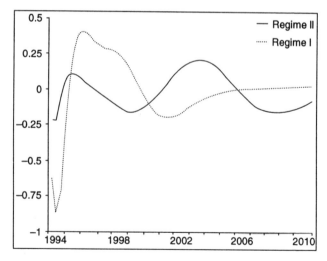

Figure 6.29   MU output, French import shock, 1994–2010

Spanish output. Once again the interest rate effect outweighs the trade effect, and in this case Spanish output rises. A similar picture emerges for inflation. Since Regime (II) reduces the size of the impact on MU interest rates and import demands, it also limits the impact of the shock on Spain

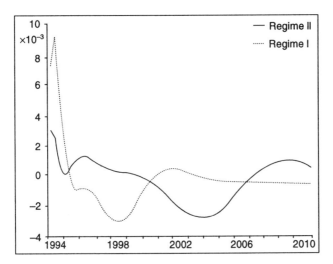

Figure 6.30   MU interest rates, German import shock, 1994–2010

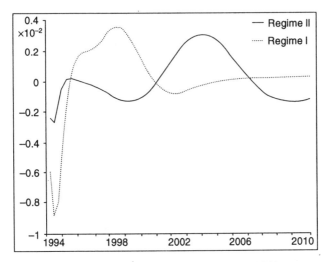

Figure 6.31   MU interest rates, French import shock, 1994–2010

(Figures 6.32 and 6.33), resulting in a much improved score based on the objective functions in Table 4.4.

For demand shocks, whether they are symmetric or asymmetric Regime (II) tends to dominate Regime (I) from the standpoint of the individual MU

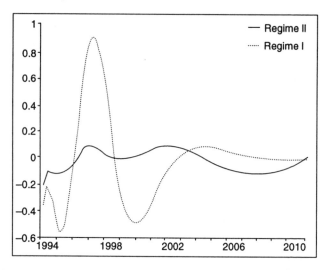

Figure 6.32   Spanish output, German import shock, 1994–2010

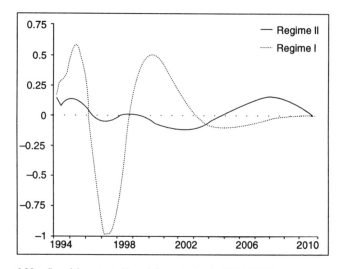

Figure 6.33   Spanish output, French import shock, 1994–2010

members, the MU as a whole and the peripheral countries. The improvement is particularly clear when the shock is asymmetric since this further reduces the efficacy of MU monetary policy. However, the size of the German economy means that German variables dominate French resulting in MU monetary policy being more responsive to the state of the German economy than the French. This becomes noticeable for asymmetric shocks.

As more countries are included in the MU the arithmetic of aggregation would reduce the importance of Germany in the ECB's reaction function. Whilst this would mean that the ECB's policy would conceivably no longer result in a rise in MU interest rates for a German import demand shock, which exacerbates the rest of the MU's recession, it would not guarantee that the ECB's response would be of any more use to the other members. On the other hand, a French import demand shock would almost certainly reduce MU interest rates, contrary to the French desire for higher rates, since by expanding membership not only is the German influence reduced, but so is the French. In short flexible fiscal policy would still have a role, indeed an enhanced role, in a MU of more than two countries, especially for asymmetric demand shocks.

Price shocks The oil shock has three main effects on France and Germany. First, the increase in imported inflation leads to higher producer prices and thus higher consumer prices. This results in the MU's interest rate being increased which depresses consumption and investment in France and Germany. The second channel is via the terms of trade. It is assumed that world and rest of ERM producer prices also increase after the oil shock, but since these regions are not fully modelled their rate of producer price inflation returns to its original value the quarter after the shock. Therefore, France, Germany, and Spain will lose competitiveness as long as their producer price inflation rate is above that of the rest of the world and the rest of the ERM. This, *ceteris paribus*, depresses exports and increases imports. Finally the shock impacts on the path of the fiscal policy variables.

The adjustment process is essentially the same in both France and Germany, the only difference being that the French adjustment takes slightly longer, explained by the nature of the French labour market. In Regime (I) the shock to prices produces an immediate increase in consumer price inflation which pushes the MU interest rate up. As interest rates rise consumption and investment fall in both core countries. Furthermore, fiscal policy becomes tighter in order to offset the effect of increased interest payments and falling tax revenues on the debt ratio. This reinforces the negative effect on output, but helps reduce the inflation rate. There is a small fall in exports due to a small inflation differential with the rest of the world and the ERM, but this is more than offset by a fall in imports due to falling domestic government and private sector demand. Inflation is brought down quickly, temporarily falling below the rest of the world's, allowing interest rates to fall and the recovery to begin. After a small increase, the debt ratio is soon returned to its base value.

Regime (II) reduces the size of the initial recession by easing fiscal policy in direct contrast to Regime (I). The impact of this is to allow inflation to remain higher for longer, which forces the ECB to increase interest rates by more than Regime (I). Since demand falls by less in Regime (II), the drop in imports is reduced whilst the increased inflation rate results in a larger and more sustained loss of exports. This prolongs the adjustment period, and even with active fiscal policy output remains below potential for longer. Ultimately inflation is brought down, but since it remains higher than Regime (I) for longer it falls below the base path by more and for longer in Regime (II). Furthermore, easier fiscal policy results in increased debt; the ratio rises by approximately 2% in France and 1.6% in Germany.

For Spain, Regime (II) produces higher interest rates than (I) in the short term, and since Spain does not have an output stabilizing fiscal policy rule, this results in a larger recession in the first few quarters than under Regime (I). However, in the medium term the recession in Spain is slightly smaller, producing an overall output cost which is less than Regime (I).

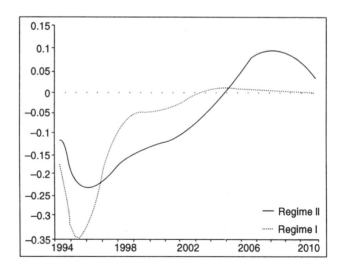

Figure 6.34   German output, oil price shock, 1994–2010

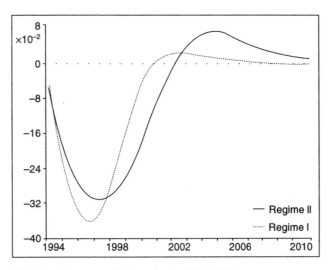

Figure 6.35   French output, oil price shock, 1994–2010

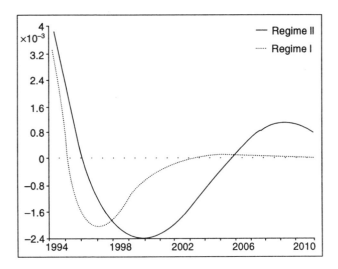

Figure 6.36   MU interest rates, oil price shock, 1994–2010

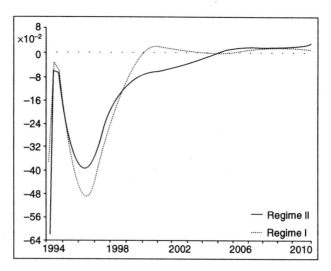

Figure 6.37   Spanish output, oil price shock, 1994–2010

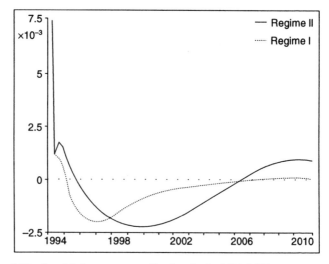

Figure 6.38   Spanish interest rates, oil price shock, 1994–2010

Regime (II) thus improves the output cost resulting from the shock in the short term for both France and Germany, but by extending the period spent away from the baseline values and by causing output to overshoot near the end of the period the Regime does less well as time elapses. Furthermore, the inflation performance of the Regime is certainly not any better than Regime (I), and in the case of Germany it is slightly worse. However the inflation cost is not large, and it must be remembered that the objective function results shown in Tables 6.2–6.5 are for deviations from the unshocked paths, for which Regime (II) is dominant. This shock exposes a weakness in fiscal policies which actively seek to stabilize output: an inflation shock under Regime (II) produces a longer adjustment period with inflation remaining further from its base path for longer. Whether the damage is enough to overturn the unshocked regime ranking will depend on the shock, the exact specification of the fiscal policy rule, and the structure of the wage–price sector.

The two asymmetric price shocks reveal the problem with Regime (II) more clearly as can be seen from the results in Tables 6.2–6.5. In each case, as domestic inflation expectations increase Regime (II) improves the output performance but worsens the shocked country's inflation performance. This is a direct result of fiscal policy's effort to stabilize output.

As inflation expectations increase in either France or Germany, the ECB increases interest rates. For the German shock, rates increase by more in both Regimes, again because of Germany's size. As interest rates rise, consumption and investment fall in both countries. Regardless of which country suffers the shock, all members experience a recession via the response of MU interest rates.

A second negative transmission mechanism to output for the shocked country is via exports, which decline as inflation increases during the shock. Finally, fiscal policy becomes tighter in both countries as output declines and interest rates rise. Whilst the unshocked countries gain competitiveness as their inflation rates fall, this is partially offset by the decline in the shocked country's demand. Whether the net impact on the unshocked country's total exports is positive or negative depends on the country's relative export shares and the shocked country's import function's sensitivity to competitiveness and domestic demand. For the German shock, the net impact on French exports is essentially neutral, whilst for the French shock, German exports increase in the short term.

As output is reduced, unemployment increases and nominal wage inflation is reduced, which feeds through into lower producer and consumer price inflation. This reduces inflation expectations and thus wage claims, setting off another round of adjustment. This is a dynamic process, and as inflation

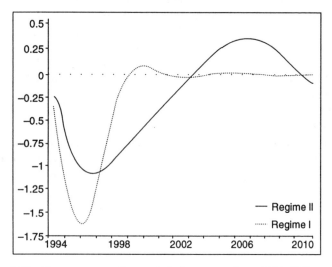

Figure 6.39   German output, German inflation expectations, 1994–2010

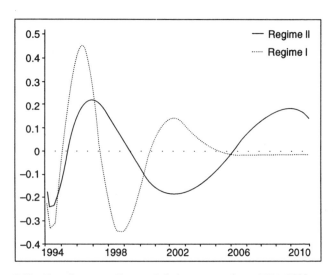

Figure 6.40   French output, German inflation expectations, 1994–2010

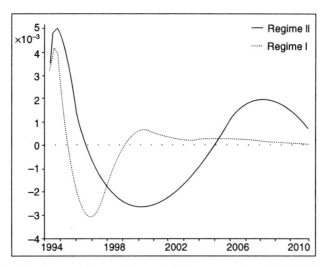

Figure 6.41   German inflation, German inflation expectations, 1994–2010

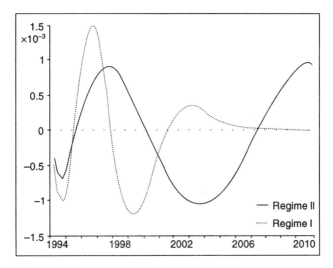

Figure 6.42   French inflation, German inflation expectations, 1994–2010

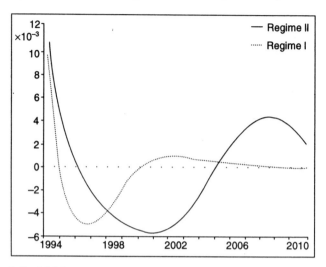

Figure 6.43   MU interest rates, German inflation expectations shock, 1994–2010

declines nominal interest rates begin to fall, competitiveness losses begin to be reversed, output starts to recover and the pace of inflation adjustment slows. By reducing the size of the initial recession in the shocked country Regime (II) also reduces the amount of inflation adjustment. This explains the worse inflation performance of the Regime for the shocked country. However, for the unshocked country the opposite is the case, by minimizing the impact of the shock Regime (II) outperforms Regime (I) for both measures. Once more, the price to pay for this is increased debt ratios in all countries for both shocks.

For Spain, the difference between the Regimes manifests itself through exports and the interest rate. By forcing short-term rates to increase by more in the core countries (since inflation is higher), the short-term impact on Spanish output is more negative under Regime (II) than (I), resulting in a larger loss as measured by the objective functions for output and inflation. It is of interest to note that the German shock has a larger impact on Spain than the French regardless of the Regime, due to the larger response of MU interest rates caused by Germany's share in MU output and inflation.

Overall, it would appear that a strict rule for fiscal policy which targets the debt ratio (and by implication, the deficit), would be less useful than one which allowed some active stabilization role for fiscal policy. Whilst this result is of course not new, the general finding has not been demonstrated for

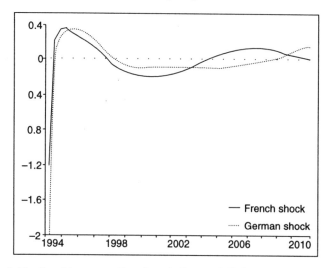

Figure 6.44 Spanish output, French and German inflation expectations shock, Regime II, 1994–2010

a MU in empirical models where the modelled states are dissimilar. One important corollary emerges, however; if monetary and fiscal policy have different objectives it is possible that the process of adjustment to a supply shock which requires price adjustment could be more extended, and therefore more painful, under this sort of rule. This is especially true for peripheral countries, if it is assumed that these countries are in the unenviable position of trying to stabilize debt and adhering to the narrow band ERM, then Regimes which result in higher core interest rates create larger short-term volatility for these countries.

Federal fiscal policy

The following discussion presents results from the federal policy regimes. Once more we start by examining the baseline paths for each regime, before moving on to consider their stabilization properties in the presence of shocks.

The federal regimes are differentiated by both the targets of national fiscal policy and the method by which the resource transfers are disbursed. The first option is for national governments to target the debt ratio exclusively, or a mix of the national output gap and the debt ratio, as in Regimes (I) and (II). The second is to affect output in the national economies through either direct

Table 6.6   Options for redistributive federal policy scheme

Regime	National fiscal target	Federal fiscal variable
(III)	Debt	Disposable income
(IV)	Debt–Output gap	Disposable income
(V)	Debt	Government spending
(VI)	Debt–Output gap	Government spending

demand or through private sector disposable income. The options are shown in Table 6.6.

The issue is to determine whether any of the federal fiscal policy schemes outperform the corresponding non-federal Regimes, and if so what particular combination of national and federal targets is appropriate. Therefore, it is legitimate to directly compare Regimes (II), (IV) and (VI), and (I), (III) and (V), since they have the same national fiscal policies. This allows us to indicate the effect of the redistributive scheme alone. It is also reasonable to compare the federal schemes on the basis of the disbursement method (compare Regimes (III) and (V) and (IV) and (VI)), and to ask whether the redistributive scheme should be supplemented with active national policy or not.

Base cases

Table 6.7 presents the baseline objective function costs for each regime as an index of Regime (I) for all countries. One immediately noticeable thing about the results is that neither of the disposable income based Regimes makes a large difference to the corresponding objective function measures in Table 6.1. The only country to suffer any appreciable change is France for Regime (III). Regime (IV) gives almost identical results to Regime (II) for all states. This is not the case for the Regimes (V) and (VI), which employ government spending. In each case the Regimes offer a gain in terms of output over their corresponding non-federal regimes, whereas for inflation the tale from the previous discussion is repeated. For France, regimes which stabilize output the most also stabilize inflation the most; for example, Regime (VI) gives the best first-year output cost, and the lowest inflation cost. For Germany this is reversed, the lowest output cost is associated with the highest inflation cost (Regime (VI)), as inflation adjustment is limited and delayed.

Table 6.7   Unshocked results: Regimes (II)–(VI); France, Germany, Spain and MU

Regime	Output			Inflation		
	Year 1	Year 5	Year 10	Year 1	Year 5	Year 10
			France			
III	104.7	109	105.5	105.2	109.6	104.7
IV	73.2	81.8	81.2	65.1	82.9	75.4
V	87.1	104.5	96.5	83.7	104.8	96.5
VI	55.6	68.6	71	48	66.7	71.5
			Germany			
III	95.6	100.7	101.9	103.7	106.1	107
IV	54.7	79.1	83	107.4	92.7	96.8
V	83.6	94.9	97.2	113.6	103.4	105.9
VI	48.6	76.4	79.6	127.1	92.7	96.3
			Spain			
III	100.7	99.7	99.6	99.7	99.5	99.4
IV	101.5	97.4	96.7	102.7	96.6	95.8
V	106.2	98.6	98.3	97	95.6	95.3
VI	108.6	97	96.3	98.7	92.9	92
			MU			
III	97.9	100.9	101.5	100.8	105	105.2
IV	59.7	74.4	76.5	74.9	82.5	78.9
V	84.8	92.9	93.9	100.7	98.5	100.5
VI	50.7	69.3	70.9	95.9	81.2	76.7

This is explained, as in the previous section, by the initial conditions in Germany and France: Germany, starting with higher inflation than the ECB's target, and France starting with a similar rate. The adjustment required in Germany is larger than that required in France. Any regime which minimizes the impact of the German adjustment on France improves the French position, whereas policies which minimize German output losses result in higher inflation in the short term, and thus, a larger inflation cost.

Let us move on to consider the implications of the federal fiscal scheme. The first point to note is that passing a fixed proportion of output to the federal budget, over and above government spending, requires higher tax rates to pay for this extra expense. In a sense, this is analogous to an insurance premium. Therefore, in all of the federal regimes, the average tax rate is higher from the outset of the simulation period. This would reduce disposable income, if not for the repayment from the federal budget. This is where the choice about how to disburse the repayment emerges. If it is passed to the private sector as a transfer, than the net effect on disposable income is dependent on the size of the tax increase and the size of the disbursement. In the case considered here, the net effect is positive. Therefore, disposable income tends to be higher, on average, for these federal Regimes than the non-federal. This is not the case for the government demand based federal Regimes, since disposable income is effected by changes in demand net of taxes, and since taxes have increased to pay for the federal transfer disposable income tends to be lower in these regimes as compared to the non-federal even though government spending is higher.

However, as seen from the unshocked results in Table 6.7, the government spending federal regimes easily dominate the income based ones. How can this be explained if the one reduces disposable income, whilst the other increases it? The answer is through the relative impact of changes in direct demand on output, and indirect changes in output caused by changes in income. The latter goes through the saving and consumption decision, and thus part of the impact on output is immediately lost. The former instantaneously changes output by the full amount of the disbursement, hence it is more powerful.

Of course, it is perfectly possible that the scheme might be financed out of current government spending with a diversion of resources, instead of appearing as a new expenditure requirement. If this were the case tax rates would not have to change since the deficit would be unaffected, *ceteris paribus*. The assumption here is that governments treat the scheme as additional spending either because it is being reimbursed immediately, or because existing spending commitments cannot be changed. Moreover, the aim is to merely give some indication of the size of the impact of such a scheme and show the sort of responses which might be expected to occur. For the shocks the results should not be materially different whichever method of financing is adopted.

Some simple analysis highlights the different effect of the two disbursement schemes on output. There are two channels: first, the negative channel due to higher taxes, which is common to both schemes; second, the positive channel from the disbursement of the funds. If we first investigate the effect of the federal Regimes on the national deficit, and thus the tax rate, we determine the size of the negative impact on disposable income. The deficit is changed to incorporate the new spending commitment, thus (in real terms) the PSBR relation becomes

$$PSBR = G + r_{t-1} B_{t-1} - SRT\, Y + x\, Y \qquad (6.6)$$

where x represents the percentage of national income given over to the federal authorities. The deficit feeds into the debt ratio

$$B = B_{t-1} + PSBR \tag{6.7}$$

which in turn affects the tax rate

$$SRT = SRT_{t-1} + \alpha_1(B/B_T - 1) + \alpha_2(B/B_{t-1} - 1) \tag{6.8}$$

Combining (6.6), (6.7) and (6.8) allows us to determine the effect of the payment to the federal authorities on national tax rates:

$$SRT = [SRT_{t-1} + (G + (1 + r_{t-1})B_{t-1} + x\,Y)(\alpha_1/B_T + \alpha_2/B_{t-1})$$
$$- \alpha_1 - \alpha_2]/[1 + (\alpha_1/B_T + \alpha_2/B_{t-1})Y] \tag{6.9}$$

which therefore differ from the non-federal scheme by the value xY. Disposable income, ignoring interest income and the inflation tax, is simply

$$YD = (1 - SRT)Y + GE \tag{6.10}$$

under the income based federal policy, where GE represents the reimbursement from the fiscal authorities. Substituting this into a simplified consumption function such as

$$C = \alpha_3 YD \tag{6.11}$$

allows us to determine the net effect of this federal scheme on output. Since the equation for GE is

$$GE = REVS(YF_{pot}/YE_{pot} + \zeta(YF_{pot}/YE_{pot} - YF/YE)) \tag{6.5}$$

where $REVS$ are determined by

$$REVS = x(YF + YG) \tag{6.12}$$

in equilibrium, where $Y = Y_{pot}$, GE will equal $x\,Y$. Therefore disposable income in equilibrium is

$$YD = (1 - [SRT_{t-1} + (G + (1 + r_{t-1})B_{t-1} + xY)\theta - \alpha_1 - \alpha_2]/$$
$$[1 + \theta Y])Y + xY \tag{6.13}$$

where $\theta = (\alpha_1/B_T + \alpha_2/B_{t-1})$
and the partial differential with respect to x is

$$\frac{\partial YD}{\partial x} = Y - \frac{\theta Y^2}{1 + \theta Y} \tag{6.14}$$

from which the impact on consumption and therefore output is

$$\frac{\partial C}{\partial x} = \alpha_3 \left[Y - \frac{\theta Y^2}{1 + \theta Y} \right] = \frac{\partial Y}{\partial x} \qquad (6.15)$$

For the income based regime, disposable income changes by the extent of the tax response only, and so the partial derivative for consumption with respect to x becomes

$$\frac{\partial C}{\partial x} = -\alpha_3 \frac{\theta Y^2}{1 + \theta Y} \qquad (6.16)$$

whilst output now changes by

$$\frac{\partial Y}{\partial x} = -\alpha_3 \frac{\theta Y^2}{1 + \theta Y} + Y \qquad (6.17)$$

since the *GE* term appears as a component of output. Since $\alpha_3 < 1$, (6.17) is greater than (6.15), indicating that the government demand method is more effective at changing output. Put another way, since tax rates rise with x in either regime, the impact on output differs due to the method of disbursement, taking the difference between the two multipliers gives

$$\frac{\partial Y}{\partial x_{Demand}} - \frac{\partial Y}{\partial x_{income}} = Y(1 - \alpha_3) \qquad (6.18)$$

so that the difference is dependent on the marginal propensity to save. The result that a government spending change has a larger multiplier than a tax change is of course well known (Karakitsos, 1992), and is confirmed here, therefore, *ceteris paribus*, we would expect the government spending disbursement method to dominate the income method. However, national fiscal policies are also reacting to the underlying adjustment going on in the model, and this is a dynamic process, but in general it would be expected that this result also holds in the simulation model.

One might assume that θ would vary in value from country to country, which is likely to be the case in the real world. In the model, however, the values assigned to α_1 and α_2 are such that the responses to a unit increase in debt are identical in France and Germany. What does vary is the marginal propensity to consume, France in particular having a relatively low short-term propensity to consume out of disposable income. Thus, for France the difference between the two disbursement methods should be larger than for Germany. This is indeed the case in the simulation results.

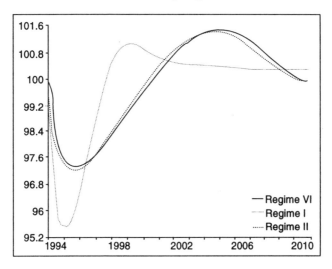

Figure 6.45   German output, Regime I, II and VI, 1994–2010

Essentially, then, the federal regimes represent an increase in government spending of *x*, which is ultimately covered by an increase in tax. Moreover, the distribution of that spending depends on the relative output situations of France and Germany. Since Germany experiences a larger recession than France in the short run, it receives a larger share of *REVS* initially. Under all Regimes, this improves German output, although the demand disbursement method has the larger effect. For France, the impact of the change to a federal regime is dependent on the disbursement method. Under the income scheme France is slightly worse off, since the combination of higher taxes, a low marginal propensity to consume, and the redistribution in favour of Germany results in a slightly increased loss of output. However, the size of this loss is small, as is shown in Table 6.7. The demand method is more successful, for two reasons. First, the higher multiplier of the method itself, and second, and related to the first, the fact that by increasing the efficiency of the transfers, less is needed in Germany allowing more to be spent in France.

Spain suffers under Regimes which are successful at mitigating Germany's output loss, since German inflation is higher, resulting in higher MU interest rates, and thus reduced domestic demand in Spain. For example, Regime (VI) gives the lowest German output cost, and the highest inflation cost; this is reflected in Spain, where this Regime creates the greatest short-term output volatility.

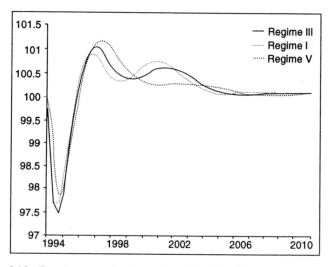

Figure 6.46   French output, Regime I, III and V, 1994–2010

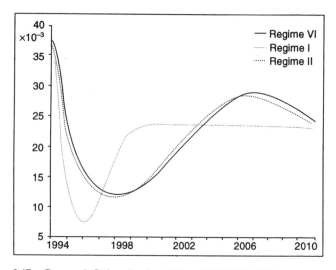

Figure 6.47   German inflation, Regime I, II and VI, 1994–2010

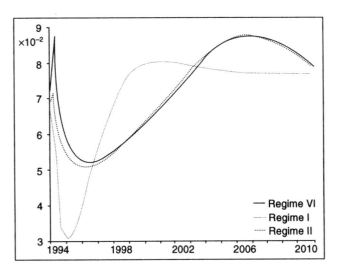

Figure 6.48   MU interest rates, Regime I, II and VI, 1994–2010

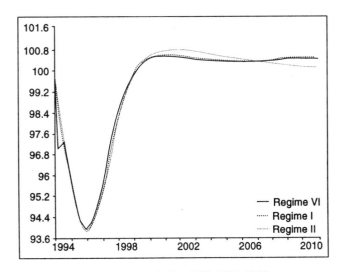

Figure 6.49   Spanish output, Regime I, II and VI, 1994–2010

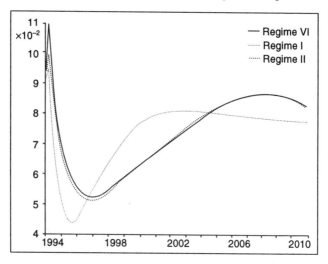

Figure 6.50   Spanish interest rates, Regime I, II and VI, 1994–2010

These results seem to indicate that the most effective distribution method is through government demand. However, there are problems with the application of this recommendation. How to implement such a disbursement method is not clear: what should the government be demanding? Moreover, there are issues pertaining to crowding out and the optimum size of government; however, these questions are beyond the scope of this book, and are left to one side. Instead, the adoption of such a disbursement method in the rest of the chapter should be thought of as an indication of the maximum effect which can be achieved for a given size of federal budget; if other disbursement methods were adopted their multipliers would be smaller.

A second interesting result from these unshocked simulations is the benefit of federal policies even in the case of active national fiscal policy. It might be argued that if flexible fiscal policy is allowed, the scope for improvements from a coinsurance scheme would be reduced. The results seem to suggest the opposite, at least for output, in the short run. For output in France the gain from using the federal scheme in line with active national policy is 32% for the first year, whereas for Germany it is 17%. These benefits erode over time, but by the end of the tenth year France is still better off by 11%, Germany by 3% and the MU region as a whole by 7%.

These gains are explained, once again, by the fact that the federal transfers represent additional government spending, targeted at the output gap. Federal transfers therefore act as a supplement to the national rules which target a mix of output and debt. Hence, it is not strictly fair to compare these federal regimes with the non-federal regimes for the unshocked simulations. It is legitimate to compare the shocked simulations for the core countries, since we are then considering differences from base, so that the effect of the increased government spending is negated. For Spain the method of modelling the ERM introduces a non-linearity which makes the results sensitive to initial conditions at the time of the shock.

Shocks

The shocks employed are the same as those used for the non-federal regimes considered above. This allows us to compare the objective function results for the federal policies directly with those for the non-federal. We are looking for results which show an appreciable change over comparable non-federal regimes. For example, Regime (II) should be compared with Regimes (IV) and (VI), since they all have active national policies; the only difference between them is the addition of the federal package, and the form that package takes. Thus, Regimes (III) and (V) can also be compared with Regime (I).

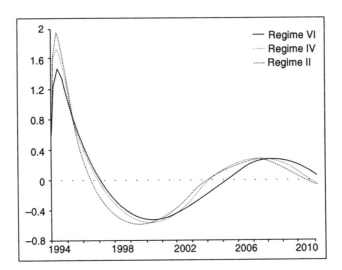

Figure 6.51   German output, German import shock, Regime II, IV and VI, 1994–2010

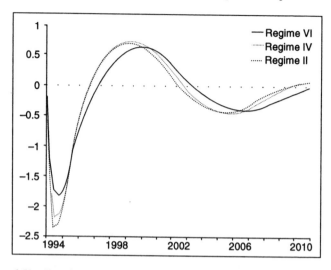

Figure 6.52 French output, German import shock, Regime II, IV and VI, 1994–2010

The results are very much as might be expected. Taking the demand shocks first, it is clear from Tables 6.8–6.11 that federal policies make no substantive difference for the symmetric shock, world trade, whatever method of disbursement is used. The output and inflation cost figures are essentially identical for the comparable regimes. For the asymmetric shocks, however, an appreciable change is made by the inclusion of the federal schemes. Both types of federal scheme, when coupled with the non-active national fiscal regimes, (III) and (V), give worthwhile improvements in both the output and inflation measures. It is also clear that the demand based federal scheme outdoes the income based by a large amount for both France and Germany.

The reason is straightforward; whichever country experiences the import shock sees an improvement in output. This results in a larger contribution to *REVS* and a smaller reimbursement, helping to reduce the increase in output. The unshocked country, on the other hand, pays less into *REVS* as its output falls, and receives a correspondingly larger reimbursement, helping to limit the fall in output. These improvements for output are reflected in the inflation cost figures; since this is a demand shock anything which reduces the deviation of output also reduces the deviation of inflation rates, and accordingly scores well.

The results for Spain are similar to the core's. None of the federal regimes cause a distinct change for the symmetric demand shock. Gains are made for the asymmetric demand shocks in terms of both output and inflation. However, the size of the gains are not as large as those experienced by the core countries. This is due to two counterbalancing effects. On the one hand,

Table 6.8   France: results with shocks

Regime	Output			Inflation		
	Year 1	*Year 5*	*Year 10*	*Year 1*	*Year 5*	*Year 10*
			Oil price			
III	102.6	98.6	99.2	99.9	99.9	99.9
IV	77.3	92.1	100	100.1	100.2	100.9
V	109.3	94.7	96.4	99.5	99.4	99.4
VI	78.7	90.3	98.9	99.8	99.9	100.6
			German inflation expectations			
III	110	92.2	96.9	113	92.5	97.1
IV	81	57.3	67.6	76.5	71.3	87.2
V	139.1	88.4	85.9	147.8	90.4	82.1
VI	93.4	57.7	60.5	91.2	62.8	68.7
			French inflation expectations			
III	97.3	100.2	100.3	100	103.3	103.8
IV	72.3	93.4	101.7	106.4	113.7	135.5
V	90.7	96.6	98.1	99.7	104.8	108.7
VI	67.8	89.7	99.7	106.9	114	140.3
			World trade			
III	100.9	97	98.8	100.8	99.1	99.6
IV	75.5	74.5	83.7	75.3	91.6	93.2
V	102.3	92.6	94.9	102.4	97.1	97.5
VI	74.8	72.9	82.3	74.9	91.3	93
			German imports from France			
III	89.7	89.9	90.1	89.4	92.6	92.7
IV	58.6	53.5	57.9	57.4	64.2	68.4
V	69.7	70.7	71.2	68.9	77.4	77.9
VI	49.8	46.4	51.6	48.8	60.4	64.4
			French imports from Germany			
III	89.9	92.6	92.9	90	96	96.4
IV	59.3	57.6	66.8	59.3	76.5	80.9
V	69.6	74.6	76.8	68.9	84.1	85.4
VI	50.3	50.7	61.1	49.9	73.5	77.4

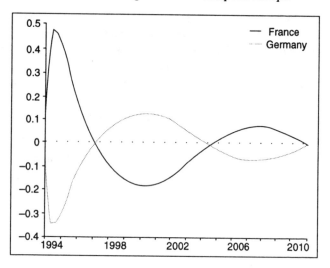

Figure 6.53   Federal spending in France and Germany, German import shock, Regime VI, 1994–2019

more stability in the core's demand for Spanish exports reduces the volatility of Spanish output and improves the objective function scores. This effect is greater for the demand disbursement than the income method. The negative transmission effect stems from the non-linearity in the Spanish interest rate reaction function.

Since the exchange rate target enters the reaction function in a non-linear fashion with a power of 3, the level as well as a change in the exchange rate will affect the interest rate. (6.19) shows the partial differential of Spanish interest rates with respect to the exchange rate with the MU. This clearly indicates the non-linear nature of the reaction function. If the base simulation values of e are smaller in one regime than another (i.e. if the currency is worth less), then for a given change in e during a shock Spanish interest rates will increase by more. Put another way, if the exchange rate starts off the simulation closer to either the upper or lower band of the ERM, interest rates will adjust by more than otherwise (ignoring devaluations or revaluations):

$$\frac{\partial r}{\partial e} = \frac{-3\alpha_{re}}{e_T}\left[\frac{e}{e_T} - 1\right]^2 \qquad (6.19)$$

Regimes which result in higher MU interest rates in the unshocked simulations cause a larger initial depreciation of the Spanish–MU exchange

Table 6.9   Germany: results with shocks

Regime	Output			Inflation		
	Year 1	Year 5	Year 10	Year 1	Year 5	Year 10
Oil price						
III	97.2	100.8	100.7	100	100.1	100.1
IV	57.3	82.1	91.4	100.9	101	101.7
V	95.4	102.5	102	99.9	99.9	99.9
VI	57.5	83.6	91.3	100.8	100.9	101.5
German inflation expectations						
III	94	99.9	100.2	103.2	105.1	106.2
IV	55.8	82.6	88.9	133.7	113.2	144.9
V	87.3	97.3	98	106.1	107.3	109.8
VI	53.6	80.8	88.4	134.7	114.3	150.5
French inflation expectations						
III	102.4	104.1	107.2	102.8	107.9	110.1
IV	58	64.3	77.1	55.1	67.1	86.9
V	106.5	106.8	109.6	107	110.4	116
VI	61.2	62	71	58.6	60.5	80.7
World trade						
III	99.3	101.4	101.1	99.3	101	101.1
IV	59.5	60.6	61.4	61	78.6	82.2
V	98.1	102.3	101.8	98.4	102.5	102.3
VI	59.9	61.6	62.3	61.5	79.7	82.3
German imports from France						
III	86.5	89.6	90.1	86.9	93.1	94
IV	49.4	45.8	50.4	51.2	57.2	63.1
V	69	72.2	73.8	69.9	78.3	81.4
VI	42.7	40.1	45.8	44.6	53.7	59.7
French imports from Germany						
III	86.7	91.8	92.7	85.9	94.2	95.7
IV	49	46.9	53.7	48.7	58.7	65.6
V	69.3	75	77.9	68.3	80.1	84.6
VI	42.5	42	49.8	42.2	56	62.7

rate. The federal regimes all do this to differing extents, Regime (VI) resulting in the highest short-run MU rates. Thus, a shock imposed on these regimes results in a larger increase in Spanish interest rates to protect the exchange rate target than Regimes with smaller base path depreciations, *ceteris paribus.* For the import shocks, core interest rates are highest in the government demand federal Regime (VI). Thus, although MU rates increase by less under this Regime than they do under the non-federal Regime, Spanish rates change by around the same amount in the short run, since the exchange rate starts off further away from its target (Figure 6.55 and Figure

Table 6.10   Spain: results with shocks

Regime	Output			Inflation		
	Year 1	*Year 5*	*Year 10*	*Year 1*	*Year 5*	*Year 10*
Oil price						
III	119.9	98.7	98.7	99.2	99.2	99.2
IV	161.6	90.2	91.7	98	97.7	97.8
V	179.1	98.9	99	97.3	97.2	97.2
VI	201	92.1	93.7	96.8	96.5	96.6
German inflation expectations						
III	115.4	110	110	121.5	105.5	104.2
IV	145.8	124.1	121.7	155.6	107.1	97.4
V	155.6	144.5	143.9	192	139.7	132.2
VI	171.3	148.3	145.3	207.7	134.9	120.8
French inflation expectations						
III	117.9	115.6	112.9	102	110.5	102.8
IV	154.9	156.7	162.1	148.5	199.2	231
V	165.5	161.9	155.8	188.1	151.1	137.5
VI	185.4	189	190.7	223.5	232.5	250.6
World trade						
III	99.9	98.7	98.8	99.4	99.3	99.2
IV	99.5	93.8	92.2	94.9	91.6	91
V	98.2	96.9	97.2	95.3	98.4	98.2
VI	99.4	93.5	92	94.2	91.5	90.9
German imports from France						
III	80.5	86.7	86.3	75.7	86.7	87.8
IV	27.2	12.2	16.9	33.6	16.1	20.6
V	74.5	76.5	75.7	71.6	75.8	78.6
VI	32.2	14.2	16.4	39.3	16.7	19
French imports from Germany						
III	77.7	88.1	87.6	71.5	86.7	88.6
IV	25	10.9	18.6	32.3	16.9	22.7
V	67.7	79.5	78.6	58.2	76.4	80.4
VI	29.2	12	16.6	37.7	16.9	19.9

6.56). Thus, by altering the base path of interest rates and the exchange rate, Regimes which improve core variables do not necessarily improve peripheral variables. However, gains are still made for the asymmetric demand shocks.

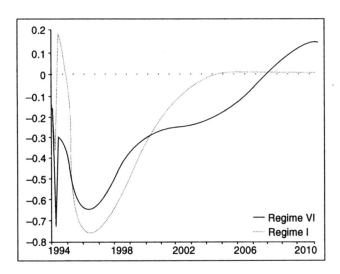

Figure 6.54 Per cent deviation of Spanish-MU exchange rate from target, unshocked simulations, Regime I and VI, 1994–2010

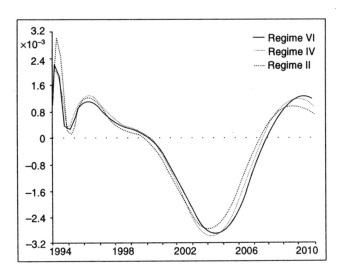

Figure 6.55 MU interest rates, German import shock, Regime II, IV and VI, 1994–2010

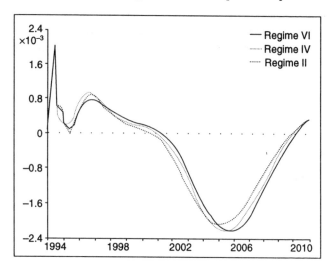

Figure 6.56   Spanish interest rates, German import shock, Regime II, IV and VI, 1994–2010

The oil price shock exhibits the same properties as the symmetric demand shock. For the core countries the introduction of a federal scheme makes little difference to the corresponding non-federal schemes. However, this is not true for Spain, where the first-year output measures exhibit some large increases in cost over their non-federal counterparts. As discussed above, the non-linearity in the Spanish interest rate equation explains the increasing cost associated with the federal regimes for this shock, especially Regime (VI). In the import shocks, MU interest rates change by less under the federal Regimes, but Spanish interest rates change by approximately the same amount.

This gives an indication as to why Spanish rates increase by more under federal Regimes with the oil shock. For the oil price shock core interest rates alter by essentially the same amount in both federal and non-federal regimes (Figure 6.57), and given the larger underlying depreciation of the peseta, Spanish interest rates increase by more (Figure 6.58). This explains the relatively larger short-term output drop indicated in Table 6.10. However, Table 6.10 shows that the output measure is similar for the comparable regimes after the first year, and that inflation is not affected; this is therefore a short-run phenomenon.

The asymmetric price shocks show, for the core countries, smaller differences between the federal and non-federal Regimes than the demand shocks. Whilst the demand shocks increase output in one member and decrease output in the other, the price shocks lead to recession in all members, and thus reduce both the total size of *REVS* and the amount of

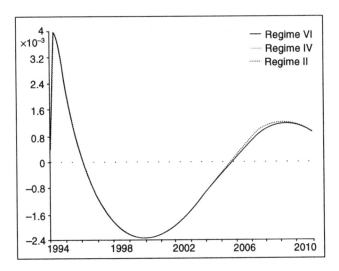

Figure 6.57   MU interest rates, oil price shock, Regime II, IV and VI, 1994–2010

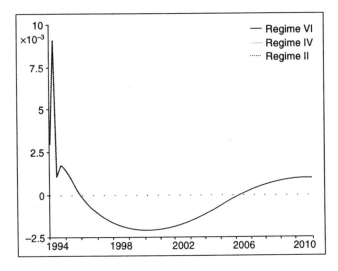

Figure 6.58   Spanish interest rates, oil price shock, Regime II, IV and VI, 1994–2010

redistribution. Thus, the opportunity for improvements by federal Regimes is reduced for these shocks. For Spain, the federal regimes increase the output and inflation cost associated with these shocks, for the same reason as the oil price shock.

Table 6.11   MU variables: results with shocks

Regime and shock	Output			Inflation		
	Year 1	Year 5	Year 10	Year 1	Year 5	Year 10
Oil price						
III	99	100	100	100	100	100
IV	63.8	89.1	97	100.6	100.8	101.4
V	100.1	99.7	99.7	99.7	99.7	99.7
VI	64.5	89.1	96.8	100.4	100.6	101.2
German inflation expectations						
III	97.8	99.9	99.9	101.8	103.8	104.4
IV	61.3	82.6	92	145.2	126.2	176.9
V	98.7	99.8	100	100	103.8	106.6
VI	62.2	82.9	91.6	143.9	125.6	175.9
French inflation expectations						
III	102.4	100.2	100.3	97.7	92.5	95.3
IV	67.5	96.6	100.7	143.5	155.1	158.6
V	103.4	99.7	99.7	94.5	87.8	90.1
VI	67.7	96.2	100.5	141.8	153.2	153.8
World trade						
III	100	100.3	100.3	99.9	100.5	100.3
IV	65.7	71.5	72.8	65.9	74.8	86.8
V	99.8	100.2	100.3	99.8	100.7	100.6
VI	65.7	71.6	73	66.1	75.2	87.3
German imports from France						
III	65.3	79.3	82.9	80.6	90.3	92.9
IV	17.4	15.5	40	35.7	38.4	50.5
V	64.7	76.1	82.7	67.8	77	85.3
VI	21.1	18.1	36.4	32.4	35.6	47.6
French imports from Germany						
III	69.5	77	82	80.7	92.7	97.5
IV	14.7	22.5	41.9	35.7	29.6	47.2
V	66.3	72	79.5	74	79.8	93.2
VI	17.5	20.5	37.3	34.6	29.1	46

The federal regimes therefore offer a gain for the core countries if asymmetric demand shocks are prevalent, whether the national authorities are allowed to practice active stabilization policy or not, and whichever disbursement method is adopted. For Spain, the results are sensitive to the initial conditions in the core and the specification of its interest rate reaction function. If the adoption of active national fiscal policy and federal policies results in higher core interest rates, and therefore depreciation pressure on the peseta, then the non-linear nature of the exchange rate target requires a larger interest rate response. If the premise that ERM members react more aggressively as the exchange rate nears its band is accepted, than this sort of the reaction function is appropriate. It is then the initial conditions which limit the applicability of the results. However, part of the effect is due to the assumption that federal financing is extra spending in the core, which increases interest rates when these policies are implemented. If this were not the case, and transfers came out of existing spending, then the adoption of federal policies would not change the initial conditions beyond the effect of the national policies alone. In this case, Spain would be no worse off with federal policies than without.

6.4 CONCLUSIONS

Chapter 6 has highlighted the lack of empirical work in the field of fiscal policy under MU. Two main themes have been developed: the need for flexible national fiscal policies, in contrast to the restrictive format set out in the Maastricht Treaty, and the possibility of some form of federal fiscal scheme.

National fiscal policies are modelled via two approaches. Member governments can target either the debt ratio, or a mix of the debt ratio and output. Regime I represents the criteria value format as advocated in Maastricht – that is, governments alter spending and taxation in order to ensure debt remains below 60% of GDP. Regime II allows debt to move beyond 60% for some time, and instead incorporates the national output gap as a partial target.

The results indicate that this second scheme offers substantial savings in lost output under various asymmetric and symmetric demand and supply shocks. The problem with this regime, however, is that it is less successful at ridding the economy of inflation after a domestic price shock than Regime (I). Since fiscal policy attempts to stabilize output, whilst monetary policy attempts to stabilize inflation, the two policies clash, resulting in a smaller output loss but a larger inflation cost. Thus, implementation of such a fiscal policy rule needs to be considered carefully in the context of the ECB's policy function.

The options for federal schemes are legion. The first possibility is a fully fledged, self-financing, centralized budget, with the federal authority able to levy taxes and issue debt. However, the current European economic and political climate makes such a large-scale transfer of power to the centre exceedingly unlikely in the short-term (Goodhart and Smith, 1993). Therefore we concentrate on an alternative scheme which, by construction, has an automatically balanced budget. It involves the transfer of resources to a centralized budget, with the size of the transfers depending on the state of the member's economy. Based on the principle that no redistribution should take place if outputs are at potential, or all members are in an equal recession, the budget re-reimburses the full amount paid in by each member in each period if these conditions occur. It is only if some members are experiencing a relative recession or boom that redistribution takes place.

Once the choice has been made to adopt such a scheme, two other decisions need to be made, the financing of the scheme, and the method of disbursement of the transfers at the national level. We have assumed that national governments pass the equivalent of 1% of their GDPs to the central authority, and that this is treated as new expenditure, not a reallocation of existing national expenditures. Under both flexible and tight national fiscal policies, this implies an increase in tax rates. There are many options for the second choice: changes in government expenditure, grants to individuals, or changes in tax rates, are examples. The book compares the first two, and finds that changes in government expenditure are more effective. Although the question of how this would actually be implemented is of obvious importance, this is beyond the scope of this book.

The federal schemes are superimposed on both national fiscal policy regimes in order to ascertain first, if the schemes are effective, and second, if they are needed when national policy is allowed to be flexible. As was expected from the way the federal schemes are constructed, they only have an appreciable impact when asymmetric shocks occur. Moreover, the schemes are more successful for demand shocks than supply. For Spain, the ERM commitment makes interest rates dependent on the level of the exchange rate; therefore regimes which cause the peseta to depreciate more in the absence of shocks force interest rates to adjust by more when shocks occur. This offsets the gains from more stable core demand, depending on the size and nature of the shock. The effect is largest for those shocks where core interest rates increase or decrease the most, for example the oil price shock or expected inflation shock. The Spanish results are therefore state dependent, the exchange rate's pre-shock position affects the post-shock response, and thus the ranking of the regimes. Overall, however, it appears that with a budget comparable in size to the Commission's existing budget, significant stabilization can be achieved by adopting a federal policy scheme.

7 Conclusions

7.1 INTRODUCTION

If the notion of a multispeed Europe is accepted, then it makes sense to consider each stage of convergence individually. This book has examined the three major phases of convergence and identified the critical issues in each phase. These are, disinflation and the timing of ERM entry in the presence of a debt constraint and uncertainty about the credibility of policy; stabilization and convergence policies in a wide and narrow band ERM; and, finally, fiscal policy in a monetary union. Although the work has concentrated on individual countries, in order to focus the discussion, the main conclusions are more widely applicable. For example, the analysis of ERM entry and disinflation would be of interest to any high inflation–high debt nation, whilst the conclusions reached for Spain about the ERM apply equally to a host of other ERM members.

The encompassing characteristic which sets this work apart is the dynamic, general equilibrium framework employed. By incorporating all the relevant dynamic processes for each of the areas studied, the results are comprehensive and thorough, something which has not been achieved in the past in these areas. The approach required the development of flexible and theoretically well understood models, with the relevant stylized facts embedded. The result is a set of practical conclusions for policy in each area, based on clear assumptions and an easily understood method of modelling policy.

7.2 A MULTISPEED EUROPE

Chapter 2 introduced compelling evidence in favour of the conclusion that the EU in its present state is made up of three groups of members. Each group was defined based on the Maastricht Treaty convergence criteria, and using cluster analysis. Treating members *en masse* therefore makes little sense. Each group has a unique set of problems to be addressed. This requires differing approaches, and a flexible convergence timetable. By identifying the groups and their problem areas, the issues covered in the book follow naturally, especially when the gaps in the literature to date are taken into account.

196

The first group comprises the core. Nominal convergence is essentially complete for this group; what emerges as a major problem area are the fiscal criteria, following the downturn of the early 1990s. This raises the question of how fiscal policy should operate within the putative MU.

The second group, the "median", is made up of those countries with persistent inflation and interest rate differentials, and either large debts or growing fiscal imbalances. For these nations, who have achieved a certain amount of nominal convergence, and experienced the ERM, the issues are: how to complete the convergence without damaging their already precarious fiscal positions? The issue boils down to policies which promote convergence, and policies which promote stabilization. Since the Maastricht criteria are not ranked in any order, achieving nominal convergence at the expense of fiscal instability will not suffice. Therefore, the unpalatable spectre of continued tight monetary policy coupled with tight fiscal policy appears. The option considered for Spain, taken as the representative of this group, was to use the wide band ERM as a way of softening the impact of tighter fiscal policy.

The final group consists of Greece. Greece has large and persistent inflation differentials, the government has until recently pursued a managed depreciation of the exchange rate, and the fiscal position has steadily worsened until recently. Greece's avowed intention is to make MU, but the scale of the adjustment required is the largest amongst the present EU members. The policy targets are therefore clear: stabilize and reduce the debt ratio, bring inflation down, and enter the ERM. The question, of course, is how to achieve these targets, at the least cost in terms of lost output. Two options have been put forward in the literature, "cold turkey", or "gradualist". The former appeals to the credibility gains to be accrued from "tying one's hands", and advocates speedy ERM entry. This, the argument runs, will not only bring inflation down rapidly, but also force the fiscal authorities to address the debt problem. The second option is to implement tight fiscal and monetary policy, with a clearly stated objective of entering the ERM when the inflation differential reaches some arbitrary value. Both these options were explored.

7.3 "OPTIMUM" DISINFLATION STRATEGIES UNDER A DEBT CONSTRAINT

Chapter 4 explored the issues raised for Greece, the peripheral country. The output cost of joining the ERM immediately was considered, based on the assumption of no change in the wage formation process or fiscal policy.

The objective was to demonstrate the effect of entry on public finances. A combination of higher interest rates, reduced output growth, and loss of the inflation tax, results in an explosive debt path. The clear message is that fiscal policy must be tightened.

Introducing a simple fiscal policy rule allows debt to be stabilized, but worsens the output cost of joining the ERM. Moreover, the danger of procrastinating was shown. If policy does not change, the debt ratio continues to climb, and if ERM entry is attempted later, the fiscal adjustment required is larger. Waiting, in this case, costs more.

A suggested policy mix was therefore examined: stabilize debt now, join the ERM later. This resulted in the lowest objective function cost with unchanged credibility. The chapter then moved on to examine the issue of credibility, and to develop a decision framework for such situations. Credibility was modelled in two ways: first, the credibility of the exchange rate target; and, second, inflation expectations. The limiting case of complete credibility was identified: where inflation expectations equal the announced policy target, German inflation in this case, and where the foreign exchange market believes the exchange rate target will be kept next period, therefore expected depreciation is zero. It is unclear how complete incredibility should be modelled, so the option was to have the model in its base state represent low credibility.

The options for the policy maker, "cold turkey" or "gradualist", were then considered under two states for the economy, credible or incredible, with the expected cost of each policy dependent on the policy makers' assessment of the likelihood of the policy being credible. The result was that Greece is better off following a gradualist path, whatever the level of credibility. This is in line with evidence in the literature.

7.4   MAASTRICHT, CONVERGENCE AND THE ERM

Chapter 5 considered the "median" group, represented by Spain. The chapter began by extending Eichengreen's (1993) political economy justification for MU, to include the argument that an excessively painful convergence framework, as measured by unemployment or output, could endanger MU and thus the Single Market.

Spain offers an informative mix of problems in this context, for example, the unemployment condition, and growing fiscal imbalances. It was first established that the fiscal deterioration during the beginning of the decade now endangers passing of the Maastricht criteria. The projected fiscal tightening will probably not be enough under current economic conditions. Therefore, as for Greece (albeit at a much reduced size), some fiscal adjustment will have to take place. However, the unemployment situation precludes an aggressive programme of fiscal consolidation. The option, therefore, is to change the priorities of monetary policy, from predominantly targeting the external target, the ERM, to internal targets, in this case output and the inflation differential with the core countries of the EU.

The chapter then demonstrates that such a move to the wide band ERM would not endanger, or reverse, the convergence achieved to date. In fact, the contrary is the case. By allowing interest rates to be more responsive to the inflation differential, such a re-prioritization actually enhances nominal convergence, and reduces the output cost associated with both the nominal convergence and fiscal adjustment.

These gains are robust over a range of shocks, and are most impressive for asymmetric shocks to German prices and demand. This is due to the hegemonic role assigned to Germany in the models. By using the 15% fluctuation bands, Spain partially insulates itself from the German shocks. Symmetric shocks are not materially different between the two monetary policy schemes.

Spain can achieve the necessary convergence of nominal variables and stabilization of fiscal variables in order to pass the Maastricht criteria under both regimes. However, by re-assigning the weights given to the targets of monetary policy, Spain can reduce the output cost associated with achieving these goals. This result is based on the assumption that the *targets* of policy do not change between regimes, merely the effective weights attached to each. Therefore, using the wider bands does not imply *easing* monetary policy, since the inflation target under both regimes is the differential with the core. The main message is that as long as policy is targeted toward convergence, fixing the exchange rate within the narrow band ERM can be counterproductive, especially if risk premia are volatile and sensitive. By adopting a less rigid external target, the likelihood of the system surviving increases.

7.5 FISCAL POLICY IN MU

The final results chapter, Chapter 6, investigated the importance of fiscal policy within MU. According to the Maastricht Treaty, fiscal policy decisions will be constrained by the numerical limits placed on debts and deficits. Since the responsiveness and effectiveness of monetary policy to regional conditions will be reduced by the formation of MU, many have argued that more fiscal freedom is required, not less, and that some form of federal fiscal package would be useful for dealing with those shocks where nominal exchange rate adjustment would have taken place.

The first set of results therefore compare a tight national fiscal policy regime where the sole target of policy is the debt ratio, with a more flexible policy which allows the debt ratio to pass the 60% limit and partially responds to the output gap. Whilst this issue has been addressed in the past (Hughes Hallett and Vines, 1993), the attempts have been exceedingly stylized and have used identically sized and symmetrical economies. Under the plausible assumption that the ECB will respond to MU averages weighted by size, Germany would dominate such a two country MU, and the impact of this is integrated into the analysis.

The more flexible national fiscal policy outperforms the tight over a variety of shocks, but does badly in terms of the inflation stabilization for the shocked country under an asymmetric price shock. This is due to the incompatibility of the ECB's policy and the national authorities' targets. Since one wants to reduce inflation, whilst the other wants to stabilize output, the result is higher inflation for longer, followed by more undershooting and overshooting of the long-run equilibrium. Thus, whilst a flexible policy can be useful, and stable (since the debt ratio is always brought close to target by the end of the simulation period), its implementation needs to be considered with care. It does not deal well with stagflation.

Finally, the federal schemes were considered. Three basic questions need to be considered in the design of such a scheme: what to use as the indicator, how to finance the scheme, and how to disburse the resources? Out of the various possible indicators, we selected each member's share of aggregate MU output, whilst the scheme was financed as extra spending on the part of national governments implying, under both national fiscal policy schemes discussed above, an increase in taxation to finance the scheme.

Two methods of disbursement were considered, direct government grants, or transfers to the private sector. It was shown that the latter method has less effect on output, the difference between the two depending on the marginal propensity to save. Therefore, if the former method is possible, it should be adopted. A fiscal transfer from each economy of 1% of national GDP was shown to give substantial improvements over non-federal regimes in output and inflation costs for asymmetric demand shocks, and to a lesser degree supply shocks. Symmetric shocks, as would be expected, do not give scope for improvement. Thus, a modest federal budget which is well designed can give useful service in redistributing resources for asymmetric shocks, either with or without flexible national fiscal policies.

7.6 FINAL POINTS

It is sometimes easy to forget that the recent doubts, questions and tensions raised in relation to MU and the ERM are largely self-imposed. Policy makers set the convergence criteria, and designed the ERM and the putative MU. For a downturn in economic activity to threaten the whole commitment begs the question of how much commitment was originally present. Surely, if the ultimate target is closer economic integration, a temporary loss of output and increase in debt ratios should not be seen as a permanent step back, but rather a delay.

This book has not questioned the desirability of MU or European integration, but instead asks how these objectives should be achieved when member states start with such large differences. The evidence in this book points toward more flexible national policies, not less, if convergence is to proceed and MU to be successful. Greece should fix its domestic problems before joining the ERM, Spain should use the full width of the ERM in order to achieve the criteria without causing excessive pain, whilst the core should contemplate a federal coinsurance scheme if national fiscal policies are placed in a straightjacket. The message is that if all members are truly committed to the ultimate target, policies which maximize the likelihood of them achieving that target should be adopted, and this includes output or unemployment stabilization, not just the Maastricht criteria. It is better that member states arrive at the destination late, but in good order, than not arrive at all.

Appendix 1: Methodology and Model

A1.1 INTRODUCTION

As discussed in the Introduction and Chapter 3, the various issues need to be examined in a coherent general equilibrium framework. Therefore an approach which allows the inspection of the effects of different policy regimes on the key variables, inflation, interest rates, exchange rates, debts and deficits, wealth and output growth in a multi-country dynamic environment is required. The model developed and described in this Appendix allows this objective to be achieved. Such a model quickly becomes intractable algebraically when we require a multi-country view point. This was the motivation for using numerical simulation models, which allow for the interactions required and combines this quality with ease of solution.

Generally, although there are obvious overlaps, one can split numerical models into three types: econometric, theoretical and computable general equilibrium. The choice between these methods depends variously on data availability, intended use (for example, forecasting or policy analysis), and to an extent on ideological preferences. These issues are discussed in more detail in Section A1.2.

A hybrid of these three approaches has been used in this research, which appears to match the requirements in the most efficient manner. The model conforms well with theory, has well understood long- and short-run properties, can be altered relatively easily, and incorporates the stylized facts of each modelled country and regime. The model is closer to the small theoretical models in spirit, but has a richer menu of variables and interactions. As such the models are not intended to represent forecasting tools for the countries studied, but rather policy regime "test beds", which are internally consistent, have proper stock-flow relationships, are multi-country, and general equilibrium in nature.

A three-country simulation framework with France, Germany, Greece or Spain, and an exogenous rest of the world and rest of the ERM is employed. Expectations are rational in financial markets, but adaptive in the goods and labour markets. In the status quo setting France and Spain are locked into the ERM through monetary policy, whilst Greece still floats. German monetary policy targets domestic German variables only, French monetary policy targets the exchange rate exclusively, whilst Spain and Greece can target a mix of domestic variables and the exchange, with varying weights.

The rest of the ERM is included, since the assumption that exchange rates are fixed between the modelled countries and this area, and that interest rates in the rest of the ERM follow German rates closely, appears valid. The model uses elasticities which are drawn from the literature, for example the European Commission's Quest model (Commission of the European Communities, 1991), the IMF's Intermod (Helliwell *et al.*, 1990) and various other sources. The models are calibrated based on data for the last quarter of 1993.

The chapter reviews different approaches to numerical modelling, before moving to a detailed description of the sort of model used in this book. The method used to calibrate and parameterize the simulation model is illustrated.

A1.2 MACROECONOMIC MODELS AND MODELLING

Empirical macroeconomic modelling is generally agreed to have started with Tinbergen's pioneering 1936 model of the Dutch economy which, although it attracted criticism from such luminaries as Keynes, set the tone for what came after the Second World War.

The post-war modelling effort stemmed from the USA with the development of the Klein–Goldberger model of the US economy. Klein featured again in the construction of the first real UK model by Klein, Ball and Vandome in 1961 which, unfortunately, was not maintained after Klein's return to the USA.

The 1960s brought a major contribution to modelling, the effects of which in terms of solution techniques and usage are still felt today. The Brookings model in the USA brought together a large team of economists to build a large disaggregated model of initially 200 equations. Once again, Klein was involved, along with Duesenberry. From the Brookings model came Ando and Modigliani's MPS which developed the financial sector. The Wharton and DRI models of the 1970s were also deeply influenced by the Brookings effort.

With the growing realization of the importance of economic interdependence, more attention was paid to the possibility of multi-country models. 1968 saw the development of Project Link at the University of Pennsylvania by Lawrence Klein. Project Link brought together independently estimated and developed country models and linked them through trade and prices. Link has 79 sub-models, each of which is fairly large, creating an extremely large complete model. Link is used mainly for forecasting purposes, and is now the official model of the United Nations.

Link paved the way, and now there are many multi-country models. The IMF's Multimod (Masson *et al.*, 1990); the OECD's Interlink (using the same methodology as Link); the EPA model of the Japanese Economic Planning Agency; the EC's Quest model operated by the Deutsches Institut für Wirtschaftsforschung (DIW); the US Federal Reserves's MCM (Multi-country Model) (Edison, 1987); the NIESR's GEM; various commercial models, for example Wharton's, Data Resources Incorporated's (DRI), and Oxford Economic Forecasting's (OEF) (Burridge *et al.*, 1991); and individual models like McKibbin and Sachs' MSG II (McKibbin and Sachs, 1991), are examples.

These models have the same spectrum of views as single-country models do. Some are monetarist, some are Keynesian in their viewpoints, although the distinction is becoming more blurred. Starting from the simple linkages of trade and prices, these models have developed complex financial market linkages between each country, some with fully determined asset demands.

As described in the introduction to this Appendix, there are many types of multi-country models, ranging from purely econometric driven, through more theoretical, to the computable general equilibrium type.

The first type tend to be reliant on the data in order to form the model's structure and dynamic responses. The second type uses structures derived from theoretical considerations, with either ad hoc "plausible" parameters, or parameters taken from the literature. The final class approaches the modelling problem from a Walrasian general equilibrium point of view, and are normally relatively highly disaggregated. "Fundamental" parameters are used to determine demands, not the reduced forms used in other approaches. Normally static and requiring the actual data to be changed in order to fit the model's assumption of equilibrium, these models have obvious drawbacks for the type of research pursued in this book.

Amongst the existing multi-country models the DRI and Wharton models lie closer to the data side, whilst Multimod resides nearer to the middle with MSG II very close to the calibrated CGE approach (see Whitley, 1994, for a discussion of these distinctions). The problems with each extreme approach is that, for purely empirical models, it is difficult to understand the "rationale" behind strange or counter-intuitive results; long-run theoretical relationships may be broken, and it can be very difficult to change the model, without wholesale re-estimation.

The purely calibrated CGE type are often static, and require data to be changed in order to fit the model's theoretical equilibrium conditions (Adams and Higgs, 1990; Henry *et al.*, 1986; Gregory and Smith, 1991; Bandara, 1991, presents a review). The theoretical simulation models (for example, Nguyen and Turnovsky, 1979, 1980; Karakitsos, 1989, 1992; Hughes Hallett and Vines, 1993; Whittaker *et al.*, 1986; Levine, 1993; Lossani and Tirelli, 1993) usually take "plausible" parameter values from the literature; as Sachs and Larrain (1993, p. 378) put it, "Unlike the other models, the equations are based on 'guesses' for the key parameters, using estimates by others, rather than new econometric estimates". The technique has also been used extensively at Imperial College as part of the PROPE research effort, where the numerical basis of the models has allowed detailed study of optimal control techniques for economies (see Becker *et al.*, 1986; Karakitsos and Rustem, 1984, 1991; Holly *et al.*, 1979). The benefits of this approach are low costs of implementation, a choice of parameter values over which to choose the most appropriate value, well understood properties, and although their usage for forecasting would seem extremely small, they do offer useful insights in policy analysis.

Since we are not attempting to forecast these economies the simulation approach used in the book is a hybrid of all three types of model. The models start with a purely theoretical structure for the behavioural equations, uses parameters derived from elasticities available in the literature, and are "calibrated" with the most recent full data set. Unlike the CGE models the initial solution is not an equilibrium but rather mirrors the case of McKibbin and Sachs' MSG II model, where the initial state of the model is "interpreted as a point on the stable adjustment path toward the steady state" (McKibbin and Sachs, 1991, p. 59). Each country has a similar structure for its behavioural equations, except where obvious differences can be discerned, but unlike MSG II each country is not constrained to have identical parameters. This approach has allowed the models to be built relatively cheaply and quickly, whilst not forcing them to be so far removed from reality as to be useless. The model used here therefore combines the best of all three types; however it also has some of each type's faults.

A1.3   A REPRESENTATIVE COUNTRY MODEL

This section sets out the general form of the models used in the research. Each modelled country has a generic structure in general, but we allow for differing wage–price sectors if the data suggests it, and of course different policy regimes call for different equations.

The issues raised in the Introduction and Chapter 3 define the variables which need to be included in the models; however, this is only the first step in the modelling process, the second is the interaction between these variables. The approach adopted in this book is to develop general equilibrium simulation models with properly specified stock–flow relationships for the current account, the government deficit and private sector wealth (Christ, 1991, provides an excellent blueprint for developing logically consistent macromodels). Since the book concentrates on policy issues, the interaction between and modelling of monetary and fiscal policy is carefully considered. The wage–price sector is treated in a standard fashion, but one which is flexible enough to allow investigations about the effect of credibility, for example, to be easily carried out. Private sector behavioural equations are general enough to encompass a variety of theoretical foundations. Imports from each region are treated separately, since this is of some obvious importance for the issues raised for the core, for example, whilst full account is taken of the difference in size between the modelled countries (which affects the ECB's reaction function). The ERM is treated in a standard fashion, except for Spanish risk premia, which receive closer attention since they are of crucial importance to the issue raised for this country. In short, whilst the models are not built on explicitly optimal micro-foundations, the functional forms used mimic those found in the literature, but the methodology used allows the models to be theoretically consistent and flexible.

The rationale behind the models developed in this book is to capture the important elements of the issues without falling into the trap of over-complicating the models. Simple theoretical models would not suffice since they are usually too small and simple to capture the relevant processes. The simple numerical models such as Hughes Hallett and Vines' (1993) usually contain a reduced form aggregate demand and supply framework, with demand dependent on interest rates, competitiveness and perhaps fiscal variables and foreign demand, and with prices determined by demand and core inflation, similar to a Lucas' surprise inflation approach. Interest rates are normally determined via uncovered interest rate parity, and as such under fixed exchange rates are equal to foreign rates. The limitations of this approach are dependent on what problem the model is being applied to. In our case, these sort of models are not informative. For instance, the evolution of government debt and private sector wealth is not considered, nor is the ability to model the ERM very rich (see p. 222 for a discussion of this problem drawn from Whitley, 1994). However, this sort of model has proved useful when applied to appropriate issues and can be a productive test bed for testing policy, since even simple models often contain too many dynamic processes for analytical solutions to be useful. As Bryant *et al.* (1993, p. 4) put it: "theoretical analysis alone, conducted in terms of highly simplified models is valuable but insufficient".

One alternative is to use the large-scale econometric models, but again there are shortcomings with the application of these models to policy analysis. Since these models were primarily designed for forecasting, they are commonly highly disaggregated, which precludes full system estimation with appropriate cross-equation restrictions. Thus, even if individual equations have consistent steady state properties, this is no guarantee that the model as a whole will: put another way, stock-flow equilibrium is often violated. However, the rich structure of these models allows them to tackle complex issues, since they incorporate many of the required variables which are missing from the simple models; unfortunately their very complexity means that ambitious policy analysis becomes very time-consuming. Indeed a common recent trend has been to produce small multi-country simulation models (Malley *et al.*, 1991) or to simplify complex econometric models (for example, Minigem from the NIESR's GEM, see Weale *et al.*, 1989) in order to examine policy analysis and design.

The approach adopted in this book represents a middle path. The models developed are much closer to the small-scale theoretical models in the tradition of Karakitsos (1989), Whittaker *et al.* (1986) and Lossani and Tirelli (1993), but are complex enough to allow the impact of fiscal and monetary policy to be fully determined, and are based on actual data in the tradition of McKibbin and Sachs (1991) and Pisani-Ferry *et al.* (1993). As such, the models should not be viewed as attempted facsimiles of the countries examined, but rather theoretical models which have similar initial conditions to the countries examined. The labels attached to the models, such as "Greece" or "France" should therefore not be taken too literally; they could equally have been "high inflation, high debt country", and "low inflation core EU country 1". As such, the results are more general than specific.

We begin by outlining the demand side of the model, move on to supply, consider identities, asset holdings, exchange rates, and finally the policy variables.

The demand side

The model is disaggregated to the level where consumption, investment, and exports and imports with each partner are determined. Government spending is treated as a policy variable, and is considered on p. 000. This level of disaggregation is reasonable given the nature of the policy regimes considered. For example, changing tax rates to control debt will directly affect disposable income, and thus consumption, but will indirectly affect investment. A further example centres around the import equations; asymmetric EU shocks would be impossible to treat properly with single import or export equations.

Consumption

The consumption function is possibly one of the most researched areas in macroeconomics. It is central to most macroeconometric models based on the national income accounts framework, and so its form is critical to any results from these models. The functional form used in the research is general enough to capture most of the underlying theories and includes what appear to be the statistically important variables.

Keynes' (1936) absolute income hypothesis was important in that it suggested a formal testable functional form for the consumption expenditure of households, namely

$$C = \alpha + \beta Y \tag{A1.1}$$

However work by Simon Kuznets (1946) highlighted a paradox in the data available at the time. Keynes' equation suggested a marginal propensity to consume (MPC) of less than one, and a declining average propensity to consume (APC) with respect to income, which is clear from (A1.1). But the data demonstrated that the savings ratio had remained relatively constant over a very long period of time.

As a result of Kuznets' work much of the early post-war research concentrated on resolving this paradox, for example Duesenberry's relative income hypothesis. The so-called intertemporal approach associated with Friedman's (1957) Permanent Income Hypothesis (PIH) and Modigliani, Ando and Brumberg's Life-Cycle Hypothesis (LCH) demonstrated a way of explaining the stylized facts in the data.

Both the life-cycle hypothesis of Modigliani and the permanent income hypothesis of Friedman are based on the assumptions that households prefer a smooth consumption stream, and that to facilitate this there exists a financial market for households to borrow or lend in. The result of this approach is that some form of long-term measure of income is important in determining the current level of consumption. This is at odds with the functional form of the original Keynesian equation, although Keynes did not ignore the affect of wealth or expectations. In the short run the intertemporal models have MPCs of less than one, whereas in the long-run, whether with respect to permanent income or "life-time" income, the MPCs are unitary.

These models fared well until the turbulent early 1970s when an obvious linkage between inflation and saving rates became apparent. Since then, research has emphasized expanding the traditional set of factors in order to explain this.

Substantial controversy still exists between the rival theories. Work by Campbell and Mankiw (1989), Carroll and Summers (1989), Flavin (1981) and many others has shown that current income may have a stronger effect than the PIH or LCH models suggest. For example, the question of liquidity constraints (see Hayashi, 1985, for an estimate of the size of this effect, and Clower[1] and Leijonhufvud, 1968, for the classic distinction between notional demand and actual, or effective, demand), bequests, and expectations formation have led to most macroeconometric models adopting a cosmopolitan approach, using consumption functions capable of encompassing many of the basic theoretical ideas. As Gowland (1983) points out about the "ever more complex" optimization models, "their role is to *point out* a number of aspects of the savings decision not explicitly captured in other analyses" (my italics), they "are not operational". Thus these models have highlighted important missing variables but cannot lead to a specific functional form unless other assumptions are made, specifically about the form of the utility function and thus consumer preferences, and the derivation of permanent income (often through an ad hoc lag structure, see Fisher, 1985, for a review).

In the light of the theoretical controversies, and the lack of explicit functional forms for the PIH and LCH, unless assumptions are made about consumer preferences, we have chosen a form which allows for most theoretical effects, and conforms with many published sources for elasticities.

Hence consumption is dependent on disposable income, the real interest rate, real wealth, and the previous period's consumption level. The functional form is

$$C = \gamma_C + \alpha_{CY}\,YD + \alpha_{Cr}\,(r - cpie) + \alpha_{Cv}\,V_{t-1}/CPI + \alpha_{CC}C_{t-1} \qquad (A1.2)$$

where C = consumption
     YD = disposable income
     r = short-term nominal interest rate
     $cpie$ = expected inflation
     V_{t-1} = *last period's nominal wealth*
     CPI = consumer price level

Disposable income is made up of wage income, the return on assets and the inflation tax on those assets. This formulation of real disposable income is now commonly accepted, with Hendry and von Ungern-Sternberg's (1981) paper highlighing its importance. Last period's wealth is included as a determinant, since as Turnovsky (1977) points out this is the appropriate measure if the consumer's budget constraint is analyzed properly. Wealth is deflated by this period's consumer price index in order to capture any Pigou effect. This formulation of disposable income and consumption would seem appropriate when disinflation and debt targeting fiscal policy are being considered.

In the long-run, when $C_t = C_{t-1}$ the equation parameters are constrained so that the long-run MPC out of disposable income is unity, following the PIH and LCH approach.

Investment

Although investment makes up a relatively small part of aggregate demand in the economy, research in this area has been extensive. According to Poindexter (1976) this is due to several reasons. First, investment is much more volatile than the other components of GDP, second, the effects of government policy are assumed to work importantly through investment, and hence policy setting needs to take investment response into account, and finally the sheer difficulty of explaining investment behaviour has "engaged the economics profession". This last point is echoed by Garganas (1991), who states, "Still, there seems to be no universally acceptable model of investment behaviour or an appropriate formulation of the empirical investment function".

The general motivation for investing is normally accepted to be the pursuit of profit. Hence early theories, for example Keynes (1936), concentrated on the discounted revenue flows from an investment project, with firms entering into any one project if either the expected present value of the net receipts are positive or the "internal rate of return", the marginal efficiency of capital in Keynes' words, exceeds the market rate. In this setting the important determinants of investment decisions are the interest rate and expected profits, which, since they are unobservable, are often proxied by output.

However, early empirical evidence, for example, Clark (1917), indicated a relatively stable relationship between the level of investment and the rate of change of output. Furthermore, early post-war evidence collected by surveys in the USA and Britain (Meyer and Kuh, 1957; Wilson and Andrews, 1951) suggested that the interest rate had little or no effect on investment decisions. For this reason, models which were independent of interest rates were tested, for example the *fixed accelerator* model.

The accelerator view relies on the idea of a fixed "engineering" relationship between the flow of output and the stock of capital. Hence for any given desired level of output flow, there is a given desired capital stock. In order to derive an investment rate, a *flow* variable, from this desired *stock* variable, one notes that this relationship exists every time period, and so investment is equal to

$$I = dK = \alpha (Y_t - Y_{t-1}) \tag{A1.3}$$

This simple accelerator view has been relatively successful, even though it is ad hoc, and if the parameter α is greater than unity it can explain the high volatility of investment in a relatively straightforward way.

However, there are several obvious criticisms of the simple accelerator model, relating to excess capacity, expectations and the role of financial variables. If firms are operating below capacity, why would they expand capacity, through investment, as soon as output growth starts to accelerate? The obverse is also true since according to the symmetry of the model the absolute value of investment will be the same regardless of the direction of change of output. But the maximum amount of aggregate disinvestment is constrained by the rate of depreciation. Therefore this approach can produce ridiculous values for disinvestment during periods of rapid decline in output.

The model also indicates that during periods of output growth, assuming no excess capacity, investment changes in order to produce the required new level of capital in the same period as the output changes itself. This requires a perfectly elastic supply of capital, and hence no increase in capital prices. Therefore for the simple accelerator model to work at the aggregate level there must be large excess capacity in the capital producing sector and zero excess capacity in all other sectors, indicating a deep flaw in the internal logic of the model.

The simple accelerator also indicates that firms respond to any changes in output, regardless of whether they are perceived as permanent or temporary, which would seem a very strong assumption (Eisner, 1963). Finally the model completely ignores the impact of availability of funds for investment or the changes in the interest rate.

Haavelmo (1960) pointed out that a theory of desired *capital stocks* is not a theory of *investment flows* unless more assumptions are made. Indeed demand for increased capital stocks can produce any rate of investment from "almost zero to infinity, depending on the additional hypothesis we introduce regarding the speed of reaction of the capital users" (Haavelmo, 1960, p. 216). This problem stems from a lack of consideration for dynamic adjustment in the model, a point closely related to the criticisms above.

In response to these criticisms the *flexible accelerator* model was developed independently by Chenery (1952) and Koyck (1954). This stipulates that any discrepancy between the desired and the actual capital stock is eliminated over a number of periods, through an ad hoc lag structure. Almon (1965, 1968) developed an even more complicated lag structure, using a parabolic structure with end points restricted to zero. The lag structures used, whilst seemingly realistic, were not derived from micro-foundations in any theoretical manner until the late 1960s, when a lag structure could be inferred from an increasing costs of adjustment approach (Fisher, 1985). However these early flexible accelerator models continued to ignore the effect of interest rates, and other variables, on the desired capital stock. There now existed a model describing investment flows in a rational model, but the argument over what determined the desired capital stock was still unclear.

Reacting to these deficiencies Jorgenson (1963) introduced the *"neoclassical"* model for desired capital spending. Jorgenson's approach was to treat demand for capital as a demand for capital services, derived from a neo-Classical production function. From profit-maximizing behaviour on the part of firms and a Cobb–Douglas production function with both constant returns to scale and shares, Jorgenson derived a negative relationship between the user cost of capital, and a positive relation between desired capital and output, as for the simple accelerator model.

$$K^* = \alpha P_Y Y / e \qquad (A1.4)$$

where K^* = desired capital (since there is an assumed one to one relationship between capital and capital services)

α = the share of capital in production

P_Y = the price of output

Y = output

e = the user cost of capital

Jorgenson spent considerable effort developing an explanation of the lag structure of investment, in order to relate K^* to actual investment spending. He concentrated on describing what he identified as five distinct stages of the investment decision: initiation of project, appropriation of funds, letting of contracts, issuing of orders and actual investment. Hence using a flexible accelerator form of the investment function, one derives a gross investment equation of the form

$$I_t = (1 - \mu)[\alpha P_Y Y_t / e - K_{t-1}] + \delta K_{t-1} \qquad (A1.5)$$

If the depreciation rate, δ, is assumed to be constant, and the user cost of capital is proxied by the interest rate, r, then in the more general form one finds that the investment equation has the signs indicated from the original Keynesian function, namely

$$I_t = f(\overset{+}{Y_t}, \overset{-}{r_t}, \overset{-}{K_{t-1}}) \qquad (A1.6)$$

With this derivation in mind, and since we use a simple Cobb–Douglas production technology, a linearized version of this equation for real gross investment is employed. Accordingly, investment is dependent on output, the real interest rate, last period's capital stock, deflated by the current producer price index, and the previous period's investment rate.

$$I = \gamma_I + \alpha_{IY} Y + \alpha_{Ir} (r - pe) + \alpha_{Ik} K_{t-1} / P + \alpha_{II} I_{t-1} \qquad (A1.7)$$

where I = investment

Y = output

K_{t-1} = last period's nominal capital stock

pe = expected producer prices

P = producer price index

Since government spending is a component of Y and monetary policy is represented in the real interest rate term, this equation shows explicitly that government policy will affect the rate of investment and thus the rate of potential output via the production function. Furthermore, the interaction between the ERM commitment and German interest rates will determine domestic interest rates; there is thus a direct link between the exchange rate target and changes in investment. Finally, since expected inflation also appears, disinflation and the speed of expectation adjustment (for example, the credibility issue for Greece) will also play a part. As for consumption, this equation therefore captures a range of processes which affect investment, and which are directly linked to the policy regime in place.

Imports

Imports, measured in foreign currency, are determined by domestic demand and a measure of competitiveness, in a relatively common approach.[2]

$$Q^{12} = \gamma_Q + \alpha_{QY} DA + \alpha_{QCOMP} \, COMP^{12} + \alpha_{QQ} \, Q_{t-1}^{12} \qquad (A1.8)$$

where DA = domestic absorption
      Q^{12} = imports of country 1 from country 2
      $COMP^{12}$ = relative prices between country 1 and 2 in domestic currency

$$Q = \sum_{i=1}^{n} Q_i$$

where Q_i represent the respective imports from each trade partner. Competitiveness is determined by relative producer prices and the exchange rate

$$COMP = Pe/P^* \qquad (A1.9)$$

where e = nominal exchange rate with trading country
     P^* = foreign producer prices

    Imports from each trade partner are considered individually, the model does not use the common approach of a single import function with constant, historically based, weights determining import shares (as in for example Malley *et al.*, 1991), rather the shares are determined endogenously. This is important for asymmetric shocks in Europe, especially shocks from Germany in the chapters on Spain and Greece, since Germany takes the hegemonic role in the ERM, so trade with the other ERM members may react differently, and for the issue of federal fiscal policy in MU considered in Chapter 7. Another importance point is that for disinflating countries, for example Greece, there is no reason to assume that trade shares will remain unchanged as inflation drops.

Exports

Exports are merely a trade partner's imports, and accordingly this is how they are determined in the model, taking into account differing country sizes

$$X = Q^* \, \alpha_{YY^*} \qquad (A1.10)$$

where X = exports
     Q^* = trade partner's imports from home country
     α_{YY^*} = scale factor to account for differing country sizes

Demand-side summary

Taken together the elements of aggregate demand are determined in a very rich manner, offering the opportunity for first and second order effects to affect the level of demand in the economy. Total demand is a function of domestic producer prices, all overseas producer prices, all overseas demand, all exchange rates, wealth, price expectations, asset values, interest income, and fiscal and monetary policy, which in turn depend on the policy regime in place and the targets of policy. Thus, we have a simple set of behavioural equations, which offers a very rich multi-country representation of demand compared to some simple numerical models, for example Hughes Hallett and Vines (1991, 1993), Levine (1993).

Each component of demand is represented as a percentage of total GDP, with the ratios gathered from the national accounts. Initial import and export shares were collected from the IMF's *Direction of Trade Statistics*. The calibration proceeds by determining the slope parameters from the literature (see Section A1.4) and then setting the intercept parameters (the γs) in the behavioural equations in order to produce the required GDP shares.

The supply side

The model has a full wage–price sector and determines potential output endogenously based on simple assumptions. We describe the determination of potential output, wages, producer, consumer and import prices, price expectations, and unemployment.

Potential output

Potential output is used in the model as a way of endogenously determining growth rates over the simulation period. The objective is not to attempt to capture all determinants of growth in an exclusive manner, but rather to have a more flexible approach than imposing a purely exogenous rate of growth of output as in, for example, Taylor (1989) and Malley *et al.* (1991).

The growth rate is determined by combining the average growth rate of the population, capital, the growth of disembodied technology and the rate of depreciation of the capital stock. These inputs produce potential output via a Cobb–Douglas production function of the form

$$Y_{pot} = Tech \, K^\alpha \, L^{(1-\alpha)} \qquad (A1.11)$$

where Y_{pot} = potential output
$Tech$ = level of technology used in production process
K = capital stock
L = natural rate of employment
α = capital's share in production (assumed fixed)

This formulation has constant returns to scale, a fixed marginal rate of substitution, and fixed shares of capital and labour coupled with disembodied technological change. This approach was favoured since the model is not estimated, and the debate about returns to scale is far from resolution.[3] Furthermore, since the CD function is a sub-set of both the Constant Elasticity of Substitution (CES) and the Transcendental-Logarithmic (Trans-Log) functions it appears to be a sensible simplification in the light of the continued controversy surrounding the question of returns to scale and rates of marginal substitution (see Fisher, 1985, for a review of the econometric evidence on this issue).

Capital grows according to the rate of gross investment and physical depreciation

$$K = (1 - \delta) K_{t-1} + I_{t-1} \qquad (A1.12)$$

where δ = rate of depreciation (fixed)[4]

whilst the labour force, L, grows at the average rate observed over the last decade.

Reliable information about the rate of technical change, and indeed capital stocks and depreciation rates, is difficult to obtain. There are, however, some approaches which can be used to proceed.

First, since we are interested in the rate of growth of an index of output, the starting level for capital, and indeed labour, is not important. It is the addition to capital which we are interested in, and as shown in (A1.13), this depends on the investment rate, which is known, and the depreciation rate, which is not. We are left with determining values for depreciation, technical change and the shares of capital and labour in production.

To derive a value for technical change note that for a constant growth rate the capital–output ratio must remain constant, hence since the rate of labour growth is known, we are left with an equation which gives technical change

$$\frac{Tech}{Tech_{t-1}} = \frac{dY}{dK\,dL} \qquad (A1.13)$$

where $dY = Y_{pot,t}/Y_{pot,t-1}$

$dK = K_t^\alpha/K_{t-1}^\alpha$

$dL = L_t^{(1-\alpha)}/L_{t-1}^{(1-\alpha)}$

and since the rates of growth of the labour supply and output, and the "required" rate of growth of capital are all known (and constant in equilibrium), we derive a constant value for the rate of technical change in equilibrium.

It is then a simple matter to derive an expression for from the equation for the evolution of capital

$$\delta = 1 - K/K_{t-1} + I/K_{t-1} \qquad (A1.14)$$

which, again, since K/K_{t-1} and I/K_{t-1} are constant in equilibrium, gives us a constant value for δ, which produces the observed *equilibrium* growth rate of output. Capital's share in production is taken from OECD data on capital income shares in the business sector.[5] The relevant data for calibrating this part of the model, along with the measures of technical change and depreciation are shown in Table A1.1.

Of course, it is perfectly possible for this potential output growth rate to be altered via the rate of investment which, as we have seen is sensitive to changes in policy; thus policy can affect the equilibrium growth rate.

The demand side of the model is detrended from this growing potential output rate for simplicity. This implies certain restrictions elsewhere in the model, for instance, whilst there is a trend productivity increase inferred from the potential output equation, detrended productivity and the real wage are stationary. Where the growth of potential output does have an important effect is in the determination of asset stocks expressed as ratios of GDP. This is, in fact, the main reason for growth being included in the model, since questions about fiscal solvency and the Maastricht debt criteria are central to the book, and the debt ratio can be reduced by increased output growth as

Appendix 1

Table A1.1 Relevant data for potential output determination

	Germany	France	Spain	Greece
Investment	18.5	16.6	20.1	19.1
Average output growth	0.51	0.47	0.6	0.36
Average labour force growth	0.19	0.13	0.25	0.3
Average capital share in output	0.346	0.337	0.377	0.34
Depreciation rate	1.8	1.6	1.9	2
Technology increase rate	0.2	0.22	0.2	0.04

Note: All growth rates are quarterly per cent. Investment is shown as a percentage of GDP for 4th quarter 1993. Averages are calculated over period from 1980–93.

well as by lowering deficits. Again, simplistic theoretical models tend to abstract from the effect of growth on the evolution of debt, and thus may overstate the effect of measured deficits on the debt ratio.

Wage–price sector

The wage–price nexus is a fundamental part of any macroeconomic model. It will determine both the model's equilibrium and the dynamic path to that equilibrium. Thus, when using a model for comparative policy analysis, this sector of the model must have plausible characteristics and be capable of capturing stylized facts for the results to have any credibility.

With this in mind standard approaches are employed in these models as found in the literature relating to empirical macro-models. To use an esoteric model would raise issues about the model's validity and deflect interest from the actual results. Moreover, the approach is capable of encompassing many of the theoretical aspects developed in the literature. Since the model is essentially in reduced form, it has nothing to say about the actual causes of, for example, sticky wages[6] or slowly adjusting expectations, instead it attempts to replicate the observed properties of the relevant time series, essentially slowly adjusting prices.

The approach draws from that found in Bartolini and Symansky (1993) as applied to Multimod. From the Cobb–Douglas production function presented above one can derive labour demand as

$$L_t^d = (Y_t/(K_t^\alpha \ Tech_t))^{1/(1-\alpha)} \tag{A1.15}$$

Viewed in this way, the production function is a simple mapping of current output onto labour demand for each level of capital and technology. Defining a "natural rate" of employment at potential output Y_{pot} as

$$L_t^n = (Y_{pot}/(K_t^\alpha \, Tech_t))^{1/(1-\alpha)} \qquad (A1.16)$$

applying logs to both equations and taking the difference of $\ln (L_t^d)$ and $\ln (L_t^n)$ gives the difference between the demand for labour and its natural level as

$$l_t^d - l_t^n = (y_t - y_{pot})/(1 - \alpha) \qquad (A1.17)$$

where lower case letters refer to the natural logarithms. By specifying a relationship between the level of actual labour supply and its natural level we can relate labour demand to labour supply and derive a reduced form for unemployment. If labour supply is

$$l_t^s - l_t^n = \nu + \gamma(w - p) \qquad (A1.18)$$

where w is the nominal wage, and p is the consumption price deflator, then combining the relationship for labour supply and demand gives

$$u = l_t^s - l_t^d = \nu + \gamma(w - p) - (y_t - y_{pot})/(1 - \alpha) \qquad (A1.19)$$

Therefore, in long-run equilibrium if real wages are constant and output is at potential, unemployment, u is equal to ν, the "natural rate". Bartolini and Symanksy then imbed this equation in a wage–price mark-up equation to relate unemployment to prices. This leaves their model as basically a Phillips curve relationship, whereas the work of, for example, Nickell (1984, 1988) stresses the theoretical problems inherent in modelling the supply side of empirical models when this approach is used. The problems with the approach have been recognized for some time (Artis, 1989). One important aspect is that an expectations augmented Phillips curve specified in rates of change cannot say anything about the level of the real wage.

One solution is to reformulate the Phillips curve to incorporate bargaining about an aspiration real wage level determined by tax rates or unemployment benefits, for example. This approach produced a rich vein of research which eventually led to a merging of the standard Phillips curve and the real wage resistance models, and ultimately the much vaunted work of Nickell and his co-workers.

Their approach (Layard, Nickell and Jackman, 1991) is to use a model of bargaining to explain the wage rate and level of employment. Unions and management pursue differing targets in an imperfectly competitive environment, the trade-off between the two producing an equilibrium which gives a non-accelerating inflation rate of unemployment (NAIRU). Generally this approach finds that the important determinants of employment and wages are taxes, and exogenous wage-push factors such as unemployment benefits and union power.

However, this approach is not without its problems (see Phelps, 1992); it relies on difficult to measure factors and since its focus is on the evolution of the natural rate itself, it describes the dynamic adjustment path of unemployment and inflation through standard hypotheses.

In this book we instead follow the suggestions in Bean (1994), who distinguishes between the Phillips curve as a disequilibrium adjustment process and the wage equation as a structural wage setting model. Combining the two Bean derives a model where the determinants of the natural rate are the factors identified in the work above, whilst the determinants of actual unemployment are price surprises and past realizations of unemployment. Real demand shocks act through these price surprises to give the actual rate of unemployment. Moreover the real wage is eliminated from the relationship, with the reservation wage subsumed into the natural rate of unemployment element of the equation.

Bearing in mind the focus of the book we have chosen to concentrate on the dynamic aspects of price determination, as typified by Bartolini and Symansky (1993), and have not attempted to explain the natural rate of unemployment. Essentially we have adopted Bean's distinction between the two, and concentrated on the price dynamics. The natural rate is assumed to be exogenous, and is set equal to the average unemployment rate observed over the last fifteen years. Whilst this is an obvious simplification, bearing in mind the structural breaks which have been recorded in European unemployment, they way the model is specified means that the natural rate has no impact on wages or prices as long as it remains constant. Thus, unemployment follows a relatively simple Okun-type equation

$$u = u_b + \alpha_{uY}\left(Y_t/Y_{pot} - 1\right) + \alpha_{uy}\left(Y_t/Y_{t-1} - 1\right) \tag{A1.20}$$

where u_b = equilibrium unemployment or the natural rate

Unemployment is dependent on the natural rate, which is exogenous, the difference between potential and actual output, and the rate of change of output around its trend to capture any hysteresis effect.

Wages Wages follow a simple model whereby expected consumer price inflation, the difference between unemployment and the natural rate, and last period's wage determine current wage inflation

$$w = \alpha_{w\,cpie}\,cpie + \alpha_{wu}(u_b - u) + (1 - \alpha_{w\,cpie})\,w_{t-1} \tag{A1.21}$$

This formulation is popular in the literature and allows for a variety of different institutional possibilities. For example, if the value of $\alpha_{w\,cpie}$ is low, this could indicate the presence of long-term contracts (see Mitchell and Kimbell, 1982, for a discussion).

Producer prices Producer prices are based on a simple mark-up equation, so that producer price inflation is determined by a weighted average of imported raw materials prices and wage costs, with $(1 - \alpha_{p\,w})$ showing the supply-side openness of the economy

$$p = \alpha_{pw}\,w + (1 - \alpha_{pw})\,(p_{rm} - (e_{rm}/e_{rm,t-1} - 1)) \tag{A1.22}$$

where p_{rm} = raw materials price inflation
e_{rm} = exchange rate with currency raw materials priced in \$

There is substantial evidence to indicate that demand conditions do not have a an effect on the mark-up itself (for instance, Masson, Symansky and Meredith, 1990), and thus capacity utilization is not included in the producer price term.

Import prices Import prices are determined by first separating imported final goods from imported raw materials with a weight derived from import categories data from the OECD. The weights for each trade partner's share stem from the import equations as shown in the equation below

$$
\begin{aligned}
p_{imp} = (1 - \alpha_{pimp\,rm}) \, &[\alpha_{pimp\,1} \, (p_1^* - (e_1/e_{1t-1} - 1)) \\
&+ \alpha_{pimp\,2} \, (p_2^* - (e_2/e_{2t-1} - 1)) + \dots \\
&\dots + \alpha_{pimp\,n} \, (p_n - (e_n/e_{nt-1} - 1))] \\
&+ \alpha_{pimp\,rm} \, (p_{rm} - (e_{rm}/e_{rmt-1} - 1))
\end{aligned}
\tag{A1.23}
$$

where p_{imp} = total import prices
$\quad\;\; p_n^*$ = import prices of finished goods from country n
$\quad\;\; e_n$ = exchange rate with country n
$\quad\;\; \alpha_{pimp\,n}$ = contribution of country n to total import prices
$\quad\;\; p_{rm}$ = raw materials prices
$\quad\;\; \alpha_{pimp\,rm}$ = ratio of raw materials to finished goods in imports

A complicating factor in a multi-country model is that careful treatment must be given to imported raw materials prices. It is normally assumed that the unmodelled countries have fixed prices or constant inflation rates. However, if an oil price shock occurs then the modelled countries are at a disadvantage as compared to the unmodelled rest of the world with this formulation. Therefore, the model counters this by incorporating a two-stage process for determining foreign export prices. Wage inflation in the *ROW* and *RERM* is assumed to be constant but producer prices in both the *RERM* and *ROW* are determined as a weighted average of their wage inflation and raw material price inflation. Therefore an increase in the oil price not only increases domestic inflation, but also foreign inflation.

Consumer prices Consumer prices are merely a weighted average of producer prices and import prices, with the weight dependent on the share of imports in final demand. The parameter $(1 - \alpha_{cpi\,p})$ therefore gives an indication of the demand-side openness of the economy:

$$
cpi = \alpha_{cpi\,p}\,p + (1 - \alpha_{cpi\,p})\,p_{imp}
\tag{A1.24}
$$

Expected consumer prices Consumer price expectations follow a simple adaptive expectations form

$$
cpie = cpie_{t-1} + \alpha_{cpie\,cpi}\,(cpi - cpie_{t-1})
\tag{A1.25}
$$

where *cpie = expected consumer price inflation for next period*

although it is perfectly possible to replace this expectations regime with a model consistent formulation in the model. Expected producer price inflation is determined with an identical equation.

Supply-side summary

Many theoretical approaches in the 1980s to explain the existence of the ERM stressed the inflationary bias when policy makers are outside the ERM and unable to credibly bind themselves to low inflation. However, the modelling approach, typified by Giavazzi and Pagano (1988), has some weaknesses which tend to throw their conclusions into doubt. In order to make their model tractable Giavazzi and Pagano are forced to assume instantly adjusting prices, and the ability of the central bank to "set" the inflation rate via money growth. It is, perhaps, not surprising that these theoretical welfare gains from joining the ERM have not materialized or appeared in the econometric evidence. Most of the evidence suggests that nominal inertia does exist for European wages and inflation (see Chapter 1). Thus, whilst the basic message of the credibility literature seems intuitively attractive, its present modelling is too restrictive, stylized and internally inconsistent to be sufficient. The approach adopted in the book is thus to incorporate the evidence which is strongly in favour of slowly adjusting inflation and inflation expectations, and to use a well understood and common wage–price sector which represents the reduced form of many underlying theories, for example Taylor's contracts hypothesis or Lucas' supply curve.

Exchange rates, identities, and assets

Exchange rates

Exchange rates follow a simple uncovered interest rate parity condition with model consistent expectations and the inclusion of a risk premium if it is appropriate:

$$e = ee/(ede + 1) \tag{A1.26}$$

where ee = expected exchange rate (model consistent)
     ede = expected depreciation

Expected depreciation is simply the interest rate differential and the risk premium

$$ede = r^* - r + risk \tag{A1.27}$$

where r^* = the foreign interest rate

This modified uncovered interest rate parity equation has been used previously as described in Whitley (1992, 1994). The risk premium is made up of a variety of indicators

$$risk = f(p, u, Y, debt, psbr, cb, nfa, shift\ term) \tag{A1.28}$$

where cb = real current account balance as a per cent of GDP
     nfa = real net foreign asset position
     shift term = exogenous shock to risk premium

Drazen and Masson (1993), Masson (1993), Stansfield and Sutherland (1995) and Cohen and Wyplosz (1989) provide some analysis of both what is important in determining the risk premium and how it impacts on monetary policy for ERM members. Drazen and Masson (1993) and Masson (1993) highlight the importance of the state of the economy as a determinant of credibility.

Masson (1993) applies this view to the UK's experience in the ERM by examining interest rate differentials with Germany. He finds that although the credibility of the UK's commitment was high by the autumn of 1991, the deteriorating unemployment situation of 1992 decreased the credibility of the peg and therefore kept interest differentials high. Drazen and Masson (1993) finds similar evidence for France.

Stansfield and Sutherland (1995) examine the dynamics of such a system in more detail. Their results are suggestive in that the presence of realignment expectations can have perverse effects. If expectations are very sensitive to the output gap then complete instability can set in; instead of stabilizing exchange rates, the EMS can become an engine of instability. Furthermore the sensitivity of realignment expectations to output can slow down the pace of the economy's adjustment, leading to larger and longer deviations of output from equilibrium. Whilst these models have some drawbacks, the approach is certainly appealing.

This view of the operation of the ERM is at odds with the "S-Band" literature as typified by the papers in Krugman and Miller (1992) and Krugman's (1991) paper. These models assume that the exchange rate target is perfectly credible, hence any deviation from the central parity, in a rational expectations world, is soon reversed since the probability of devaluation–revaluation declines as the exchange rate approaches its margins (due to perfectly offsetting intervention). Tests of this type of model are not encouraging as to its ability to explain the functioning of exchange rates in bands (Bertola and Caballero, 1990).

The approaches of Masson, Drazen, Stansfield and Sutherland and the evidence on inflation credibility indicate an ERM modelling approach where credibility is not garnered instantaneously. Attaching a risk premium which reflects the "pain" of the disinflation process represents a stylized way of capturing the private sector's view about the government's determination to defend the parity. Whilst this approach has gained some credence in the literature, it has not been applied in a general equilibrium simulation model of this kind; instead only partial equilibrium analysis has been attempted with the onus on explaining the risk premium itself, not on the feedback from the risk premium to the rest of the economy and fiscal policy. Thus, where this approach is incorporated in the book the results are new.

The risk premium is most important for Greece and Spain in the book. The Greek and French premiums are simply determined by the current account deficit, following Whitley (1992), whereas the treatment for Spain needs to be richer because of the focus of the research for the median countries. The evidence on interest rate differentials in the ERM indicates that they persist for some time; this has been explained by a mix of continuing devaluation expectations and a risk premium. The approach adopted for Spain exploits the apparent time path of the risk premium: slow reductions in the interest rate differential.

The method used to formulate the risk premium is to first postulate a set of policies which it is assumed would result in a steadily declining risk premium and interest rate differential as observed in the data. The risk premium follows an autoregressive path,[7] declining over time as the "credible" policy is pursued. This policy mix is one where nominal convergence proceeds, whilst the debt ratio is kept close to its Maastricht target (this policy mix is discussed in depth in Chapter 6). The evolution of the risk premium is then related via an OLS regression to the values from the simulation of variables which are assumed to be of importance for Spain. These are the debt ratio, unemployment, the inflation differential with Germany, and the rate of change of German inflation expectations.

The reasoning is as follows. Market perceptions are assumed to take into account the possibility that the higher unemployment is, the more likely is a relaxation of monetary policy and a devaluation. For the current account, it could be argued that a devaluation may be used to help reduce the deficit, whilst the inclusion of debt represents a mix of fears about default, attempts to inflate away the debt, or reductions in interest rates to ease debt interest payments. Finally, changes in German inflation are included to capture concern about diverging business cycles and tighter German monetary policy. The path of these variables for the "declining risk premium" simulation is in keeping with a steadily declining expectation of devaluation. The base risk premium equation is

$$risk_{t+1} = 0.975^* risk_t \qquad (A1.29)$$

where the risk premium at $t = 0$ is determined by the quarterly interest rate differential between Germany and Spain with initial exchange rate expectations equal to the ERM target rate. Therefore, at the beginning of the base simulation period the interest rate differential is enough, *ceteris paribus*, to avoid downward pressure on the exchange rate. The full equation for the rest of the simulations is then given by

$$risk = 0.0053 - 0.4(cpiG - cpiS) + 4.2(cpieG - cpieG_{t-1})$$
$$+ 0.07\, ugapS - 0.002\, cbS/YS + 0.00025\, (bS - bS_{t-1}) \qquad (A1.30)$$

This equation when used with the "high credibility" policy mix results in the same path as the autoregressive equation (4.29). If any of these variables vary from their baseline "low" risk path, the risk premium will increase, putting pressure on the peseta to depreciate as compared to the base path. Therefore, if any one of the following occurs: increased inflation differential, increased unemployment gap, increased rate of growth of the debt to GDP ratio, higher German inflation expectations, or a worsening of the current account, then Spanish interest rates will have to increase to combat the pressure for depreciation.

Identities

The government budget deficit is described by

$$psbr = G + r_{t-1}debt_{t-1} - T - inftax = \Delta m + \Delta debt \qquad (A1.31)$$

where Δm = change in real base money supply
       $\Delta debt$ = change in real government debt
       T = tax revenues
       $inftax$ = the inflation tax

Tax revenues are derived from an income tax and a tax on interest income

$$T = srt\,(Y_L + opi) \qquad (A1.32)$$

where srt = tax rate
       opi = other personal income, interest income on domestic and foreign assets.
       Y_L = labour income

The inflation tax is the loss on the real value of domestic assets due to inflation

$$inftax = cpi\,(m + debt) \qquad (A1.33)$$

Disposable income is simply GDP plus other personal income net of tax, *less* the inflation tax and capital gains/losses on foreign bond holdings due to exchange rate changes

$$YD = (Y + opi)\,(1 - srt) - inftax - caplos \qquad (A1.34)$$

Other personal income includes domestic interest income, and income from overseas

$$opi = r_{t-1}\, debt_{t-1} + osi \qquad (A1.35)$$

where *osi* is net overseas income, dependent on the foreign interest rate, and the exchange rate.

$$osi = r^*_{t-1}\, nfa_{t-1}/e \qquad (A1.36)$$

The nominal current account balance is determined by the trade balance, in home currency, and the net flow of interest income

$$CB = PX - (P^*e)Q + osi \qquad (A1.37)$$

Finally, output, *Y*, is equal to government spending, *G*, consumption, *C*, investment, *I*, and exports, *X*, *less* imports, *Q*

$$Y = G + C + I + X - Q \qquad (A1.38)$$

Asset stocks

The determination of demand for money holdings is discussed on p. 000, which leaves domestic bond holdings to be determined by the budget deficit. The change in total bond holdings are thus

$$\Delta debt = psbr - \Delta m \qquad (A1.39)$$

the residual of the budget deficit *less* the change in money supply, given by the demand for money equation. It is permissible to not include a demand for bonds via Walras' law.

Net foreign assets (in domestic currency) follow the deficit/surplus on the balance of payments

$$NFA = NFA_{t-1} + CB \qquad (A1.40)$$

Attempts to incorporate a full explanation of demand for domestic bonds, foreign bonds and domestic money in a multi-country environment led to very complicated asset demand structures. To incorporate this sort of structure properly would require the introduction of at least one new asset, private sector bonds and/or equities, and this was felt to unnecessarily complicate the model.

Total wealth, V, is defined as the sum of all "outside" assets held by the private sector, including physical capital.

$$V = M + DEBT + NFA/e + K \qquad (A1.41)$$

Ricardo's equivalence theorem is therefore not accounted for in the wealth identity, and bonds act as a net positive source of wealth to the private sector.

Monetary and fiscal policy

Bearing in mind the objectives of the book dynamic optimization techniques were not felt to be appropriate. Instead, simple reaction functions where used to capture the stylized facts and responses of the alternative monetary and fiscal policy regimes.[8]

Since we are comparing between different regimes compared *ex post* through an objective function, this is in a sense optimal control in reverse. Optimal control theory first specifies the objective function and then determines the policy rule for the instruments (at least in a linear model). Since we *know* what policies are available the optimal control approach is not appropriate. In short we are not determining the "optimal" policy mix in the usual sense, but finding the "best" policy regime between the available choices. What is important is that the model is capable of capturing the stylized facts of the different regimes.

As Whitley (1994) discusses, the issue of how one goes about modelling different regimes throws up some interesting operational problems. Whitley chooses an example where the exchange rate is to be fixed. There are three approaches to this, simply assume the exchange rate is exogenous, use residual adjustment, denoted as a type 1 fix, or adjust some other variable, to which the target variable is linked, the type 2 fix. If one assumes an exchange rate equation of the form

$$e_t = e_{t-1} + (r_t - r_t^*) - (P_t - P_t^*) + RES_t \qquad (A1.42)$$

where the exchange rate is determined by its lagged value, the nominal interest rate differential, relative prices and other influences (the residual RES_t), then the three methods of fixing e_t are easily compared.

Exogenization	fix $e_t = e_{T,t}$
Type 1 fix	Set RES_t so that $e_t = e_{T,t}$
Type 2 fix	Set r_t so that $e_t = e_{T,t}$

(where $e_{T,t}$ is the target)

The first point Whitley makes is that all three methods will have the same effect on e_t, that is to fix the exchange rate at its target level. However the full impact of which method is used will be felt elsewhere in the model. For example, the effect of exogenization and the type 1 fix on the price level will be the same: the price level will change to the extent that there exists a relationship between the exchange rate and price levels; the type 2 fix will however have an additional transmission channel, through the impact of changed interest rates on prices. As Whitley (p. 206) puts it,

> The type 1 fix and exogenisation methods do not explain how the exchange rate has attained its given level, whereas the type 2 method is explicit about the scale of required adjustment to policy variables, and also indicates the scale of additional policy changes required if there is a shock to the system.

This clearly indicates the importance of ensuring that any model which purports to capture the stylized facts of a particular regime is a realistic interpretation of how that regime requires policy to react. By avoiding control techniques this research has been able to concentrate on a more realistic policy environment which takes account of the biases introduced by assuming exogeneity or type 1 fixes of target variables.

The other aspect of the book, the determination of plausible convergence policies, again precludes the use of full dynamic optimization, for a variety of reasons. First, the model is non-linear and employs rational expectations in the asset markets leading to exceedingly complex calculations to derive the optimal path, not to mention the problem of time inconsistency (see Blackburn, 1987, for a survey of the literature), and solutions for the instruments which are not normally in the form of an easily understood policy rule, but instead are a series of values for the instruments for each period. It is of course possible to translate these results into feedback rules which are approximations of the fully optimal path, but this tends to defeat the purpose of the exercise.

With the objectives of the book in mind it was felt that straightforward policy reaction functions, which are easily manipulated and easily understood, were appropriate

Monetary policy

The monetary policy rule depends on the policy regime in place. If a country is in the ERM then its monetary policy is to set interest rates with the exchange rate, output and inflation as targets. The resultant equation takes the form:

$$r = \alpha_{rY} (Y/Y_{pot} - 1) + \alpha_{rp} (cpi - cpi_T) \\ + \alpha_{re} (ee/e_T - 1 + r^* + risk) + (1 - \alpha_{re})r_b \tag{A1.43}$$

where cpi_T = inflation target, for example EU average
$\quad\ \ e_T$ = exchange rate target, i.e. ERM parity
$\quad\ \ ee$ = expected exchange rate
$\quad\ \ r^*$ = German interest rate
$\quad\ \ r_b$ = base interest rate

so that if complete exchange rate targeting is the policy the only α to remain non-zero is α_{re}. Of course, the country can follow any combination of targets with this equation by changing the relative weights. In the long run, if one assumes homogeneity of degree one between the exchange rate and the price level, the inclusion of both the exchange rate level and the rate of change of the price level can be viewed in terms of Phillips' proportional and derivative feedback laws. However, in the short term if the authorities want to target the exchange rate precisely then its inclusion is warranted. Furthermore, since there are margins of fluctuation within the ERM, there is the option to target other variables when the exchange rate is within the band. One important facet of the equation is the non-linearity of the exchange rate target: the further the exchange rate is from its target the larger the reaction of interest rates. This allows the other variables to play a larger role when the exchange rate is close to its parity, or well inside its band, but as it approaches the band's edges the other targets become less important.

This sort of interest rate reaction function has been widely used in research on MU and the ERM, for example the Multimod exercise in "One Market, One Money" (Commission of the European Communities, 1990), Masson and Symansky (1993), Whitley (1992), and in wider terms Bryant *et al.* (1993) (which also provides an excellent summary of policy analysis with reaction functions of this type). One problem with adopting this approach is the selection of values for the reaction parameters. As these coefficients reflect the state of the economy and the priorities of the policy makers, they can be chosen to suit the policy exercises while ensuring the stability of the system. For this book we followed the rankings and elasticities observed in the literature where similar equations have been used (for example Annex E "One Market, One Money" and Bryant *et al.*, 1993), and adopted values which normally resulted in stable solution paths.

If interest rates are used as the policy instruments then money demand follows the following equation which is in line with most econometric evidence (see Laidler, 1985; Fisher, 1985; Karakitsos, 1992)

$$M = CPI[\alpha_{Mr}r + \alpha_{MY}Y + \alpha_{Mv}V_{t-1}/CPI + \gamma_M] + \alpha_{MM}M_{t-1} \tag{A1.44}$$

How does this interest rate reaction function ensure that the exchange rate target is hit every period? If France, for example, decides to fix the Franc/DM rate unilaterally, this would be achieved by inverting the exchange rate equation and solving for the interest rate. Hence, given the variables outside the French central bank's control, interest rates will be set in order to clear the market at the target exchange rate. Since, in this instance, the interest rate is exclusively determined by the exchange rate, the authorities must stand ready to satisfy whatever level of money demand is generated at that interest rate or, in other words, the money supply becomes infinitely elastic with respect to the interest rate. This formulation of exchange rate targeting represents a type 2 fix under Whitley's (1994) definition, and follows the spirit of Branson's (1990) formulation (Branson adjusts the money supply to target the exchange rate, but still uses the principal of an inverted exchange rate equation).

Of course, other variables could be used to target the exchange rate, for example reserves (sterilized intervention in the foreign exchange market) or open market operations in the money market. As Branson (1990) points out, the first method is unsustainable: at some point, interest rates will have to change. Furthermore in a quarterly model, since interventions are normally important on a day-by-day basis (see Whitley, 1994, p. 253), it would appear more plausible to follow the "ultimate" change, that is interest rates. Unsterilized foreign exchange intervention or domestic money market interventions result in only small differences in simulation results when compared with using the interest rate as the policy variable, since they are, strictly speaking, identical. The required change in the money supply for the exchange rate target to be hit is the same whether it is achieved via the interest rate or foreign exchange market operations.

The reaction function for monetary policy allows tight exchange rate targeting (which we define as the "narrow band" ERM, looser exchange rate targeting (the "wide band" ERM), or a free float (where the exchange rate is dropped as a target completely). This is all achieved by simply changing the relative parameter values in the function. In order to model MU, however, some changes are required. Since MU implies a ECB the reaction function becomes common to all MU members.

Empirical papers which compare MU with the ERM and floating regimes, for example, Masson and Symansky (1993), Annex E of "One Market, One Money", Minford *et al.* (1992), and Whitley (1992) have assumed that the ECB will target some weighted average of the national economies' inflation rates which, if the consumer price index is used, is wrong. This becomes clear when one examines the determinants of each country's CPI inflation rate and the effect of taking a weighted average of all the members. (A1.45) shows CPIs for a two-member MU

$$CPI_1 = \alpha P_1 + (1 - \alpha)(\beta_1 P_2 + \beta_2(P_{ROW}e_{ROW}))$$
$$CPI_2 = \alpha P_2 + (1 - \alpha)(\beta_1 P_1 + \beta_2(P_{ROW}e_{ROW})) \tag{A1.45}$$

so that each members CPI is a weighted average of domestic and foreign producer prices. It is clear from these relationships that each member's CPI inflation rate will depend on the others. Taking a GDP weighted average of these two relations, as has been the case, gives

$$CPI_{MU} = CPI_1\gamma_1 + CPI_2\gamma_2 = P_1(\gamma_1\alpha + \gamma_2\beta_1(1-\alpha)) + P_2(\gamma_1\beta_1(1-\alpha) + \gamma_2\alpha)$$
$$+ P_{ROW}e_{ROW}\beta_2(1-\alpha)(\gamma_1 + \gamma_2) \tag{A1.46}$$

and since $(\gamma_2 + \gamma_1) = 1$ by definition, this collapses to

$$CPI_{MU} = P_1(\alpha\gamma_1 + (1 - \alpha)\gamma_2\beta_1) + P_2(\alpha\gamma_2 + (1 - \alpha)\beta_1\gamma_1)$$
$$+ (1 - \alpha)\beta_2 P_{ROW} e_{ROW} \tag{A1.47}$$

or, if the βs and αs differed between countries, the same equation but with some weighted average of demand-side openness, coefficient α, and the relative import weights, β. Contrast this equation with one determined from the real income accounting identity for the MU,

$$Y_{MU} = C1 + I1 + G1 + X12 + X1W - Q12 - Q1W + C2 + I2 + G2$$
$$+ X21 + X2W - Q21 - Q2W \tag{A1.48}$$

since country 1's imports are country 2's exports, this equation can be restated as

$$Y_{MU} = C1 + I1 + G1 + X1W + C2 + I2 + G2 + X2W - (Q1W + Q2W) \tag{A1.49}$$

which, if one attaches the proper price deflators to each flow, leads to the conclusion that MU prices depend on a mix of each country's production deflators and import deflators, as in (A1.47) above, but that the extra term which appears in (A1.47) due to the imports of each member from each other should not appear. Instead CPI_{MU} should be made up of a straight weighted average of each country's share in MU output and extra-MU import prices, the weight for which should be determined by the MU's total imports, not the individual state's. Thus, the proper measure is

$$CPI_{MU} = \alpha(P_1\gamma_1 + P\gamma_2) + (1 - \alpha)P_{ROW} e_{ROW} \tag{A1.50}$$

which varies from (A1.47) depending on the openness of the economies and the weight each member has in the other's total imports. This measure is used both in the ECB's interest rate reaction function and when regimes are being compared in terms of MU inflation performance. The ECB's reaction function is therefore

$$r = \alpha_r Y(\mu(Y^1/Y_{pot}^1 - 1) + (1 - \mu)(Y^2/Y_{pot}^2 - 1)) + \alpha_{rp} cpiE \tag{A1.51}$$

Fiscal policy

Fiscal policy is one of the main areas of research in the book, and so an in-depth look at the various policies and reaction functions is left to the results chapters. This section serves to give a flavour of the sort of approach used. There are two fiscal instruments available: taxes and government spending. Fiscal policy can follow a variety of target combinations, ranging from the debt level to output depending on the application; therefore we present the general form of the government spending and tax rate equations.

$$F = f(F_{t-1}, Y, p, psbr, \Delta psbr, debt, \Delta debt) \tag{A1.52}$$

where F = fiscal policy instrument
$psbr$ = government budget deficit

$\Delta psbr =$ change in government deficit
$debt =$ *outstanding government debt*
$\Delta debt =$ *change in outstanding government debt*

Note that the rate of change of a target variable can also enter, as can the lagged value of the instrument. These derivative and integral rules[9] reduce the possibility of instrument instability, and are a more realistic approach to fiscal policy setting.

These rules close the model by ensuring that the government solvency condition is met, for example that the ratio of debt to GDP is constant. In a growing economy this requires that the relative growth rates of debt and GDP are equal, or for a reduction in the ratio, that debt is growing more slowly. Therefore the simple PSBR equation above should be altered in a growing economy by dividing through by current output. (A1.29) transformed to continuous time is

$$PSBR = G + rDEBT - T - INFTAX = \Delta M + \Delta DEBT \qquad (A1.53)$$

which becomes, with lower case letters representing ratios of a variable to GDP

$$g + (r - y)debt - t - inftax - \Delta m = \Delta debt \qquad (A1.54)$$

where y is the rate of growth of output.

Monetary and fiscal policy summary

The model has a well developed fiscal and monetary policy aspect which is essential to the process of understanding the issues and to investigating alternatives. By deliberately avoiding optimal control techniques the aim is to provide a clear description of what sort of policies are being pursued, and how. Whilst large-scale econometric models are capable of much more detailed descriptions of the workings of monetary and fiscal policy, this is not always the case (for example Quest does not have well developed monetary or fiscal sectors, whilst the HERMIN models – see Bradley *et al.*, 1995 – do not consider monetary policy). But the lessons learned from these models when they are used to investigate alternative simple monetary policy rules indicates that the approach adopted here is superior to either money growth or nominal income targets (see Bryant *et al.*, 1993).

Whilst many simple numerical models are also capable of modelling similar monetary policy regimes, they rarely cover the fiscal policy targets adequately, if at all. Furthermore, the method adopted for modelling monetary policy in the ERM is not only intuitively appealing, it also conforms to Whitley's type 2 fix, whilst the risk premium is treated in a novel manner. It would become increasingly difficult to achieve these twin objectives if the model where simplified.

A1.4   CALIBRATION, ELASTICITIES AND DATA SOURCES

The parameters used in the models are derived from a variety of sources. Where a range of values is available either an average is taken, or the most reasonable. It must be stressed, however, that these sources are used as *guides* to finding plausible parameter values, since these models are not meant for forecasting, but must have theoretically sound parameters.

For each country there were at least two sources in the literature, and although the coverage of each study may not have complemented ours, there was often enough information to derive the required parameter estimates. Table A1.2 shows the elasticities and parameters used. All the wage–price–unemployment sector numbers shown are parameter values, all other values are elasticities or semi-elasticities as defined in the note to Table 4.2. Where a range of values is shown, those highlighted in bold are the ones used. In the instances where mid-range values are not adopted (for example, Spanish MPC) this is due to a closer correspondence between the model in the book and the published source, or a more recent estimate. In many cases elasticities from Quest are used since its structural equations are similar to the models used in the book.

The parameters can be derived from published point elasticity estimates due to the following relationship for elasticity

$$\varepsilon = \frac{\partial Y}{\partial X} \frac{X}{Y} \qquad (A1.55)$$

and since we require $\frac{\partial Y}{\partial X}$ one simply rearranges to find

$$\frac{\partial Y}{\partial X} = \varepsilon \frac{Y}{X} \qquad (A1.56)$$

For example, if the elasticity related disposable income to consumption, then $\frac{\partial Y}{\partial X}$ represents the marginal propensity to consume, whilst $\frac{Y}{X}$ is the average propensity to consume.

Y and X or, continuing the example, consumption and disposable income, can be derived from the most recent data set available. The data used is from a variety of sources, mainly the IMF's *Financial Statistics and Direction of Trade Statistics*, the OECD's *Country Reports* and various publications of the European Commission. The data and the derived parameter values used in the models are shown in Appendix 2.

A1.5 SIMULATION SOFTWARE AND METHODS

E-STAT, the simulation software used in this book, was developed at Imperial College for the PROPE research effort in the 1980s by Robin Becker (1990). The software provides a variety of solution techniques, for example, Newton–Raphson, or Gausss–Seidel,[10] and supports model consistent expectations solutions.

The models to be solved are first coded in an ASCII editor, after which they are compiled, and finally called by E-STAT. Data files for the models are then loaded into E-STAT before the simulations begin. The software allows output through printing the results numerically, or plotting the results to screen or printer. E-STAT solves relatively large models relatively quickly.

Table A1.2 Elasticities used in the models

Parameter	Spain	Greece	Germany	France
	Consumption function (A1.2)			
α_{cy}	0.23, 0.494, **0.66**	0.21, 0.28, **0.3**	0.39, **0.4**, 0.7	0.15, **0.29**
α_{cr}^1	**-6.26**[2], 0.34, -0.15	-0.12, **-10.6**[2]	-0.4, **-13.4**[2]	-0.41, **-3.3**[2]
α_{cv}	0.03	0.12	0.05	0.17, **0.026**
	Investment function (A1.7)			
α_{iy}	**1**, 0.625	0.83	0.65	0.722
α_{ir}^1	-0.55, **-25**[2]	**-34**[2]	-0.19, **-8.4**[2]	-0.15, **-7.4**[2]
α_{ir}	-0.15	-0.045, **-0.082**	-0.111	-0.117, **-0.07**
	Import function (A1.8)			
α_{oy}	0.69, **0.96**, 0.98	0.38, 0.41, **0.88**	0.696, **0.72**, 0.862, 1.24	0.41, **1.2**, 1.3
α_{ocomp}	0.1, **0.44**	0.91	0.21, 0.44	**0.22**, 0.24
	Wage–price sector (A1.20–A1.25)			
α_{wr}^2	0.31	0.212	0.63	0.64
$\alpha_{w\,cpie}^2$	0.5	0.5	0.5	0.5
α_{wu}^2	0.13, 0.23, 0.29, **0.31**[3]	0.086, **0.2**	0.09, 0.11, 0.29, **0.35**, 0.47	0.14, **0.25**, 0.29
$\alpha_{p\,w}^2$	0.7	0.79	0.71, **0.81**	0.46, **0.8**
$\alpha_{pimp\,rm}^2$	0.099	0.098	0.083	0.087
α_{cpip}^2	0.79	0.673	0.714	0.798
	Money demand function (A1.43)			
α_{mr}^1	-0.54	-1.3	**-0.275**, -0.36, -0.4	-0.32
$\alpha_{m\,y}$	0.289	0.48	0.48	0.35
$\alpha_{m\,v}$	0.107	0.196	0.122	0.125

Notes: 1. Semi-elasticity
2. Parameter
3. Represents effect of total unemployment on wages. Chapter 6 discusses in more detail the treatment of the Spanish labour market, which is segmented between workers with permanent and temporary contracts.

Sources: Edison *et al.* (1987), Mauleon (1988), Bentolila and Blanchard (1990), Helliwell *et al.* (1990), Burridge *et al.* (1991), Commission of the European Communities (1991), Garganas (1991), Layard *et al.* (1991), Egebo and Englander (1992), Ballabriga *et al.* (1993), Bartolini and Symansky (1993), ... M... (199...), Ela... and M.Eries (199...), Sakellaion and Hawland (1993), Turner *et al.* (1993), Bradley *et al.* (1995).

A1.6   CONCLUSIONS

Appendix 1 has introduced the model used in the research and justified the simulation approach adopted. Each equation has been described and put into context *vis-à-vis* the literature. Consumption and investment are perhaps two of the most important demand-side behavioural equations. Recent theoretical work has led to a wealth of results which should be taken into account when model building. The approach in this book is to incorporate the inflation tax and wealth effects into the determination of private sector income and spending, since these are important variables when considering disinflation for high inflation countries. The background to these functions were analyzed and the actual functional forms used were described and justified.

On the supply side, it was explained that the model attempts to endogenize growth of potential output in a simple manner. The alternatives are to have a complicated, estimated model giving full account to the micro-foundations of firm's and household's decisions, or to use a simple time-trend as a proxy. By taking the middle line, and noting that this model is not estimated, growth has been incorporated in a simple, yet plausible manner.

The wage–price sector is relatively straightforward. Wages and prices are sticky, since producer prices are determined as a mark-up on a weighted average of import prices and wages. The framework, which encompasses many approaches to explaining sticky prices, for example Taylor's contracts, or frictions in the labour market, but does not attempt to explain the natural rate, or the determinants of real wage aspirations. Instead the focus is on the dynamic evolution of inflation, consistent with the objectives of the research.

The treatment of exchange rates and risk premia was demonstrated, before the chapter moved on to discuss the determination of the policy variables. Policy setting in the model is crucial, and hence some time was spent on this aspect of the model. The approach of simple, and ad hoc, policy rules was compared to full dynamic optimizations. The former where chosen for a variety of reasons.

The modelling approach adopted is therefore a hybrid of the three main forms of simulation model, CGE, theoretical and large-scale econometric. The model is basically a Mundell–Fleming open economy model with secular inflation. It is calibrated for a base data quarter, and its parameters are garnered from plausible estimates in the literature. The approach is flexible, as for theoretical models, and yet capable of capturing the important stylized facts of the economies considered and complex interactions of the issues raised in this book, as large econometric models can. It thus represents an important extension over similar theoretically based, but simplistic simulation models in the literature, whilst avoiding the lack of stock-flow relationship in larger econometric models and the implausible equilibrium assumptions of CGE models.

Appendix 2: Parameters and Data Used in the Models

Appendix 2 presents the data and parameters (see Table A2.1–A2.8) used for the base simulation runs. The data are taken from IMF and OECD sources for 1993:4.

The trade matrix tables (Tables A2.6 and A2.7) show the split of imports as a per cent of domestic GDP; for example, German imports from France are 2.91% of German GDP, wheras Greek imports from the rest of the world (*ROW*) are 12.25% of Greek GDP. The *RERM* and *ROW* figures represent the corresponding country's exports to these areas as a per cent of GDP, for example, German exports to the rest of the ERM (*RERM*) are 12.9% of German GDP.

Table A2.1   Initial parameter values

	Germany	France	Spain	Greece
α_{CY}	0.48	0.21	0.467	0.23
α_{Cr}	−13.35	−3.3	−6.26	−10.6
α_{Cv}	0.009	0.006	0.007	0.027
α_{CC}	0.26	0.71	0.34	0.7
α_{IY}	0.12	0.12	0.2	0.16
α_{Ir}	−8.44	−7.43	−25	−34
α_{Ik}	0	−0.006	−0.015	−0.005
α_{II}	0.94	0.86	0.01	0.17
α_{QQ}	0.417	0.686	0.56	0
α_{uY}	−0.63	−0.64	−0.39	−0.212
$\alpha_{w\,cpie}$	0.5	0.5	0.5	0.5
$\alpha_{w\,u}$	−0.35	−0.25	−0.31	−0.2
$\alpha_{p\,w}$	0.81	0.8	0.7	0.79
$\alpha_{cpi\,p}$	0.714	0.798	0.79	·0.673
$\alpha_{cpie\,cpi}$	0.25	0.25	0.25	0.25
$\alpha_{r\,Y}$	1.5	–	0.5	0.5
$\alpha_{r\,p}$	2.36	–	0.9	0.9
$\alpha_{r\,e}$	–	–	50,000	–
$\alpha_{SRT\,B1}$	0.0105	0.01	0.097	0.02
$\alpha_{SRT\,dB/dt}$	0.291	0.315	0.3	0.637

Table A2.2   German import parameters

	France	Spain	Greece	ROW	RERM
α_{QY}	0.021	0.006	0.001	0.117	0.062
α_{QCOMP}	0.61	0.17	0.031	3.4	1.81

Table A2.3   French import parameters

	Germany	Spain	Greece	ROW	RERM
α_{QY}	0.055	0.014	0.0007	0.099	0.075
α_{QCOMP}	1.65	0.43	0.02	2.96	2.24

Table A2.4   Spanish import parameters

	Germany	France	ROW	RERM
α_{QY}	0.038	0.036	0.072	0.055
α_{QCOMP}	1.76	1.64	3.29	2.5

Table A2.5   Greek import parameters

	Germany	France	ROW	RERM
α_{QY}	0.075	0.029	0.123	0.101
α_{QCOMP}	7.48	2.85	12.25	10.12

Table A2.6   Trade matrix: Germany, France, Greece model

	Germany	France	Greece	RERM	ROW
Germany	–	4.58	7.48	12.9	19.76
France	2.91	–	2.85	8.79	9.95
Greece	0.146	0.057	–	6.32	11.88
RERM	9.34	7.36	10.12	–	–
ROW	16.2	8.19	12.25	–	–

Table A2.7   Trade matrix: Germany, France, Spain model

	Germany	France	Spain	RERM	ROW
Germany	–	4.58	4	12.14	19.8
France	2.91	–	3.73	7.55	10.02
Spain	0.823	1.18	–	7.37	6.95
RERM	8.66	6.25	5.69	–	–
ROW	16.2	8.19	7.48	–	–

Table A2.8   Data used for calibration

	Germany	France	Spain	Greece
Y	100	100	100	100
C	55.8	61.1	62.9	71.7
I	18.5	16.6	20.1	19.1
G	18	19.6	17.1	19.1
X	36.3	22.9	20.8	22.8
Q	28.6	20.2	20.9	32.7
cpi	0.038	0.021	0.047	0.122
r	0.065	0.0683	0.09	0.215
Debt	48.5	52.5	59	106.1
PSBR	3.3	5.8	7.2	12.8
K	200	200	200	200
M	23.6	21.4	26.4	15.5
NFA	16.7	−6.6	−17	−17.8
Wealth	288.8	267.3	268.4	303.8
opi	3.98	3.12	4.17	20.15
inftax	2.7	1.54	3.95	14.2
SRT	0.145	0.153	0.107	0.11
YD	86.2	83.2	85.4	74.8
u	0.089	0.117	0.227	0.098
NAIRU	0.069	0.0935	0.18	0.071

Notes

Introduction

1. An exception is the EC's Quest model, but, in its current published form Commission of the European Communities (1991) it has undeveloped fiscal and monetary sectors. 1995 brought the publication of a set of papers describing models of the periphery (Bradley *et al.*, 1995), which were developed as part of the EC's HERMIN programme. Whilst these models are well constructed for their task (examining transfers and supply-side responses) they are not appropriate for this sort of policy analysis.
2. See Karakitsos *et al.* (1993, 1994, 1995).

1 European Integration, the ERM and Maastricht

1. The domination of the US economy in the early post-war world is graphically indicated by Hobsbawm (1994). The USA suffered no damage during the war, increased GNP by two thirds and ended the war with two thirds of the world's industrial production.
2. A direct result of this was that intra-European trade increased more quickly than trade with the USA.
3. Haas (1958) gives a detailed history of the setting up of this body, whilst Mayne (1970) gives an entertaining insider's view of the state of European politics at the time.
4. Drummond (1987) and Kenen (1994) provide interesting analyses of the functioning and collapse of the gold standard.
5. See Russo and Tullio (1988) for a discussion of the weaknesses of the Bretton Woods system, US policy over the period, and a comparison with the gold standard, and Crockett (1989) who describes the problems of coordination in the Bretton Woods era.
6. After some extended discussions and arguments between the "monetarists" and "economists" on the appropriate strategy to be adopted in the transition. On the one hand, the economists wanted policy coordination before MU, on the other the monetarists wanted exchange rate discipline with less emphasis on prior convergence (Tsoukalis, 1993; El-Agraa, 1994; Goodhart 1990; and Denton, 1974).
7. For a description of the provisions and operating practices of the EMS De Grauwe (1992), Tsoukalis (1993), El-Agraa (1994) and Giavazzi and Giovannini (1989) are especially good. Alternatively, Vaubel (1979) presents a succinct summary.

8. Vaubel starts his discussion with a description of the new EMS, "before it is abolished". As Coffey (1984) and Currie (1992) point out, this attitude was common place at the time; the longevity of the EMS surprised many.

9. See De Grauwe (1992), Giavazzi and Giovannini (1989) and Flanders (1974) for a general discussion and Vaubel (1979) for reasoning on Germany's ultimate role.

10. Giovannini (1989) presents the counter argument and points out the weaknesses in some of the tests used.

11. The *National Westminster Bank Economic Review* (December 1992, p. 2) is indicative of the market's view: "The asymmetric structure is now virtually cast in stone, and it is unrealistic to think that it can now be changed".

12. Previously, intra-marginal intervention was made in dollars, without the access to the unlimited amounts of the partner's currency as was available under the VSTFF.

13. For a fine history and analysis of the re-unification see Akerlof *et al.* (1991), for a general review see Owen (1991). Chauffour *et al.* (1992), using an econometric model, assess the impact on the rest of Europe.

14. In the sense that the adjustment required by the Single Market could be exacerbated by wide exchange rate fluctuations, leading to private sector lobbying for the rescinding of the SEA. It is interesting to compare this to the recent announcements from Paris and Brussels about the beggar-thy-neighbour devaluations of the UK and Italy and the suggestions of "fines" commensurate with competitiveness gains.

15. See Thygesen (1989, 1990) for an in-depth analysis of the various stages and proposals in the report.

16. This was allowed only if the member had a derogation before 31 December 1993.

17. The qualified majority at this stage does will include the member state with a derogation, only those who are in MU.

2 Convergence in the EU – A Multispeed Europe?

1. The analysis excludes those members which joined the EU in 1995.

3 Issues in the Three Stages of Convergence

1. Estimates vary as to the size of the offset, from less than 10% in von Hagen (1991) to 40% in Sachs and Sala-i-Martin (1991); see Eichengreen (1993), Goodhart and Smith (1993) and Pisani-Ferry *et al.* (1993) for reviews.

2. The literature in this area is large. See Barro and Gordon (1983a, 1983b), and Kydland and Prescott (1977). Persson (1988) provides an excellent survey. In essence, whenever there is a congruence of fixed nominal wages (over a contract period, for example), and below optimal output (normally explained by some market imperfection), there is a temptation on the part of the government to engineer a surprise inflation, thereby reducing real wages and increasing employment. The logical basis for this approach has been attacked by many (for example, Goodhart, 1990).

3. "Conservative" in the sense that the banker's aversion to inflation is higher than society's average.
4. As Giavazzi and Giovannini (1989, p. 196) put it, "the EMS is just one element of a much wider set of agreements among European countries in the trade, industrial and agricultural areas. Leaving the EMS is perceived as a move that would endanger other spheres of cooperation as well."
5. And from the negative influence on reserve requirements as financial markets are liberalized.
6. Whittaker *et al.* (1986) show the limitations of analytical solutions when the dynamic complexity of a model is high.

4 Timing of ERM Entry, Disinflation and Debt: Greece

1. For correlations of growth rates, not levels, of GDP.
2. Whitley (1992) employs a similar approach.

5 The ERM and the Maastricht Criteria: Spain

1. This dates back to the 1970 Preferential Trade Agreement with the EC.
2. See the *OECD Country Report* (1993).
3. See Hooper and Bryant (1993) for a discussion of the properties of these measures.

6 Fiscal Policy Regimes in a Monetary Union

1. This is a common approach, see for example Masson and Melitz (1990), Whitley (1992), Gagnon and Tryon (1993) and Bradley *et al.* (1995).
2. Or an environment where members' growth rates are the same.
3. Chosen to reflect the average German inflation rate during the 1980s and early 1990s.

Appendix 1: Methodology and Models

1. Reproduced in Surrey (1976).
2. See Commission of the European Communities (1987) for a discussion of the underlying theoretical foundations and an application for the Quest model.
3. Commission of the European Communities (1986) found the estimated long-run elasticity of substitution between labour and capital for the then EU-10 was 0.967, which is statistically different from 1, but does suggest that for aggregate EU data the Cobb–Douglas unitary elasticity hypothesis is a good approximation. Helliwell *et al.* (1990) employ the same approach.
4. The importance of the fixed depreciation assumption is related to the investment function adopted and discussed on p. 208.
5. OECD, *Economic Outlook*, 56 (December 1994), Annex Table 23.
6. For an in-depth look at the theoretical explanations for sticky wages, for example, implicit contracts, efficiency wages and insider–outsider models, see

Haley (1990) or Timbrell (1989). Bean (1994) examines the background and explanations on offer for the European unemployment experience.

7.   Gagnon and Tryon (1993) also use an autoregressive risk premium term.

8.   See Weale *et al.* (1989), Chapter 11, Bryant *et al.* (1993), Chapters 1 and 4, and Whitley (1994) for a discussion of the relative merits of optimal policies derived from control techniques and simple policy feedback rules. Anderson and Enzler (1987) discuss some interesting refinements and applications.

9.   See Peston (1974) and Turnovsky (1977) for a description of Phillips' proportional, integral and derivative rules.

10.   Burden and Faires (1989) is an excellent introduction to numerical solution techniques and their applications.

References

ADAMS, P.D. and P.J. HIGGS (1990) "Calibration of Computable General Equilibrium Models from Synthetic Benchmark Equilibrium Data Sets", *The Economic Record*, 66, 110–26.

AKERLOF, G.A., A.K. ROSE, J.L. YELLEN and H. HESSENIUS (1991) "East Germany in from the Cold: The Economic Aftermath of Currency Union", *Brookings Papers on Economic Activity*, 1, 1–105.

ALDENDORFER, M.S. and R.K. BLASHFIELD (1984) *Cluster Analysis*, (New York: Sage).

ALLEN, R.G.D. (1970) *Macro-Economic Theory* (London: Macmillan).

ALMON, S. (1965) "The Distributed Lag Between Capital Appropriations and Expenditures", *Econometrica*, 33, 178–96.

ALMON, S. (1968) "Lags Between Investment Decisions and their Causes", *Review of Economics and Statistics*, 50, 193–206.

ALOGOSKOUFIS, G.S. (1992) "Monetary Accommodation, Exchange-Rate Regimes and the Inflation Persistence", *The Economic Journal*, 102, 461–80.

ALOGOSKOUFIS, G.S. (1993) "Greece and European Monetary Unification", in H. J. Psomiades, and S. B. Thomadakis (eds), *Greece, the New Europe, and the Changing International Order* (New York: Pella Publishing).

ALOGOSKOUFIS, G.S. and A. MANNING (1988) "On the Persistence of Unemployment", *Economic Policy*, 7, 427–69.

ALOGOKOUFIS, G.S. and R. SMITH (1991) "The Phillips Curve, the Persistence of Inflation, and the Lucas Critique: Evidence from Exchange Rate Regimes", *The American Economic Review*, 8, 1254–75.

ANDERSEN, T. and O. RISAGER (1988) "Stabilization Policies, Credibility, and Interest Rate Determination in a Small Open Economy", *European Economic Review*, 32, 669–79.

ANDERSON, R. and J.J. ENZLER (1987) "Toward Realistic Policy Design: Policy Reaction Functions That Rely on Economic Forecasts", in R. Dornbusch, S. Fischer and J. Bossons, *Macroeconomics and Finance: Essays in Honor of Franco Modigliani*, Cambridge, MA: MIT Press.

ANDERTON, B., R. BARRELL and J. WILLEM in't VELD (1992) "Forward Looking Wages and the Analysis of Monetary Union", in Barrell and Whitley (eds) (1992).

ARTIS, M.J. (1989) "Wage Inflation", in D. Greenaway (e.d.), *Current Issues in Macroeconomics* (London: Macmillan).

ARTIS, M.J. and M.P. TAYLOR (1988) "Exchange Rates, Interest Rates, Capital Controls and the European Monetary System: Assessing the Track Record", in Giavazzi *et al.* (eds) (1988).

ARTIS, M.J. and M.P. TAYLOR (1994) "The Stabilizing Effect of the ERM on Exchange Rates and Interest Rates: Some Non-Parametric Tests", *IMF Staff Papers*, 41, 123–48.

BALLABRIGA, F.C., C. MOLINAS, M. SEBASTIAN and A. ZABALBA (1993) "Demand Rationing and Capital Constraints in the Spanish Economy", *Economic Modelling*, 10, 96–112.

BANDARA, J.S. (1991) "Computable General Equilibrium Models for Development Analysis in LDCs", *Journal of Economic Surveys*, 4, 3–69.

Bardays Bank – Country Report: Greece (1994)

BARRELL, R. (1992) *Economic Convergence and Monetary Union in Europe*, (London: Sage).

BARRELL, R. and J. WHITLEY (1992) *Macroeconomic Policy Coordination in Europe* (LONDON: NIESR and Sage).

BARRO, R.J. and D.B. GORDON (1983a) "Rules, Discretion, and Reputation in a Model of Monetary Policy", *Journal of Monetary Economics*, 12, 101–21.

BARRO, R.J. and D.B. GORDON (1983b) "A Positive Theory of Monetary Policy in a Natural Rate Model", *Journal of Political Economy*, 91, 589–610.

BARRO, R.J. and X. SALA-I-MARTIN (1991) "Convergence Across States and Regions", *Brookings Papers on Economic Activity*, 1, 107–82.

BARTOLINI, L. and S. SYMANSKY (1993) "Unemployment and Wage Dynamics in MULTIMOD", *Staff Studies for The World Economic Outlook* (December) (Washington, DC: IMF), 76–85.

BAYOUMI, T. (1992) "The Effect of the ERM on Participating Economies", *IMF Staff Papers*, 39, 330–56.

BAYOUMI, T. and M.P. TAYLOR (1992) "Macro-Economics Shocks, the ERM, and Tri-Polarity" IMF Research Department (mimeo).

BAYOUMI, T. and A. THOMAS (1995) "Relative Prices and Economic Adjustment in the United States and the European Union: A Real Story About EMU", *IMF Staff Papers*, 42, 108–33.

BEAN, C.R. (1994) "European Unemployment: A Survey", *Journal of Economic Literature*, 32, 573–619.

BECKER, R.G. (1990) "EEL: A System For Specifying and Evaluating Econometric Models" in N. Christodoulakis (Ed.), *Modelling and Control of National Economies* (Oxford: Pergamon Press).

BECKER, R.G., B. DWOLATZKY, E. KARAKITSOS and B. RUSTEM (1986) "The Simultaneous use of Rival Models in Policy Optimisation", *The Economic Journal*, 96, 425–48.

BEGG, D. (1988) "Comment on 'The Advantage of Tying One's Hands: EMS Discipline and Central Bank Credibility' by F. GIAVAZZI and M. PAGANO", *European Economic Review*, 32, 1075–77.

BEGG, D. and C. WYPLOSZ, (1987) "Why the EMS? Dynamic Games and the Equilibrium Policy Regime", in: R. Bryant and R. Portes (eds), *Global Macroeconomics, Policy Conflict and Cooperation* (London: Macmillan).

BENTOLILA, S. and O.J. BLANCHARD (1990) "Spanish Unemployment", *Economic Policy*, 10, 233–81.

BERTOLA, G. and R. J. CABALLERO (1990) "Targets Zones and Realignments", *CEPR Discussion Paper*, 398.

BHANDARI, J.S. and B.H. PUTNAM (eds) (1983) *Economic Interdependence and Flexible Exchange Rates* (Cambridge, MA: MIT Press).

BIGMAN, D. and T. TAYA (eds) (1980) *The Functioning of Flexible Exchange Rates* (Cambridge, MA: Ballinger).

BILSON, J.F.O. and R.C. MARSTON (eds) (1984) *Exchange Rate Theory and Practice* (Chicago: NBER and University of Chicago Press).

BINI SMAGHI, L. and S. MICOSSI (1990) "Monetary and Exchange Rate Policy in the EMS with Free Capital Mobility", in De Grauwe and Papademos (eds), (1990).

BLACKBURN, K. (1987) "Macroeconomic Policy Evaluation and Optimal Control Theory: A Critical Review of Some Recent Developments", *Journal of Economic Surveys*, 1, 113–48.

BLANCHARD, O. and P.A. MUET (1993) "Competitiveness Through Disinflation: An Assessment of the French Macroeconomic Strategy", *Economic Policy*, 16, 11–56.

BLANCHARD, O., J. CHOURAQUI, R.P. HAGEMANN and N. SARTOR (1990) "The Sustainability of Fiscal Policy: New Answers to an old Question", *OECD Economic Studies*, 15, 7–36.

BLUNDELL-WIGNALL, A., F. BROWNE and P. MANASEE (1990) "Monetary Policy in Liberalised Financial Markets", *OECD Economic Studies*, 15, 145–78.

BOVENBERG, A.L., J.J.M. KREMERS and P.R. MASSON (1991) "Economic and Monetary Union in Europe and Constraints on National Budgetary Policies", *IMF Staff Papers*, 38, 374–98.

BRADA, J.C. and J.A. MENDEZ (1988) "Exchange Rate Risk, Exchange Rate Regime and the Volume of International Trade", *Kyklos*, 41, 263–80.

BRADLEY, J., L. MODESTO and S. SOSVILLA-RIVERO (1995) "HERMIN: A Macroeconometric Modelling Framework for the EU Periphery", *Economic Modelling*, 12, 221–47.

BRANSON, W.H. (1990) "Financial Market Integration, Macroeconomic Policy and the EMS", *CEPR Discussion Paper*, 385.

BRYANT, R.C., P. HOOPER and C.L. MANN (eds) (1993) *Evaluating Policy Regimes: New Research in Empirical Macroeconomics* (Washington DC: The Brookings Institution).

BRYANT, R.C., D.A. CURRIE, J.A. FRENKEL, P.R. MASSON, and R. PORTES (eds) (1989) *Macroeconomic Policies in an Interdependent World* (Washington, DC: The Brookings Institution).

BUITER, W., G. CORSETTI and N. ROUBINI (1993) "Excessive Deficits: Sense and Nonsense in the Treaty of Maastricht", *Economic Policy*, 16, 57–90.

BUITER, W.H. and R.C. MARSTON (eds) (1984) *International Economic Policy Coordination* (Cambridge: Cambridge University Press)

BURDEN, R.L. and J.D. FAIRES (1989) *Numerical Analysis* (Boston, MA: PWS–Kent).

BURRIDGE, M., S. DHAR, D. MAYES, G. MEEN, E. NEAL, N. TYRELL and J. WALKER (1991), "Oxford Economic Forecasting's System of Models", *Economic Modelling*, 8, (3), 227–413.

CAMPBELL, J.Y and N.G. MANKIW (1989) "Consumption, Income, and Interest Rates: Reinterpreting the Time Series Evidence", *NBER Macroeconomics Annual*, 4, 185–216.

CANZONERI, M.B. and D.W. HENDERSON (1991) *Monetary Policy in Interdependent Economies: a Game Theoretic Approach* (Cambridge, MA: MIT Press).

CARROLL, C. and L.H. SUMMERS (1989) *Consumption Growth Parallels Income Growth: Some New Evidence* (Cambridge, MA: Harvard University Press).

References 241

CHADHA, B., P.R. MASSON and G. MEREDITH (1992) "Models of Inflation and the Cost of Disinflation", *IMF Staff Papers*, 39, 395–431.
CHAUFFOUR, J., H. HARASTHY and J. LE DEM (1992) "German Re-unification and European Monetary Policy", in Barrell and Whitley (eds) (1992).
CHENERY, H.B. (1952) "Overcapacity and the Acceleration Principle", *Econometrica*, 20, 1–28.
CHIRINKO, R.S. (1993) "Business Fixed Investment Spending: Modelling Strategies, Empirical Results, and Policy Implications", *Journal of Economic Literature*, 31, 1875–1911.
CHRIST, C.F. (1991) "Pitfalls in Macroeconomic Model Building", in T.K. Kaul, and J.K. Sengupta (eds), *Essays in Honor of Karl A. Fox* (Amsterdam: Elsevier Science Publishers).
CLARK, J.M. (1917) "Business Acceleration and the Law of Demand: A Technical Factor in Economic Cycles", *Journal of Political Economy*, 25, 217–35.
COCKERLINE, J., J.F. HELLIWELL and R. LAFRANCE (1988) "Multi-Country Modelling of Financial Markets", *NBER Working Paper*, 2736.
COFFEY, P. (1984) *The European Monetary System – Past, Present, and Future* (Dordrecht: Martinus Nijhoff).
COHEN, D. and C. WYPLOSZ (1989) "The European Monetary Union: An Agnostic Evaluation", in Bryant *et al.* (eds) (1989).
COHEN, D., J. MELITZ and G. OUDIZ (1988) "The European Monetary System and the Franc–Mark Asymmetry", *CEPR Discussion Paper*, 245.
COLLINS, C.D.E. (1994) "History and Institutions of the EC", in El-Agraa (ed.) (1994).
COLLINS, S.M. (1988) "Inflation and the European Monetary System", in Giavazzi F *et al.* (eds) (1988).
COMMISSION OF THE EUROPEAN COMMUNITIES (1986) "Compact: A Prototype Macroeconomic Model of the European Community in the World Economy", *European Economy*, 27.
COMMISSION OF THE EUROPEAN COMMUNITIES (1987) "Estimation and Simulation of International Trade Linkages in the Quest Model", *European Economy*, 31.
COMMISSION OF THE EUROPEAN COMMUNITIES (1990) "One Market, One Money", *European Economy*, 44.
COMMISSION OF THE EUROPEAN COMMUNITIES (1991) "Quest: A Macroeconomic Model for the Countries of the European Community as Part of the World Economy", *European Economy*, 47, 170–236.
COMMISSION OF THE EUROPEAN COMMUNITIES (1993) "Report and Studies on the Economics of Community Public Finance", *European Economy, Supplement.*
COMMITTEE ON THE STUDY OF ECONOMIC AND MONETARY UNION (the Delors Committee) (1989) *Report on Economic and Monetary Union in the European Community (Delors Report)* (with Collection of Papers), Luxembourg: Office for Official Publications of the European Communities).
COOPER, R.N. (1985) "Economic Interdependence and Coordination of Economic Policies", in R.W. Jones, and P.B. Kenen, (eds), *Handbook of International Economics*, Vol. II. (Amsterdam: North-Holland).
CROCKETT, A. (1989) "The Role of International Institutions in Surveillance and Policy", in Bryant *et al.* (eds) (1989).

242 *References*

CURRIE, D. (1992) "European Monetary Union: Institutional Structure and Economic Performance", *The Economic Journal*, 102, 248–64.

CURRIE, D., P. LEVINE and J. PEARLMAN (1990) "European Monetary Union or Hard-EMS?", *CEPR Discussion Paper*, 472.

DALZIEL, P.C. (1991) "Theoretical Approaches to Monetary Disinflation", *Journal of Economic Surveys*, 5, 329–57.

DE CECCO, M. and A. GIOVANNINI (1989) *A European Central Bank? Perspectives on Monetary Unification after Ten Years of the EMS* (Cambridge: Cambridge University Press).

DE GRAUWE, P. (1990) "Is the European Monetary System a DM- Zone?", in De Grauwe and Papademos (eds) (1990).

DE GRAUWE, P. (1992) *The Economics of Monetary Integration* (Oxford: Oxford University Press).

DE GRAUWE, P. and L. PAPADEMOS (eds) (1990) *The EMS in the 1990's* (London: Longman).

DENTON, G. (ed.) (1974) *Economic and Monetary Union in Europe*, (London: The Federal Trust).

DORNBUSCH, R. (1988a) *Exchange Rates and Inflation* (Cambridge, MA: MIT Press).

DORNBUSCH, R. (1988b) "The European Monetary System, The Dollar and the Yen", in Giavazzi *et al.* (eds) (1988).

DORNBUSCH, R. (1989) "Ireland's Disinflation", *Economic Policy*, 8, 173–209.

DORNBUSCH, R. (1990) "Two-Track EMU, Now!", in K.O. Pool *et al.* (eds), *Britain and EMU* (London: Centre for Economic Performance, LSE).

DORNBUSCH, R. (1991) "Problems of European Monetary Integration", in Giovannini, and Mayer (eds) (1991)

DORNBUSCH, R., S. FISCHER and J. BOSSONS (1987) *Macroeconomics and Finance: Essays in Honour of Franco Modigliani* (Cambridge, MA: MIT Press).

DRAGHI, M. (1989) "Comment on 'The Exchange Rate Question in Europe' by Francesco Giavazzi", in Bryant *et al.* (eds).(1989).

DRAZEN, A. (1989) "Monetary Policy, Capital Controls and Seigniorage in an Open Economy" in De Cecco, and Giovannini (eds) (1989).

DRAZEN, A and P.R. MASSON (1993) "Credibility of Policies Versus Credibility of Policymakers", IMF Research Department (mimeo).

DRIFFILL, J. (1988) "The Stability and Sustainability of the European Monetary System with Perfect Capital Markets", in Giavazzi, *et al.* (eds) (1988).

DRIFFILL, J. and M. MILLER (1992) "Is the Road to Monetary Union Paved with Recession?", in Barrell and Whitley (eds) (1992).

DRUMMOND, I.M. (1987) *The Gold Standard and the International Monetary System 1900–1939*, (London: Macmillan).

DUESENBERRY, J.S. (1949) *Income, Saving and the Theory of Consumer Behaviour*, (Cambridge, MA: Harvard University Press)

EDISON, H.J., J.R. MARQUEZ and R.W. TRYON (1987) "The Structure and Properties of the Federal Reserve Board Multicountry Model", *Economic Modelling*, 4, 115–315.

EGEBO, T. and A.S. ENGLANDER (1992) "Institutional Commitments and Policy Credibility: A Critical Survey and Empirical Evidence from the ERM", *OECD Economic Studies*, 18, 45–84.

EICHENGREEN, B. (1993) "European Monetary Unification", *Journal of Economic Literature*, 31, 1321–57.

References 243

EISNER, R. (1963) "Investment: Fact and Fancy", *American Economic Review*, 53, 237–46.
EL-AGRAA, A.M. (ed.) (1994) *The Economics of the European Community* (Brighton: Harvester Wheatsheaf).
ELMESKOV, J. and M. MACFARLAN (1993) "Unemployment Persistence", *OECD Economic Studies*, 21, 37–86.
FAIR, R.C. (1974) *A Model of Macroeconomic Activity* (Cambridge, MA: Ballinger).
FAIR, R.C. (1979) "On Modelling the Economic Linkages Among Countries", in R. Dornbusch and J.A. Frenkel (eds), *International Economic Policy: Theory and Evidence* (Baltimore: Johns Hopkins University Press.
FISHER, D. (1985) *Macroeconomic Theory: A Survey*, (London: Macmillan).
FLANDERS, M.J. (1974) "Some Problems of Stabilization Policy Under Floating Exchange Rates", in G. Horwich and P.A. Samuelson (eds), *Trade, Stability, and Macroeconomics: Essays in Honor of Lloyd A. Metzler* (New York: Academic Press).
FLAVIN, M.A. (1981) "The Adjustment of Consumption to Changing Expectations About Future Income", *Journal of Political Economy*, 89, 974–1009.
FLOOD, R.P. and A.K. ROSE (1993) "Fixing Exchange Rates: A Virtual Quest for Fundamentals", *LSE Financial Markets Group Discussion Paper*, 163.
FRANKEL, J.A. (1979) "On the Mark: A Theory of Floating Exchange Rates Based on Real Interest Differentials", *American Economic Review*, 69 (4,), 611–22.
FRATIANNI, M. and J. VON HAGEN (1990) "Asymmetrical realignments in the EMS", in De Grauwe and Papademos (eds) (1990).
FRENKEL, J.A. and M. GOLDSTEIN (1991) "Monetary Policy in an Emerging European Economic and Monetary Union: Key Issues", *IMF Staff Papers*, 38, 356–73.
FRENKEL, J.A., M. GOLDSTEIN and P.R. MASSON (1989) "Simulating the Effects of Some Simple Coordinated Versus Uncoordinated Policy Rules", in Bryant, *et al.* (eds) (1989).
FRIEDMAN, M. (1957) *A Theory of the Consumption Function* (Princeton: Princeton University Press).
FROOT, K.A. (1988) "Credibility, Real Interest Rates, and the Optimal Speed of Trade Liberalization", *Journal of International Economics*, 25, 71–93.
GAGNON, J.E. and R.W. TRYON (1993) "Stochastic Behaviour of the World Economy under Alternative Policy Regimes", in Bryant *et al.* (eds) (1993).
GALY, M., G. PASTOR and T. PUJOL (1993) "Spain, Converging with the European Community", *IMF Occasional Paper*, 101.
GANDOLFO, G., P.C. PADOAN and G. PALADINO (1990) "Exchange Rate Determination: Single-Equation or Economy-Wide Models? A Test Against the Random Walk", *Journal of Banking and Finance*, 14, 965–92.
GARDNER, E.H. and W.R.M. PERRAUDIN (1993) "Asymmetry in the ERM: A Case Study of French and German Interest Rates Before and After German Unification", *IMF Staff Papers*, 40, 427–50.
GARGANAS, N.C. (1991) *The Bank of Greece Econometric Model of the Greek Economy* (Athens: Bank of Greece).
GARTNER, M. (1993) *Macroeconomics Under Flexible Exchange Rates*, LSE Handbooks in Economics (Brighton: Harvester Wheatsheaf).
GHOSH, A.R. and P.R. MASSON (1991) "Model Uncertainty, Learning, and the Gains from Coordination", *The American Economic Review*, 81, (3), 465–79.

244   *References*

GIAVAZZI, F. (1989) "The Exchange Rate Question in Europe", in Bryant, *et al.* (eds) (1989).

GIAVAZZI, F. and A. GIOVANNINI (1989) *Limiting Exchange Rate Flexibility: The European Monetary System* (Cambridge: Cambridge University Press).

GIAVAZZI, F. and M. PAGANO (1988) "The Advantage of Tying One's Hands: EMS Discipline and Central Bank Credibility", *European Economic Review*, 32, (5), 1055–82.

GIAVAZZI, F. and L. SPAVENTA (1989) "Italy: The Real Effects of Inflation and Disinflation", *Economic Policy*, 8, 133–71.

GIAVAZZI, F. and L. SPAVENTA (1991) "Fiscal rules in the European Monetary Union: A No Entry Clause", *CEPR Discussion Paper*, 516.

GIAVAZZI, F., S. MICOSSI and M. MILLER (eds) (1988) *The European Monetary System* (Cambridge: Cambridge University Press).

GIOVANNINI, A. (1990) "European Monetary Reform: Progress and Prospects", *Brooking Papers*, 2, 217–91.

GIOVANNINI, A. (1991) "On Gradual Monetary Reform", *European Economic Review*, 35, 457–66.

GIOVANNINI, A. and C. MAYER (1991) *European Financial Integration.* (Cambridge: Cambridge University Press).

GOODHART, C. (1990) "Economists' Perspectives on the EMS: A Review Essay", *Journal of Monetary Economics*, 26, 471–87.

GOODHART, C. (1992a) "The ECSB After Maastricht", *LSE Financial Markets Group Special Paper*, 44.

GOODHART, C. (1992b) "National Fiscal Policy Within EMU: The Fiscal Implications of Maastricht", *LSE Financial Markets Group Special Paper*, 45.

GOODHART, C. (1994) "European Monetary Union: A Progress Report", *LSE Financial Markets Group Special Paper*, 63.

GOODHART, C. (1995) "European Monetary Integration", *LSE Financial Markets Group Special Paper*, 73.

GOODHART, C. and E. HANSEN (1990) "Fiscal Policy and EMU", *LSE Financial Markets Group Special Paper*, 31.

GOODHART, C. and S. SMITH (1993) "Stabilization" in *Reports and Studies on the Economics of Community Public Finance, European Economy*, 5, 417–56.

GORDON, R.J. (1990) "What is New-Keynesian Economics?", *Journal of Economic Literature*, 28, 1115–71.

GOWLAND, D.H. (ed.) (1983) *Modern Economic Analysis 2* (London: Butterworths).

GREGORY, A.W. and G.W. SMITH (1991) "Calibration as Testing: Inference in Simulated Macroeconomic Models", *Journal of Business and Economic Statistics*, 9, 297–303.

GRILLI, V. (1986) "Buying and Selling Attacks on Fixed Exchange Rate Systems", *Journal of International Economics*, 20, 143–56.

GRILLI, V. (1989) "Seigniorage in Europe", in De Cecco and Giovannini (eds) (1989).

GROS, D. (1990) "Seigniorage and EMS discipline", in De Grauwe and Papademos (eds) (1990).

GRUB, D., R. JACKMAN and R. LAYARD (1983) "Wage Rigidity and Unemployment in the OECD Countries", *European Economic Review*, 22, 11–39.

HAAS, E.B. (1958) *The Uniting of Europe, Political, Social and Economic Forces 1950–1957* (Stanford: Stanford University Press).

HAAVELMO, T. (1960) *A Study in the Theory of Investment* (Chicago: University of Chicago Press).

HADJIMICHALAKIS, M.G. (1982) *Modern Macroeconomics* (Englewood Cliffs, NJ: Prentice-Hall).

HAGEMANN, H. and O.F. HAMOUDA (1991) "Hicks on the European Monetary System", *Kyklos*, 44, 411–29.

HALEY, J. (1990) "Theoretical Foundations for Sticky Wages", *Journal of Economic Surveys*, 4, 115–55.

HALL, S.G. and A. GARRATT (1995) "Model Consistent Learning and Regime Switching in the London Business School Model", *Economic Modelling*, 12, 87–95.

HALL, S.G., D. ROBERTSON and M.R. WICKENS (1992) "Measuring Convergence of the EC Economies", *The Manchester School: Proceedings of the Money, Macroeconomics and Finance Research Group 1991*, 60, Supplement, 99–111.

HAMADA, K. (1979) "Macroeconomic Strategy and Coordination under Alternative Exchange Rates", in R. Dornbusch and J.A. Frenkel (eds), *International Economic Policy, Theory and Evidence* (Baltimore: Johns Hopkins University Press).

HAYASHI, F. (1985) "Tests of Liquidity Constraints: A Critical Survey", *NBER Working Paper*, 1720.

HELLIWELL, J.F., G. MEREDITH, Y. DURAND and P. BAGNOLI (1990) "Intermod 1.1: A G7 Version of the IMF's MULTIMOD", *Economic Modelling*, 7 (1), 3–63.

HENDRY, D.H. and T. von UNGERN-STERNBERG (1981) "Liquidity and Inflation Effects on Consumers' expenditure", in A.S. Deaton (ed.), *Essays in the Theory and Measurement of Consumer Behaviour* (Cambridge: Cambridge University Press).

HENRY, J. and J. WEIDMANN (1994) "Asymmetry in the EMS Revisited: Evidence From the Causality Analysis of Daily Eurorates", paper presented at *Forecasting Financial Markets: New Advances for Exchange Rates, Interest Rates and Stock Prices* (London: Chemical Bank and Imperial College).

HENRY, K.R., R. MANNING, E. McCANN and A.E. WOODFIELD (1986) "Implementing General Equilibrium Models: Data Preparation, Calibration and Replication", *New Zealand Economic Papers*, 20, 101–20.

HOBSBAWM, E. (1994) *Age of Extremes, The Short Twentieth Century 1914–1991* (London: Michael Joseph).

HOLDEN, K., D.A. PEEL and J.L. THOMPSON (1982) *Modelling the UK Economy: An Introduction* (Oxford: Martin Robertson).

HOLLY, S., B. RUSTEM and M.B. ZZARROP (eds) (1979) *Optimal Control for Econometric Models* (London: Macmillan).

HOOPER, P. and R.C. BRYANT (1993) "Deterministic Simulations with Simple Policy Regimes", in Bryant *et al.* (eds) (1993).

HORN, H. and T. PERSSON (1988) "Exchange Rate Policy, Wage Formation and Credibility", *European Economic Review*, 32, 1621–36.

HUGHES HALLETT, A.J. and D. VINES (1991) "Sheet Anchors, Pöhl Anchors and Price Stability in a Monetary Union", paper presented at the Open

Economy Macroeconomics Conference, organized the by Institute for Advanced Studies, Internation Economic Association and the Austrian Economic Association (May–June).

HUGHES HALLETT, A.J. and D. VINES (1993) "On the Possible Costs of European Monetary Union", *The Manchester School*, 61, 35–64.

HUGHES HALLETT, A.J., P. MINFORD, and A. RASTOGI (1993) "The European Monetary System: Achievements and Survival", in Bryant *et al.* (eds) (1993).

ITALIANER, A. and M. van HEUKELEN (1993) "Proposals for Community Stabilization Mechanisms: Some Historical Applications", in *Reports and Studies on the Economics of Community Public Finance, European Economy*, 5, 495–506.

JONES, R.W., and P.B. KENEN (eds) (1985) *Handbook of International Economics, Vol. 2.* (Amsterdam: Elsevier Science Publishers).

JORGENSON, D.W. (1963) "Capital Theory and Investment", *American Economic Review*, 53, 247–59.

KARAKITSOS, E. (1989) "Monetary Policy, Exchange Rate Dynamics and the Labour Market", *Oxford Economic Papers*, 41, 408–33.

KARAKITSOS, E. (1992) *Macrosystems: The Dynamics of Economic Policy* (London: Basil Blackwell).

KARAKITSOS, E. (1994) *Currency Turbulence in the EMS: Smart Speculators or Fool Central Bankers?*, Inaugural Lecture, Imperial College of Science, Technology and Medicine.

KARAKITSOS, E. and B. RUSTEM (1984) "Optimally Derived Fixed Rules and Indicators", *Journal of Economic Dynamics and Control*, 8, 33–64.

KARAKITSOS, E. and B. RUSTEM (1991) "Min–Max Policy Design with Rival Models", *PROPE Discussion Paper*, 116.

KARAKITSOS, E., K. GAYNOR, S. BRISSIMIS and J. LEVENTAKIS (1993) *Disinflation and the Exchange Rate Regime: Greece and the ERM*, Report to DGII of the European Commission.

KARAKITSOS, E., K. GAYNOR, S. BRISSIMIS and J. LEVENTAKIS (1994) *Spain on the Road to EMU: Problems, Policies and Prospects*, Report to DGII of the European Commission.

KARAKITSOS, E., K. GAYNOR, S. BRISSIMIS and J. LEVENTAKIS (1995) *Portugal, Policies for Macroeconomic Convergence with the EU*, Report to DGII of the European Commission.

KATSELI, L. (1989) "Economic Integration and Standard Adjustment in the Greek Economy" in CEPR Bulletin, No. 36, Dec. 1989, pp. 3–5.

KENEN, P. (1969) "The Theory of Optimum Currency Areas: An Eclectic View", in R. Mundell and A. Swoboda (eds), *Monetary Problems of the International Economy* (Chicago: University of Chicago Press).

KENEN, P. (1989) *Exchange Rates and Policy Coordination* (Manchester: Manchester University Press).

KENEN, P. (1994) *The International Economy* (Cambridge: Cambridge University Press).

KENEN, P. and D. RODRIK (1986) "Measuring and Analyzing the Effects of Short-term Volatility in Real Exchange Rates", *Review of Economics and Statistics*, 68, 311–15.

KEYNES, J.M. (1936) *The General Theory of Employment, Interest and Money* (New York: Harcourt Brace).

KNIESNER, T.J. and A.H. GOLDSMITH (1987) "A Survey of Alternative Models of the Aggregate US Labor Market", *Journal of Economic Literature*, 25, 1241–80.

KOYCK, L.M. (1954) *Distributed Lags and Investment Analysis* (Amsterdam: North-Holland).

KREMERS, J. (1990) "Gaining Policy Credibility for a Disinflation", *IMF Staff Papers*, 37 (1), 117–44.

KRUGMAN, P.R. (1990) "Policy Problems of a Monetary Union", in De Grauwe and Papademos (eds) (1990).

KRUGMAN, P.R. (1991) "Target Zones and Exchange Rate Dynamics", *The Quarterly Journal of Economics*, 106, 669–82.

KRUGMAN, P.R. and M. MILLER (eds) (1992) *Exchange Rate Targets and Currency Bands* (Cambridge: Cambridge University Press).

KUZNETS, S. (1946) *National Product Since 1869* (New York: National Bureau of Economic Research).

KYDLAND, F.E. and E.C. PRESCOTT (1977) "Rules Rather than Discretion: The Inconsistency of Optimal Plans", *Journal of Political Economy*, 85, 473–92.

LAIDLER, D.W. (1985) *The Demand for Money: Theories, Evidence, and Problems* (New York: Harper & Row).

LAMBERTINI, L., M. MILLER and A. SUTHERLAND (1992) "Inflation Convergence with Realignments in a Two-Speed Europe", *The Economic Journal*, 102, 333–41.

LARRE, B. and R. TORRES (1991) "Is Convergence a Spontaneous Process? The Experience of Spain, Portugal and Greece", *OECD Economic Studies*, 16, 169–98.

LAYARD, P.R.G., S.J. NICKELL and R.A. JACKMAN (1991) *Unemployment: Macroeconomic Performance and the Labour Market* (Oxford: Oxford University Press).

LEIJONHUFVUD, A. (1968) *On Keynesian Economics and the Economics of Keynes* (Oxford: Oxford University Press).

LEVINE, P. (1993) "Fiscal Policy Co-ordination Under EMU and the Choice of Monetary Instrument", *The Manchester School, Proceedings of the Money, Macroeconomics and Finance Research Group 1992*, 61, Supplement, 1–12.

LEVINE, P. and J. PEARLMAN (1992) "Fiscal and Monetary Policy Under EMU: Credible Inflation Targets or Unpleasant Monetary Arithmetic?", *CEES Discussion Papers in European Economic Studies*, 92/11 (University of Leicester).

LINDERT, P.H. (1986) *International Economics* (Homewood, IL: Irwin).

LOSSANI, M. and P. TIRELLI (1993) "Correcting Macroimbalances in a Monetary Union: An Evaluation of Alternative Fiscal Policy Rules", *The Manchester School, Proceedings of the Money, Macroeconomics and Finance Research Group 1992*, 61, Supplement, 248–269.

LUCAS, R.E. (1976) "Econometric Policy Evaluation: A Critique", *Carnegie–Rochester Conference Series on Public Policy*, 1, 19–46.

LUCAS, R.E. (1977) "Understanding Business Cycles", *Carnegie–Rochester Conference Series on Public Policy*, 5, 7–30.

MacDONALD, R. and M.P. TAYLOR (1992) "The Monetary Approach to the Exchange Rate: Rational Expectations, Long-Run Equilibrium and Forecasting", *IMF Research Department Working Paper*, WP/92/34.

MALLEY, J.R., D. BELL and J. FOSTER (1991) "The Specification, Estimation, and Simulation of a Small Global Macroeconomic Model", *Economic Modelling*, 8, 546–59.

MANKIW, N.G. (1987) "The Optimal Collection of Seigniorage: Theory and Evidence", *Journal of Monetary Economics*, 20, 327–41.

MANKIW, N.G. (1990) "A Quick Refresher Course in Macroeconomics", *Journal of Economic Literature*, 28, 1645–60.

MASSON, P.R. (1993) "Gaining and Losing ERM Credibility: The Case of the United Kingdom", IMF Research Department (mimeo).

MASSON, P.R. and J. MELITZ (1990) "Fiscal Policy Independence in a European Monetary Union", *IMF Working Paper*, WP/90/24.

MASSON, P.R. and S. SYMANKSY (1993) "Evaluating the EMS and EMU Using Stochastic Simulations: Some Issues", *IMF Working Paper*, WP/93/28.

MASSON, P.R., S. SYMANKSY and G. MEREDITH (1990) "MULTIMOD Mark II: A Revised and Extended Model", *IMF Occasional Paper*, 71.

MASTROPASQUA, C., S. NICOSSI and R. RINALDI (1988) "Interventions, Sterilization and Monetary Policy in the EMS Countries (1979–1987)", in Giavazzi *et al.* (eds) (1988).

MAULEON, I. (1988) "A Quarterly Econometric Model for the Spanish Economy", in H. Motamen (ed.), *Economic Modelling in the OECD Countries* (London: Chapman & Hall).

MAYES, D.G. (1994) "The European Monetary System", in El-Agraa (ed.) (1994).

MAYNE, R. (1970) *The Recovery of Europe, From Devastation to Unity* (London: Weidenfeld and Nicolson).

McKIBBIN, W.J. and J.D. SACHS (1991) *Global Linkages: Macroeconomic Independence and Cooperation in the World Economy* (Washington, DC: The Brookings Institution).

McKINNON, R.I. (1963) "Optimum Currency Areas", *American Economic Review*, 53, 717–25.

McKINNON, R.I. (1990) "Public Debt in Italy and the European Community: Some Thoughts on the Monetary Consequences", *LSE Financial Markets Group Special Paper*, 30.

MELITZ, J. (1988) "Monetary Discipline, Germany and the European Monetary System", in Giavazzi *et al.* (eds) (1988).

MELITZ, J. (1991) "German Reunification and Exchange Rate Policy in the EMS", *CEPR Discussion Paper*, 520.

MEYER, L.H. and E. KUH (1957) *The Investment Decision: An Empirical Study* (Cambridge, MA: Harvard University Press).

MILES, (1994)

MILLER, M. and A. SUTHERLAND (1991) "The 'Walters Critique' of the EMS – A Case of Inconsistent Expectations?", *The Manchester School* 89, Supplement, 23–37.

MINFORD, P., M. BRECH and K. MATTHEWS (1980) "A Rational Expectations Model of the UK Under Floating Exchange Rates", *European Economic Review*, 14, 189–219.

MINFORD, P., A. RASTOGI and A. HUGHES HALLETT (1992) "ERM and EMU – Survival, Costs and Prospects", in Barrell and Whitley (eds) (1992).

References   249

References   249

References   249

Clearing.

MITCHELL, D.J.B. and L.J. KIMBELL (1982) "Labour Market Contracts and Inflation" in M.N. Baily (ed.), *Workers, Jobs, and Inflation* (Washington, DC: The Brookings Institution).

MOORE J. (1989) "Deflationary Consequences of a Hard Currency Peg", *Greek Economic Review*, 11 (1), 119–30.

MUNDELL, R. (1961) "A Theory of Optimal Currency Areas", *American Economic Review*, 51, 657–65.

National Westminster Bank (1992) *Economic Review* (December) (London).

NGUYEN, D.T. and S.J. TURNOVSKY (1979) "Monetary and Fiscal Policies in an Inflationary Economy: A Simulation Approach", *Journal of Money, Credit and Banking*, 11 (3), 259–83.

NICKELL, S.J. (1984) "The Modelling of Wages and Employment", in D.F. Hendry and K.F. Wallis (eds), *Econometrics and Quantitative Economics* (Oxford: Basil Blackwell).

NICKELL, S.J. (1988) "The Supply Side and Macroeconomic Modelling", in R.C. Bryant, D. Henderson, G. Holtham, P. Hooper and S. Symansky, *Empirical Macroeconomics for Interdependent Economies* (Washington, DC: Brookings Institution).

OBSTFIELD, M. (1988) "Comment on 'Inflation and the European Monetary System' by S. COLLINS", in Giavazzi *et al.* (eds) (1988).

OECD (various years) *Country Reports* (Greece and Spain).

OECD (1994) *Economic Outlook*, 56.

OWEN, R.F. (1991) "The Challenges of German Unification for EC Policymaking and Performance", *AEA Papers and Proceedings*, 81, 171–5.

PADOA SCHIOPPA, T. (1984) "Policy Coordination and the EMS Experience", in W.H. Buiter and R.C. Marston (eds), *International Economic Policy Coordination* (Cambridge: Cambridge University Press).

PADOA SCHIOPPA, T. (1988) "The European Monetary System: A Long Term View", in Giavazzi *et al.* (eds) (1988).

PAPADEMOS, L. (1990) "Greece and the EMS: Issues, Prospects and a Framework of Analysis", in De Grauwe and Papademos (eds) (1990).

PAPADEMOS, L. (1993) "European Monetary Union and Greek Economic Policy", in H.J. Psomiades and S.B. Thomadakis (eds), *Greece, the New Europe, and the Changing International Order* (New York: Pella Publishing).

PERSSON, T. (1988) "Credibility of Macroeconomic Policy: An Introduction and Broad Survey", *European Economic Review*, 32, 519–32.

PESTON, M.H. (1974) *The Theory of Macroeconomic Policy* (Oxford: Philip Allan).

PHELPS, E.S. (1992) "A Review of *Unemployment*", *Journal of Economic Literature*, 30, 1476–90.

PISANI-FERRY, J., A. ITALIANER and R. LESCURE (1993) "Stabilization Properties of Budgetary Systems: A Simulation Analysis", in *Reports and Studies on the Economics of Community Public Finance, European Economy*, 5, 511–38.

van der PLOEG, F. (1988) "International Policy Coordination in Interdependent Monetary Economies", *Journal of International Economics*, 25, 1–23.

van der PLOEG, F. (1991) "Macroeconomic Policy Coordination Issues During the Various Phases of Economic and Monetary Integration in Europe", *European Economy, Special Edition*, 1, 136–64.

POINDEXTER, J.C. (1976) *Macroeconomics* (Hinsdale, IL: The Dryden Press).

RIEKE, W. (1990) "Alternative Views of the EMS in the 1990s", in De Grauwe and Papademos (eds) (1990).

ROGOFF, K. (1985) "The Optimal Degree of Commitment to an Intermediate Monetary Target", *Quarterly Journal of Economics*, 100, 1169–90.

ROSE, A.K. and L.E.O. SVENSSON (1993) "European Exchange Rate Credibility Before the Fall", *LSE Financial Markets Group Discussion Paper*, 164.

RUSSO, M. (1989) The Prospects for European Central Bank in D. CECCO M and A. Giovannini (eds).

RUSSO, M. and C. TULLIO (1988) "Monetary Policy Coordination within the European Monetary System: Is there a Rule?", in Giavazzi *et al.* (1988).

SACHS, J.D. and F. LARRAIN (1993) *Macroeconomics in the Global Economy* (Brighton: Harvester Wheatsheaf).

SACHS, J.D. and X. SALA-i-MARTIN (1991) "Federal Fiscal Policy and Optimal Currency Areas – Evidence from Europe and the United States", *NBER Working Paper*, 3855.

SAKELLARIOU, C.N. and D.J. HOWLAND (1993), "An Expenditure Determined Macroeconometric Model of Greece", *Economic Modelling*, 10, 35–56.

SIEBERT, H. (1991) "German Unification: the Economics of Transition", *Economic Policy*, 13, 287–340.

SIMMS, C. (1993) "Invited Contributors: Selected Comments and Reflections", in Bryant *et al.* (eds) (1993).

SOLNIK, B. (1978) "International Parity Conditions and Exchange Risk: A Review", *Journal of Banking and Finance*, 2, 281–93.

SOMERS, F. (ed.) (1992) *European Economies: A Comparative Study* (London: Pitman).

STANSFIELD, E. and A. SUTHERLAND (1995) "Exchange Rate Realignments and Realignment Expectations", *Oxford Economic Papers*, 47, 211–28.

SURREY, M.J.C. (1976) *Macroeconomic Themes* (Oxford: Oxford University Press).

TAYLOR, J. (1989) "The Treatment of Expectations in Large Multicountry Econometric Models", in Bryant *et al.* (eds) (1989).

THYGESEN, N. (1989) "The Delors Report and European Economic and Monetary Union", *LSE Financial Markets Group Special Paper*, 22.

THYGESEN, N. (1990) "Institutional Developments in the Evolution of the EMS towards EMU", in De Grauwe and Papademos (eds) (1990).

TIMBRELL, M. (1989) "Contracts and Market-Clearing in the Labour Market", in D. Greenaway (ed.), *Current Issues in Macroeconomics* (London: Macmillan).

TOBIN, J. and W.C. BRAINARD (1977) "Asset Markets and the Cost of Capital", in B. Balassa and R. Nelson (eds), *Economic Progress, Private Values, and Public Policy. Essays in Honour of William Fellner* (Amsterdam: North-Holland).

TSOUKALIS, L. (1993) *The New European Economy: The Politics and Economics of Integration* (Oxford: Oxford University Press).

TURNER, D. (1995) "Speed Limits and Asymmetric Inflation Effects from the Output Gap in the Major Seven Economies", *OECD Economic Studies*, 24, 57–88.

TURNER, D., P. RICHARDSON and S. RAUFFET (1993) "The Role of Nominal Rigidities in Macroeconomic Adjustment: A Comparative Study of the G3", *OECD Economic Studies*, 21, 87–136.

TURNOVSKY, S.J. (1977) *Macroeconomic Analysis and Stabilisation Policy* (Cambridge: Cambridge University Press).

TURNOVSKY, S.J. and D.T. NGUYEN (1980) "Perfect Myopic Foresight and the Effects of Monetary and Fiscal Policy in a Simple Inflationary Model: Some Analytical and Numerical Results", *European Economic Review*, 14, 237–69.

VAUBEL, R. (1979) "Choice in European Monetary Union", *Ninth Wincott Memorial Lecture*, The Institute of Economic Affairs (London).

VINALS, J. (1990) "The EMS, Spain and Macroeconomic Policy", in De Grauwe and Papademos (eds) (1990).

VON HAGEN, J. (1992) "Fiscal Arrangements in a Monetary Union: Evidence from the US", in D.E. Fair and C. De Boissieu (eds), *Fiscal Policy, Taxation and the Financial System in an Increasingly Integrated Europe* (Dordrecht: Kluwer Academic).

WEALE, M., A. BLAKE, N. CHRISTODOULAKIS, J. MEADE and D. VINES (1989) *Macroeconomic Policy: Inflation, Wealth and the Exchange Rate* (London: Unwin Hyman).

WEBER, A.A. (1992) "The Role of Policymaker's Reputation in the EMS Disinflations", *European Economic Review*, 36, 1473–92.

WHITLEY, J.D. (1992) "Aspects of Monetary Union–Model Based Simulation Results", in Barrell and Whitley (eds) (1992).

WHITLEY, J.D. (1994) *A Course in Macroeconomic Modelling and Forecasting* (Brighton: Harvester Wheatsheaf).

WHITTAKER, R., S. WREN-LEWIS, K. BLACKBURN and D. CURRIE (1986) "Alternative Financial Policy Rules in an Open Economy under Rational and Adaptive Expectations", *Economic Journal*, 96, 680–95.

WILSON, T. and P.W.S. ANDREWS (eds) (1951) *Oxford Studies in the Price Mechanism* (Oxford: Oxford University Press).

WYPLOSZ, C. (1991) "Monetary Union and Fiscal Policy Discipline", in *European Economy, The Economics of EMU: Background Studies for European Economy, No. 44, One Market, One Money* (Commission of the European Communities).

Index